Assertiveness in the Context of Human Rights, Ethics, and Classical Virtues

Susana Castaños-Cervantes
Connie Atristain-Suárez
Editors

Assertiveness in the Context of Human Rights, Ethics, and Classical Virtues

palgrave
macmillan

Editors
Susana Castaños-Cervantes
Escuela de Psicología
Facultad de Ciencias de la Salud
Universidad Panamericana
Ciudad de México, Mexico

Connie Atristain-Suárez
Facultad de Ciencias Económicas y Empresariales
Universidad Panamericana
Ciudad de México, Mexico

ISBN 978-3-031-60961-9 ISBN 978-3-031-60962-6 (eBook)
https://doi.org/10.1007/978-3-031-60962-6

This Palgrave Macmillan imprint is published by the registered company Springer Nature Switzerland AG.
The registered company address is: Gewerbestrasse 11, 6330 Cham, Switzerland

Preface

"All human beings are born
free and equal in dignity and rights.
They are endowed with reason
and conscience
and should act towards one another
in a spirit of brotherhood."

- United Nations, Charter, 1945

Assertiveness is an attitude and a way of relating to the outside world, backed up by a set of skills for effective communication. To be truly assertive, we need to see and embrace ourselves as being of worth and as having a right to enjoy life. At the same time, we must regard others as equally valuable, respecting their right to an opinion and to enjoy themselves.

Thus, the philosophy of assertiveness is based on the premise that we are all equal and we possess the same basic rights. As such, the goal of assertiveness is to stand up for our rights without infringing the rights of others.

Ciudad de México, Mexico

Susana Castaños-Cervantes
Connie Atristain-Suárez

Contents

Notes on Contributors

Mary Paz Agudín-Colmenares holds an LLB from the Universidad Panamericana's School of Law in Mexico City Campus, where she is Professor of Roman Law. She received her PhD from her *alma mater* with a dissertation on the "Legal Regime of the International Distribution Agreements". She is also a Roman and Integration Law specialist studying at the Università degli Studi di Roma Tor Vergata. She combines tax and administrative litigation with teaching interests in law and philosophy. Her lines of research include negotiation and ethics for lawyers, systemic thinking, and pedagogical and technological innovations in educational legal institutions.

Sandra Rubí Amador-Corral has a Doctorate in Philosophy with an Orientation in Social Work and Comparative Social Welfare Policies from the Autonomous University of Nuevo León, Nuevo León, Mexico. She is a research professor at the Faculty of Social Work and Human Development, Autonomous University of Nuevo León, Mexico. She is a member of the National System of Researchers Level 1. She leads the academic body of social work and vulnerable groups. Her lines of study are health and nutrition, social work, and vulnerable groups.

Francisco José Argüello-Zepeda, originally from the State of Chiapas, Mexico, is married and has two children. He completed undergraduate studies in Economics at the National Autonomous University of Mexico (1972–1976) and a Master's in Social Anthropology at the National School of Anthropology and History (1983–1985). He holds a PhD in

Anthropology from the Université Laval, Québec, Canada. He investigates rural anthropology, environmental education, sustainability, and economic ethics. Currently, he is a researcher at the Center for Multidisciplinary Research in Education (CIME) of the Autonomous University of the State of Mexico. He is a National System of Researchers (SNI) Level I and has a Desirable Profile PRODEP/SEP member. He has worked in budget areas of Public Administration and higher education institutions in teaching, thesis advisory, and research activities. He has been the Director of the *Psychology Magazine* of the Autonomous University of the State of Mexico. He is part of the internal editorial board of the magazine *Con Texto Humano*. He is the author and co-author of 5 books, 33 scientific articles, 37 book chapters, technical reports, and reviews.

Connie Atristain-Suárez is the Director of the Business Science PhD and a full-time professor and researcher at the Universidad Panamericana, Campus Mexico City. She holds undergraduate and graduate degrees in Administration from the Instituto Tecnológico Autónomo de México (ITAM) and a doctoral degree in Administrative Sciences from the EGADE Business School at the Instituto Tecnológico y de Estudios Superiores de Monterrey (ITESM), Campus Mexico City. Her interest and professional and teaching experience include the areas of competitiveness, strategic planning, and business management and development. She has taught training courses to senior executives. She has carried out over 25 management development programmes on relevant topics of current importance, not only for the academic world but also for the business sector. Her research includes measuring and modelling competitiveness, theoretical and empirical models of micro and macro competitiveness, cluster competitiveness, Family Business Firm competitiveness, strategy, and operational efficiency in small and medium enterprises (SMEs). She has published research studies in prestigious international refereed journals. In addition, she has a chapter on "Entrepreneurship, Micro, Small and Medium Enterprises" in the book *Administration, an Interdisciplinary Approach* and two books entitled *Organisational Performance and Competitiveness: Analysis of Small Firms* and *Strategy, Power and CSR: Practices and Challenges in Organizational Management*.

Susana Castaños-Cervantes, the Social Service Coordinator of Psychology at the School of Psychology of the Faculty of Health Sciences at Universidad Panamericana and the Coordinator of Psychology at the Sociedad de Asistencia Panamericana, I.A.P., is a cognitive-behavioural art therapist and play therapist. With a wealth of experience and expertise, she holds undergraduate and graduate degrees in Health and Social Psychology from the Faculty of Psychology of the Universidad Nacional Autonoma de Mexico and a postdoctoral degree in Intervention Programs for Vulnerable Groups from the Psychology Doctoral Research Program of the Psychology Department at Universidad Iberoamericana of Mexico City. She is a specialist in positive psychology, resilience, personal development, mental health prevention and promotion, and personal strengths. Her expertise extends to vulnerable populations, particularly foster children and youth. She has collaborated in designing Comprehensive Intervention Models for these groups, and her research includes designing Social and Emotional Intervention Models. As an oral speaker at various international conferences and a published author in scientific journals indexed in SCImago, Scopus, and JCR, she has shared her knowledge and experiences. She has also taught in several undergraduate and graduate psychology and pedagogy programmes and given more than 20 workshops for vulnerable groups, families of vulnerable groups, and employees working at institutions that serve vulnerable populations as their primary function. Her collaboration with the Mexican government in developing intervention programmes for foster children, youth, and older people placed in residential care from a human rights perspective, a gender perspective, a strengths-based approach, and a quality care approach is a testament to her extensive experience and expertise.

Nadia Saraí Corral-Frías an accomplished psychologist from the Technological Institute of Higher Studies of the West (ITESO), graduated with honours. Her academic journey continued in the Graduate Interdisciplinary Neurosciences Program (GIDP in Neurosciences) at the University of Arizona. She is currently a researcher at Washington University in St. Louis, where she has made significant contributions to understanding the neurogenetic bases of stress-related psychopathologies. Furthermore, she is a full-time professor at the University of Sonora, where she has been instrumental in advancing the research on the biopsychosocial basis of stress-related psychopathologies.

Marlene Del Toro-Granados has a Doctorate in Philosophy with an Orientation in Political Science from the Autonomous University of

Nuevo León, Nuevo Leon, Mexico, a master's degree in International Relations from the Autonomous University of Nuevo León, and a Degree in Language Teaching from the Autonomous University of Baja California. She has a certificate in the Teaching Knowledge Test by Cambridge English at the University of Cambridge. The research lines are human rights, migration, and governance.

Juan Francisco Díez-Spelz is a PhD candidate at Universidad Panamericana's Law School. His dissertation concerns the relationship between "time" and "human rights". He holds an MA in Theory and Practice of Human Rights from the University of Essex (United Kingdom), where he participated in the Essex Business and Human Rights Project. He also holds a Master's in Legal Science and an LLB from Universidad Panamericana in Mexico City. He is an associate professor at Universidad Panamericana's Law School. He teaches and researches the theory of human rights, International human rights law, especially business and human rights, legal philosophy, and legal logic. He participates in different projects as an advisor on these topics and holds a certification in Environmental, Social, and Governance (ESG).

Luz Alejandra Escalera-Silva has a Doctorate in Conflict Resolution Methods from the Autonomous University of Nuevo León, Nuevo León, Mexico. She is a professor at the Faculty of Social Work and Human Development, Autonomous University of Nuevo León, a member of the National System of Researchers Level 1, and a member of the Academic Body Social Work and Vulnerable Groups. Her primary research areas are conflict management, alternative justice, and vulnerable groups.

Jennifer Lizeth Espinoza-Romero holds a PhD in Social Sciences and is Professor of Criminology and Psychology. She is interested in studying bio-psycho-social factors of antisocial behaviour in adolescents and young adults, specifically on personality, such as the dark triad. Her current focus is on psycho-legal factors related to violating and promoting children and adolescents' rights. She has participated in national and international conferences and an academic exchange at a university in the United States. She brings several indexed publications and is an assistant editor of the *PSICUMEX* Journal.

Martha Frías-Armenta holds a PhD in Psychology and Law and is a professor at the University of Sonora, Sonora, Mexico. She is a member of the National Researcher System of Mexico. She has published seven books and several articles in national and international journals. She was the General Director of the Institute for Treatment and Application of Measures for Delinquent Adolescents in Sonora State from 2009 to 2011. She is an editor of Mexican and international scientific journals and editor-in-chief of the Mexican journal *PSICUMEX*.

César Augusto García-Avitia holds a bachelor's degree in Psychology, a master's degree in Applied Psychology from the Faculty of Psychology of the University of Colima, and a PhD in Psychology from the University of Guadalajara of Mexico. An intern for the Master's in Bioethics from the University of Colima, with Diploma in Ethics for Psychologists from the Colombian Association of Psychology Faculties and the Colombian College of Psychologists, he is undergraduate and postgraduate professor at the University of Colima, Mexico Faculty of Psychology, and member of the National System of Researchers (candidate level). He is developing research lines on competencies and professional, ethical behaviour, attitudes and psychosocial meanings, and welfare and human rights. He authorises various chapters for academic books and articles published in scientific journals.

Abraham Alfredo Hernández-Paz has a PhD in Management and Educational Policy from the Center for University Studies of Baja California, a Master's in International Relations from the Faculty of Political Sciences and International Relations of the Universidad Autónoma de Nuevo León, Nuevo León, Mexico, and a Specialty in Educational Management and Policies at the Latin American Faculty of Social Sciences (FLACSO). Hernández-Paz is a full-time professor with PRODEP profile and a member of the SNI level 1, and Director of the Faculty of Political Science and International Relations at Universidad Autónoma de Nuevo Leon (UANL). Research interests include educational policies and leadership.

Dave Alexander López-Mejía is a PhD candidate in Political Science at the Faculty of Political Science and International Relations, Universidad Autónoma de Nuevo Leon (UANL), Nuevo León, Mexico; holds Master's in Political Science from the Faculty of Political Science and International Relations of the UANL and Law Degree from the Polytechnic University of Nicaragua (UPOLI); is professor of bachelor's and master's courses at the Faculty of Political Science and International Relations of the UANL and Coordinator of the Graduate and Research Quality Management

System at the Faculty of Political Sciences and International Relations of the UANL. Lines of research include human rights, citizen participation, and citizen security.

Rogelio López-Sanchez is a research professor at the Faculty of Political Sciences and International Relations of the Autonomous University of Nuevo León, Nuevo Leon, Mexico. He specialises in human rights and legal argumentation and has ten books published by internationally renowned publishers such as Thomson Reuters, Dykinson, and Civitas.

Laura Mejías-Rojas is a psychologist with more than 12 years of experience in health, human rights, values and formation, emotion management, and group interventions. Her research and work focus on the quality of life in paediatrics, pain, therapeutic adherence, social support, access to justice and health in cancer patients, and human health rights. She has teaching experience in value formation workshops and social skills in children, adolescents, and adults. She successfully performs in preventing risk behaviours in social and health matters.

Ramón C. Rocha-Manilla, MD and Sociologist, Specialist and Master's in Development, PhD in Physical Anthropology, with publications and awards as a researcher, is Head of Teaching, Head of Science Laboratory at ISSSTE Hospital in Orizaba, Veracruz; Director of Rehabilitation Center in Tequila, Veracruz; researcher in project planning at the Ministry of Health; research professor at the Intercultural Universidad Veracruzana, Open and Distance (online) University of the SEP. He has been a visiting professor at the Universidad Mayor de San Andrés (Bolivia), the University of Viña del Mar (Chile), the National University of Pilar (Paraguay), and the Federal University of Rio de Janeiro (Brazil). The line of research is reflectivity, bio-cultural diversity, metabolic syndrome, and human development. He is a member of the Pierre Bourdieu Reflective Research Group.

José Enrique Siqueiros-Fernández has a Bachelor of Philosophy and Master of Government from Universidad Panamericana (UP) and Bachelor's in Marketing from Universidad Tecnológica de México. He teaches rhetoric and social philosophy at UP and AI ethics in data science at ITAM. He specialises in classical rhetoric, behavioural sciences, and tech ethics. His last publications are *Neuro-rights and Ethical Ecosystems. The Chilean Legislation Attempt* (Springer, 2022) and *Gentrification and Education in Mexico. Possibilities of Data Science* (McGraw Hill, 2021).

He coordinates the book *AI Ethical-Legal Ecosystems* (Tirant lo Blanch, 2023, in press). Since 2017, he founded Rētor, a soft management and business ethics agency, where he researches and teaches assertive communication to businesspeople and politicians. Since 2015, he has been the Director of Política de a Pie, an NGO about citizen skills against social isolation and misinformation.

Gerardo Tamez-González is a Doctor in Management and Educational Policy and has a master's degree in Public Policy from Universidad Autónonoma de Nuevo León (UANL), Nuevo León, Mexico; he also has a speciality in Educational Policy and Management from FLACSO; he has two bachelor's degrees from UANL, a bachelor's degree in International Relations and a bachelor's degree in Political Science and Public Administration. During his academic training, he performed excellently, obtaining different recognitions such as the Academic Merit Award granted by the University Council, the Best Students of Mexico award granted by the El Universal Group, and the Outstanding New Students Award. León, awarded by the Federation of Professional Colleges of Nuevo León A.C. He is currently a Member of the National System of Researchers Level 1 (SNI) and has the PRODEP 2019–2024 Desirable profile recognition; he has made academic stays at universities such as the Autonomous University of Barcelona and the George Washington University, among others. Tamez-González has to his credit 13 published books, 14 book chapters, and 7 articles, all in editorials and quality magazines; he has also participated as a speaker at national and international conferences. In the professional field, Tamez-González has held positions as a Citizen Counsellor of the Government of the State of Nuevo León in the Faculty of Political Sciences and International Relations. He was Director from 2012 to 2018 and is currently Director of Undergraduate Studies at the Autonomous University of Nuevo León.

Elio Francisco Vázquez-Luna is a PhD candidate in Alternative Conflict Resolution Methods at the Autonomous University of Nuevo León, Nuevo León, Mexico. He is also a Law and Social Sciences Professor at Emiliano Zapata University. His primary research interests are the culture of peace and human rights.

Alejandro Ernesto Vázquez-Martínez is a full-time professor and researcher at the Departamento de Ciencias Jurídicas of the Instituto de Ciencias Sociales y Administración at Universidad Autónoma de Ciudad

Juárez, Chihuahua, Mexico. He has a PhD in Social Anthropology from the Escuela Nacional de Antropología e Historia and a master's degree in Criminology and Criminal Policy from the Instituto Nacional de Ciencias Penales. He is a National System of Researchers Level I member. He has a PRODEP SEP Profile. He belongs to the Consolidated Academic Body 101 Studies in discourses, cultures, and gender. Among his lines of research are (a) victimisation processes and critical public policies and (b) victimological discursive construction and pedagogy of memory and conflict.

List of Figures

List of Tables

CHAPTER 1

"I'm OK, You're OK" Philosophy: Promoting a Culture of Respect, Equity, Justice, and Peace Through Assertiveness—An Introduction

Susana Castaños-Cervantes
and Connie Atristain-Suárez

> Assertiveness is a behaviour which enables a person to act in his/her own best interest, to stand up for him/herself without undue anxiety, to express honest feelings comfortably, or to exercise his/her own rights without denying the rights of others.
>
> —Alberti and Emmons (1974, p. 2).

S. Castaños-Cervantes (✉)
Escuela de Psicología, Facultad de Ciencias de la Salud, Universidad Panamericana, Mexico City, Mexico
e-mail: scastanos@up.edu.mx

C. Atristain-Suárez
Facultad de Ciencias Económicas y Empresariales, Universidad Panamericana, Mexico City, Mexico
e-mail: connie.atristain@up.edu.mx

S. Castaños-Cervantes, C. Atristain-Suárez (eds.), *Assertiveness in the Context of Human Rights, Ethics, and Classical Virtues*,
https://doi.org/10.1007/978-3-031-60962-6_1

Have you ever undermined someone by talking about them behind their back? Have you always been late for appointments with an excuse in hand? Have you ever done a household chore so poorly that someone else takes over? Have you ever experienced frustration when trying to communicate your views and feelings? Have you felt powerless in a situation? Have you ever been influenced to do one thing when you wanted to do something else? Have you found yourself quiet in cases where you wish you had said something? Have you felt conflicted between speaking up and being a decent, nice person? Have you stated your views verbally attacking the other person, or have you let the other person have their way? Have you often felt that you needed to hear your opinions or that people readily dismissed or undermined your views? Have you found yourself giving in to unreasonable demands or going along with the crowd? Have you a habit of obtaining what you want through aggression? Or have you just failed to see the negative consequences of aggression? You probably answered yes to many of these questions because we live in an ever-changing world where our lives are settled around other people who may have very different ideas or ways of doing things than we do ourselves. It is difficult to think of aspects of our lives that do not involve other people in one way or another. Therefore, we have all faced the abovementioned circumstances, and most of us wonder if there could have been better ways of reacting, behaving, and being.

Since we were little, parents have taught us that we should always please and defer to others (passive behaviour), that it is selfish and not lovely to place our personal needs above those of others, or that we should just be quiet and try to stay away from that person in the future. Furthermore, when facing conflict, we were taught to defend ourselves the best way we could, possibly paving the way for a habit of handling situations aggressively. Seldom were we taught to make sure that our rights are respected in our everyday interactions and that our actions do not infringe on the rights of others or to be assertive.

The ever-increasing complexity of the environment in which we live puts us under the most diverse difficulties. The most complex problems originate from interpersonal relationships and require assertiveness for a solution to be found. You have probably heard the term "assertiveness" many times, most likely in contexts that address practical behavioural and communication skills. Nevertheless, what exactly is assertiveness? What does it mean to be assertive? Moreover, why should assertiveness be a core part of one's life?

Assertiveness is a healthy, prosocial behaviour in the middle of a continuum. While no one enjoys being walked on, many dislike being overly aggressive. Respect comes from standing up for oneself. Others will not only respect us, but we will also respect ourselves for speaking up. Assertiveness is knowing when and how to demonstrate our views. It requires being forthright about our wants and needs while still considering the rights, needs, and wants of others. When we are assertive, we are self-assured and draw power from this to get our point across firmly, fairly, and empathetically. It means to voice our needs and wants confidently, calmly, and respectfully while considering the needs and wants of others. However, it is not a trait with which people are born. It is a behavioural and communication skill learned and developed through training and practice. It also depends upon the individual, context, and situation—people react differently to different situations. The same incident may cause one person to respond aggressively, while someone else may be passive, and yet another person may be assertive.

Since it is an acquired ability, we must begin by learning our fundamental assertive rights. To do so, we must ask ourselves: Are we afraid of sounding mean, aggressive, or rude when standing up for ourselves? What do we value enough to stand up for? What for are we willing to speak up? What are we willing to advocate for or remain firmly?

Fundamental assertive rights are all those people possess by virtue of being. Nonetheless, this also means others have the same assertive rights as us. To comprehensively understand assertiveness from a human rights perspective in the context of emerging and developing countries, this chapter will introduce you to this edited collection by beginning with the understanding of the "*I am OK; You are OK*" philosophy, seeking to promote a culture of respect, equity, justice, and peace through assertiveness. It will provide knowledge about assertiveness as a human right and guide you through assertive rights as the foundation and key to developing assertive behaviour to being assertive the right way. Lastly, it will offer a general overview of the complete book focused on assertiveness in the context of human rights, ethics, and classical virtues since one core component of being and behaving assertively, in addition to wisely choosing what to say and how to say it, lies in believing that individuals have certain fundamental rights as human beings which include expressing ourselves. Many people have forgotten or may have never been told that these fundamental human rights exist. We brought together this edited collection about assertiveness as a human right to pave the way to a culture of respect, equity, justice, and peace, especially in emerging and developing countries or low- and middle-income countries. Reminding ourselves of these rights can validate our own needs, opinions, and boundaries with others and, in doing so, make it easier to assert and express ourselves.

Understanding Assertiveness as a Core Life Skill

As social beings, humans constantly interact with others to meet their physiological, social, and emotional needs. Whether in everyday disagreements, bargaining episodes, or high-stakes disputes, people typically see a spectrum of possible responses to dealing with differences with others, ranging from avoidance and accommodation to competition and aggression. While coming across such circumstances, it is crucial to advocate for oneself to achieve personal goals, overcome difficulties, and be determined—but control aggressive impulses without harming the rights and interests of others. Assertiveness is a core skill that implies managing oneself, people, and situations better. It is the ability to communicate personal needs, feelings, desires, and thoughts fairly, openly, firmly, and empathetically. It is a fundamental skill based on balance since it requires being forthright about individual wants and needs while still considering the rights, needs, and wants of others. It is needed in all areas of life, from work situations, social interactions, relationships with friends and family to buying something in the supermarket. It is the foundation for creating healthier societies based on respect for self and others and developing direct, confident communication skills. Thus, assertiveness is a fundamental pillar for promoting a culture of respect, inclusion, diversity, equity, justice, and peace.

Assertiveness has numerous benefits. It keeps people from taking advantage of others and prevents individuals from acting like a bully. It aids people to understand and acknowledge their feelings. It is considered a means of self-development, social competence, and accomplishment of maximum self-actualisation (Parray & Kumar, 2016). It is associated with higher self-confidence and self-esteem (Manesh et al., 2015), professional success, and personal development (Phillips, 2013). It helps gain self-respect and a sense of empowerment. It encourages self-care, social commitment, and self-worth (Ibrahim, 2011). It increases job satisfaction, productivity, work performance, teamwork, healthy team relationships, and commitment (Omura et al., 2016). It diminishes work bullying through self-assertiveness (Fang et al., 2020). It reduces anxiety, stress, burnout, and depression (Eslami et al., 2016). It increases self-efficacy, thus reducing aggression (Khademi Mofrad & Mehrabi, 2015). It fosters healthy relationships. It improves decision-making skills, problem-solving skills (Avşar & Ayaz Alkaya, 2017), and communication. It creates win-win situations and induces health-promoting lifestyles (Jiménez-Bernardino et al., 2017). It is one of the critical features for establishing a patient safety culture in health-related scenarios (Francis, 2013), protecting the patients' rights in clinical settings, and advocating their rights, safety, and welfare (Vincent et al., 2015). Lastly, it promotes social co-existence and healthy and sustainable behaviours (Cantero-Sánchez et al., 2021).

Despite the many benefits of assertiveness, several common barriers prevent individuals from behaving assertively. These include fear of conflict and rejection and a lack of self-confidence. Many struggle with being too passive or aggressive in their communication style, which can harm relationships and mental health. When individuals struggle to assert themselves, they can be taken advantage of quickly. Low assertiveness can take on multiple forms, such as timid proposals to others, a readiness to accommodate others' positions, and avoiding making requests in the first place. These can lead an individual to worse material or instrumental outcomes for themselves, failing to get the resources or support they seek.

On the other hand, people can adopt an aggressive communication style when interacting with others. High assertiveness can jeopardise instrumental outcomes (e.g., by provoking resistance, impasses, or retaliation), can undermine relationship outcomes (e.g., by damaging trust), and can hamper well-being (e.g., by stoking stress-inducing conflicts) (Ames et al., 2017). Ethnic, cultural, and family norms and social identity elements may influence an individual's willingness to be assertive in everyday interactions and communication, determining perceptions of social appropriateness (Pfafman & McEwan, 2014). Therefore, assertive communication is considered more effective when it is adaptive assertiveness (Ames et al., 2017) or deliberately controlled according to specific social situations and frames (Ames & Wazlawek, 2014).

The goals of behaving assertively include increasing awareness of personal rights, a differentiation between non-assertiveness and assertiveness, understanding passive-aggression and aggression, and the opportunity to learn more about how persons communicate verbally and non-verbally. Hence, assertiveness is based on mutual respect as it is a practical and diplomatic communication style. Being assertive shows that individuals respect themselves because they are willing to stand up for their interests and express their thoughts and feelings. It also demonstrates that they acknowledge and are aware of others' rights and are willing to work on resolving conflicts. For purposes of this book, assertiveness is defined as a human right in which people appropriately and objectively express their ideas, feelings, and boundaries without resorting to manipulation or pretence while respecting others' rights, maintaining positive affect in the receiver, and considering potential consequences of the expression. Assertiveness can then be synthesised in the expression "*I am OK; you are OK*" philosophy—promoting a culture of respect, equity, justice, and peace through assertiveness.

Further, assertiveness is learned through education, training, and practice. People are not born assertive; they become assertive. One way to explain why individuals learn to be assertive is with Albert Bandura's Social Cognitive Theory (1986, 1989). This theory states that people learn new behaviours by observing socially relevant models. By practising these new behaviours, they develop self-efficacy or confidence in achieving the intended results. It posits that learning occurs in a social context with a dynamic and reciprocal interaction of the person, environment, and behaviour. Its unique feature is the weight on social influence and its emphasis on external and internal social reinforcement. It considers the unique way individuals acquire and maintain behaviour while also considering the social environment in which individuals perform it. The theory considers a person's past experiences, which factor into whether behavioural action will occur. These past experiences influence reinforcements, expectations, and expectancies, all of which shape whether a person will engage in a specific behaviour and why a person engages in that behaviour. Social Cognitive Theory aims to explain how people regulate their behaviour through control and reinforcement to achieve goal-directed behaviour that can be maintained over time. Individuals learn to be assertive by observing others, considering the social and cultural context, self-reflecting on their capabilities (e.g., self-efficacy and motivation), and receiving positive or negative reinforcements due to the displayed behaviour.

Finally, this chapter aims to qualitatively analyse assertiveness and assertive rights and responsibilities through a lens of the philosophy "*I am OK, you are* OK" and as a constructive and critical communication and behaviour style. The chapter focuses on assertiveness from a community systems approach, highlights the need to educate assertively to cultivate a culture of respect, peace, enrichment, and thriving, and forge social well-being, and gives the reader a general overview of the present book.

"*I am OK; You are OK*" Philosophy: Promoting a Culture of Respect, Equity, Justice, and Peace Through Assertiveness

Communicating and behaving assertively is the most valuable life skill that leads to personal and professional success. Especially nowadays, in a world immersed in violence and human rights infringement, in which individuals are exposed every day to more and more brashness and insensitivity, going over the basics of healthy and respectful assertive communication and behaviour will help people in improving their corner of the world, the quality of their relationships with family, friends, co-workers, and others they encounter in everyday life, their well-being, mental health, and self-development (Belmont, 2016). It will also help them fully exercise their assertive rights and corresponding responsibilities for personal development, empowerment, thriving, intercultural competence, and social well-being.

The concept of assertiveness originated in social skills training and behaviour therapy in North America (Wolpe, 1958), and it initially referred to standing up for one's rights with respect and consideration for others' rights (Alberti & Emmons, 1970). Since then, assertiveness has evolved into a construct that implies being able to express personal opinions, thoughts, ideas, wants, needs, desires, and emotions in a clear, direct, and honest way, taking into account the situation, surroundings, people involved, and other's thoughts, emotions, needs, and desires (Lee et al., 2023). Hence, assertiveness means to communicate firmly and fairly. It is an essential social skill associated with multiple benefits. It improves competence (Kim, 2016), speaking up for oneself and others (Anim-Sampong et al., 2022), and self-esteem and emotional intelligence (Niyogi et al., 2020). It diminishes social anxiety (Ahmadi et al., 2017), stress (Noh & Kim, 2021), and social victimisation (Avşar & Ayaz Alkaya, 2017). It is associated with more social adaptation and adjustment (Eguchi & Hamaguchi, 2015) and a more effective and satisfactory professional life (Pades Jiménez et al., 2023). It promotes mental resilience (Ramadhan et al., 2019), effective communication, positive behaviours, and a healthy workplace (Aul et al., 2023) and helps build healthy interpersonal relationships. As an effective communication style, assertiveness also significantly impacts teamwork, reducing risks, preventing significant errors at the workplace, and increasing productivity, quality, and proficiency. It fosters a positive work environment with a culture of open communication based on effective team relationships (Nakamura et al., 2017). As such, assertiveness, a key determinant of adult well-being (Plantade-Gipch et al., 2023), goes hand in hand with a health-promoting lifestyle, spiritual development, and interpersonal relationships (Jiménez-Bernardino et al., 2017), and with a higher degree of psychological well-being (Abdelaziz et al., 2020). Therefore, assertiveness means respecting the worth, value, and dignity of oneself and others, all of which define and determine the "*I am OK, you are* OK" philosophy.

"*In lak-ech-hala ken*" is a Mayan saying that traditionally means "*I am you, and you are me*". This Mayan greeting is a statement of honouring each other, respect, unity, and oneness. It could be understood as an epitome of assertiveness in which the philosophy "*I am OK, you are* OK" takes place because assertiveness represents an interpersonal behaviour that involves relatively honest and direct expression of thoughts and feelings that are socially appropriate, that is, the degree to which a person is seen as standing up, speaking out and advocating for common interests, while taking into account the feelings and welfare of other people (Ames et al., 2017; Okbani et al., 2019), and since assertiveness is also considered to be a mean of self-development and accomplishment of maximum self-actualisation in various communication fields, in conjunction with the increased demands of personal social competence (Parray & Kumar, 2016). However, the appropriateness of the "*I am OK, you are* OK" philosophy requires assertiveness to be contextually and culturally sensitive (Kılıç & Sevinç, 2018) for it to be functional and practical so that both speaker and listener perceive that their communication is adequate and that their objectives are achieved (Mitamura, 2018). Likewise, assertiveness entails sharing awareness of selfhood and otherness, paving the way for intercultural competence (Yılmaz & Göçen, 2013) by forging societies based on inclusion and diversity, which leads to belonging (Allen et al., 2021) and enhancing justice, equity, and peace. Consequently, assertiveness is a transformative tool for interacting constructively with individuals to bridge differences, solve conflicts, and set the foundations of peaceful co-existence. As the African word "*Ubuntu*" refers to a philosophy of human interconnectedness and relationship, assertiveness provides a vision in which human beings are connected and reciprocal relationships are valued for establishing a culture of peace, equity, and justice.

Learning to live together, one of the foundations of education (Delors, 1996), has become essential in a globalising world. As such, intercultural competencies are a requisite response for building and forging inclusive and diverse societies based on equity, justice (The Organization for Economic Cooperation and Development [OECD]/Open Society Foundations, 2019), and peace in which all members learn to shape a positively shared future for humankind at all levels (United Nations Educational, Scientific and Cultural Organization [UNESCO], 2013). Then, assertiveness drives sustainable development and harmonious coexistence by connecting meaning conducive to self and mutual understanding and contesting or accommodating differences. As a pillar of intercultural competencies, assertiveness facilitates relationships and interactions among diverse people who must learn to live together in peace amidst an environment of justice and equity.

Intercultural competencies are abilities to adeptly navigate complex environments marked by a growing diversity of people and lifestyles (Leeds-Hurtwitz, 2013). It is the skill to perform effectively and appropriately when interacting with others different from oneself (Fantini & Tirmizi, 2006). It includes the following basic set of skills (Deardorff, 2011), which are at the heart of assertiveness:

- Respect (valuing oneself and others)
- Self-awareness/identity (understanding the lens through which each person views the world)
- Seeing from other perspectives/world views (how these perspectives are both similar and different)
- Listening (engaging in authentic intercultural dialogue)
- Adaptation (being able to shift temporarily into another perspective)
- Relationship building (forging lasting cross-cultural personal bonds)
- Cultural humanity (combines respect with self-awareness)

Social actors need to produce meaningful speech and behaviours in ways that will be understood as relevant in context by other participants in an interaction. Individuals need to learn when to say what to whom (Celce-Murcia, 2007). Therefore, assertiveness helps cultivate a diverse, equitable, and inclusive society where everyone is valued. Diversity helps generate a wealth of ideas and perspectives that enhance a society's collective ability to solve global problems, strengthen its capabilities, and work on its weaknesses to enrich itself and be more productive and harmonious (United Nations Children's Fund, n.d.). Inclusion enables individuals to express their whole selves safely and productively (United Nations Office for Project Services [UNOPS], 2022). To build a society that is both diverse and inclusive, people must ensure equitable treatment of its members and engage in a sustained effort to create a culture of attentive curiosity, compassionate action, and self-reflection. Assertiveness, through intercultural competence, helps create an environment that actively welcomes diversity and ensures inclusion. Consequently, equity and justice are established, which, in turn, harness belonging (see Fig. 1.1).

To be able to understand how assertiveness helps cultivate a culture of justice, peace, equity, respect, diversity, and inclusion, leading to

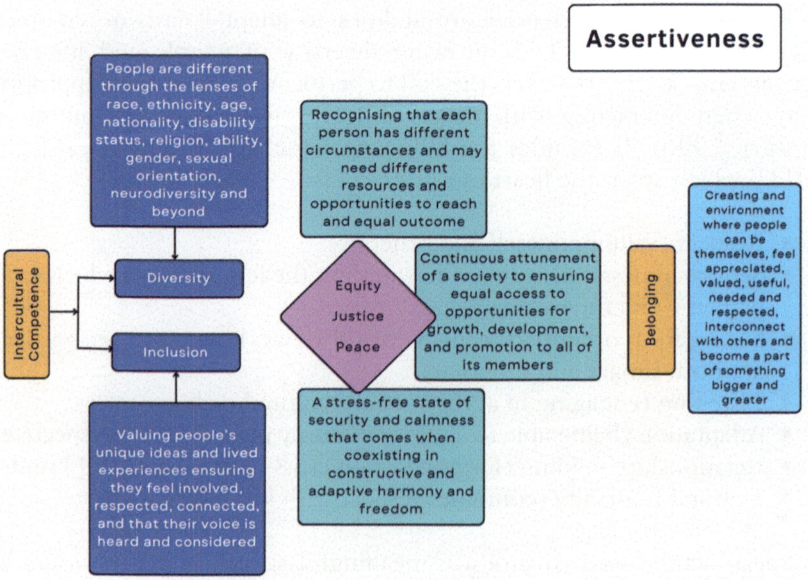

Fig. 1.1 How assertiveness helps cultivate a culture of enrichment and thriving. *Note.* As an intercultural competence based on diversity and inclusion, assertiveness paves the way for equity, justice, and peace needed for building and forging a culture of enrichment and thriving. Source: Authors' elaboration

enrichment and thriving, it is necessary to adopt a community systems approach (Sousa & Costa, 2017) since people live and develop among multiple scenarios and are in constant contact with each other. Human beings are influenced by their surroundings, and they, in turn, affect their environments. The account and study of these reciprocal relations are crucial for fostering assertiveness and creating communities based on respect and understanding of self and others. As such, a community systems approach helps recognise the interactions and interconnectedness among individuals and their community systems. A system dynamics approach accounts for individuals' and their communities' dynamic and adaptive nature when developing and behaving assertively. Assertiveness occurs among multiple personal, institutional, socio-economic, environmental, and infrastructure systems. Hence, a person's background and the various environments he/she develops are necessary to study and harness assertiveness. To behave assertively, people consider their capabilities, the context, the situation, and the ones involved to learn what to say, how to say it, and how to behave accordingly. A community systems approach of assertiveness would provide the foundation to nurture the potential of individuals, self-care, self-worth, self-development, and a sense of empowerment, encourage self-actualisation and professional success, facilitate human interactions, and create opportunities based on human rights for conflict solution, mutual respect, social connection, social cohesion, social competence, and social awareness. As a result, social co-existence and healthy and sustainable behaviours would be promoted, and social well-being would be fostered.

To sum up, a community systems approach provides the background for understanding and assessing the living conditions of people and the social, political, economic, institutional, personal, and cultural contexts in which assertiveness takes place and leads to social well-being. Social well-being is building healthy relationships based on human rights and meaningful interactions. It is having a sense of belonging while valuing diversity. It involves open communication, boundary setting, and mutual respect regardless of personal differences. It is the ability to achieve tolerance and interdependence, co-exist peacefully in communities by building collaborative relationships and trust, and gain social cohesion. Social well-being is a process through which people move to a shared future, fostering intergroup understanding and strengthening non-violent conflict resolution mechanisms. Its components are (Keyes, 1998):

- Social integration: Evaluation of the quality of one's relationship to society and community. Healthy individuals feel that they are a part of society. Integration is, therefore, the extent to which people feel they have something in common with others who constitute their social reality (e.g., their neighbourhood) and the degree to which they feel they belong to their communities and society.
- Social acceptance: Construal of society through the character and qualities of other people as a generalised category. Individuals who illustrate social acceptance trust others, think that others are capable of kindness, and believe that people can be industrious.
- Social contribution: Evaluation of one's social value. It includes the belief that one is a vital member of society with something of value to give to the world.
- Social contribution reflects whether and to what degree people feel that whatever they do in the world is valued by society and contributes to the commonwealth.
- Social actualisation: Evaluation of the potential and the trajectory of society. It is the belief in the evolution of society and the sense that it has potential, which is realised through its institutions and citizens. Healthier people are hopeful about the condition and future of society, and they can recognise society's potential. Socially healthier people can envision that they, and people like them, are potential beneficiaries of social growth.
- Social coherence: Perception of the social world's quality, organisation, and operation. It includes a concern for knowing about the world. Healthier people not only care about the kind of world in which they live but also feel they can understand what is happening around them since they have maintained or promoted the desire to make sense of life.

Hence, assertiveness from a community systems approach entails optimal social functioning as the foundation for social well-being. Furthermore, by being assertive, individuals can craft strong and reasonable responses, calmly and respectfully disagree, and stand their ground. The bottom line is that the "*I am OK, you are* OK" philosophy promotes a culture of peace, respect, inclusion, diversity, equity, and justice through assertiveness. Thus, assertiveness is our human right for equality and fairness in our lives and relationships and as a society based on virtue as it relentlessly seeks greatness through constant collaborative and critical construction.

Assertiveness as a Human Right

Assertiveness has been strongly emphasised as a human right (Alberti & Emmons, 1970). Since it is an acquired form of communication and behaviour, people must begin by learning their fundamental assertive rights and responsibilities to behave and communicate assertively.

Assertive rights and their corresponding responsibilities (see Fig. 1.2) are the keys to developing assertive behaviour and communication because assertiveness is the ability every human being has to defend their rights non-aggressively (the aggressive philosophy is "*I am OK, you are not*") and non-passively (the passive or non-assertive philosophy is "*You are OK, but I am not unless you like me*") and to carry out the responsibilities associated with their rights appropriately. While all human beings have fundamental human rights, it is frequently forgotten that each person with whom an interaction is established also has rights. It is important to remember this when communicating with others. Often, when a conflict arises with someone, it can be resolved by looking at the fundamental assertive rights and examining if one of these has been infringed. The first

My Human Bill of Rights and Corresponding Responsibilities	
I have a right to:	***I have a responsibility to:***
Be treated with respect	Treat others respectfully
Not let others control me	Not control others
Accept my feelings without judgment	Accept the feelings of others
Stand up for my rights	Respect the rights of others
Express my needs and wants	Accept the wants and needs of others
Love myself unconditionally	Love others unconditionally
View my needs as important	Accept the needs of others
Accept myself for who I am	Accept others for who they are
Change myself	Not try to change others
Set boundaries and limits with others	Respect the boundaries of others
Accept my feelings without judgment	Be non-judgmental with others
Make mistakes and even fail	Not critique the failings of others
Ask for help	Offer help
Have privacy and my own personal space	Respect the personal space of others
Set my priorities	Respect the priorities of others
Say "no" without feeling selfish	Accept "no" from others
Follow my dreams, interests and passions	Support other's dreams and interests
Feel weak	Accept other's weaknesses
Not live up to others' expectations	Not place demands on others
Be forgiving of myself	Forgive others
Seek others that support my growth	Support the growth of others

Fig. 1.2 Assertiveness rights and their corresponding responsibilities, as mentioned by Belmont (2016). Source: Belmont (2016)

step is identifying the communication breakdown and healing the relationship (Belmont, 2016).

People have a right to be who they are, express their thoughts and feelings, and do it with the utmost respect for themselves and others. Individuals can be assertive when they know their rights and alternatives to protect them. Fundamental assertive rights are all those people possess just by virtue of being, which means that others have the same assertive rights. When people behave assertively, they affirm that they have rights and responsibilities, as do those with whom they interact. Consequently, assertiveness is the human right for equality and fairness in people's lives and relationships. It is a crucial ingredient for promoting human dignity in which the speaker and the listener are *OK* because they make sure that their rights are respected during their interaction, that their actions do not infringe on the rights of the other, and that they take responsibility for their decisions, actions, thoughts, emotions, and mistakes (see Fig. 1.3).

Human rights are norms that aspire to protect all people everywhere from political, legal, and social abuses (Nickel, 2021). In 1948, the Universal Declaration of Human Rights was the first international instrument to establish a comprehensive list of rights for all individuals in all societies and settings, thus providing a basis for managing relations between various peoples and their multiple groups. People are born with rights, so human rights are innate or inherent in human beings (Morsink, 2009), and legal enactment at the national and international levels provides them with a secure status. Human rights include the following:

1. Civil and political rights (life, security, integrity, fundamental freedoms, access to justice)
2. Economic, social, and cultural rights (education, health, work, food, housing, participation in economic, social, and cultural life)
3. Fundamental principles such as universality and inalienability; indivisibility, interrelatedness, and interdependence; equality and non-discrimination (women's rights, rights of indigenous people, children's rights, rights of persons with disabilities, rights of migrant workers); participation and inclusion, accountability and the rule of law
4. Individual and collective rights (free determination, development, environment, rights belonging to such groups as indigenous peoples; freedom of religious expression)

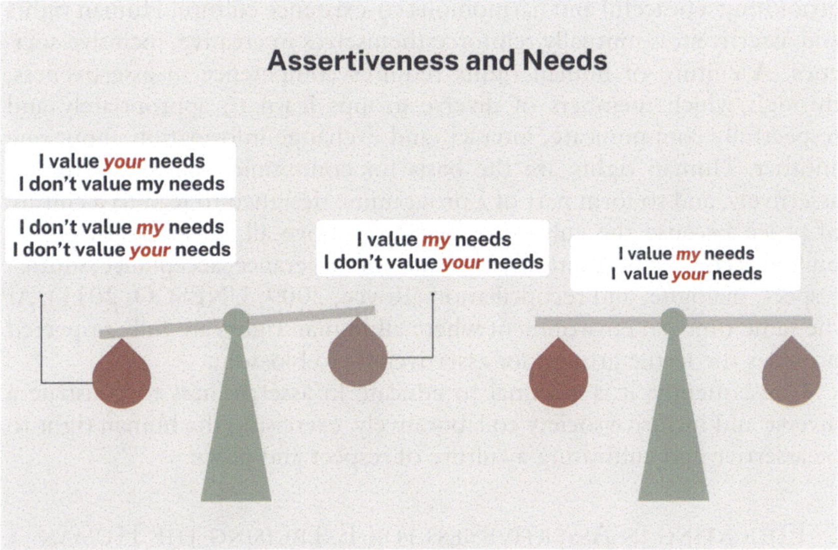

Fig. 1.3 Assertiveness rights based on balance of needs. Source: HEE Workbook (2020)

5. Elements and dimensions such as availability, accessibility, adaptability, acceptability, quality, and appropriateness

Security rights protect people against murder, torture, and genocide. Due process rights protect people against arbitrary and excessively harsh punishments and require fair and public trials for those accused of crimes. Liberty rights protect people's fundamental freedoms in beliefs, expression, association, and movement. Political rights protect people's liberty to participate in politics by assembling, protesting, voting, and serving in public office. Equality rights guarantee equal citizenship, equality before the law, and freedom from discrimination. Social rights require that governments ensure the availability of work, education, health services, and an adequate standard of living. Minority and group rights protect women, racial and ethnic minorities, indigenous peoples, children, migrant workers, and the disabled (Nickel, 2021). Assertiveness is a human right embedded mainly in liberty rights and individual and collective rights. Hence, assertiveness complements human rights as a catalyst for promoting a peaceful and harmonious co-existence culture. Human rights and assertiveness mutually reinforce themselves in creative, inclusive societies. A culture of human rights requires competence in assertiveness, through which members of diverse groups learn to appropriately and respectfully communicate, interact, and exchange information about one another. Human rights are the basis for communicating and behaving assertively, and so form part of a programme designed to lead to a culture of peace because the culture of peace is, above all, a culture of peace-building, conflict prevention and resolution, tolerance, acceptance, mutual respect, dialogue, and reconciliation (Royce, 2009; UNESCO, 2011). At the same time, an environment where all human rights are fully respected provides the fertile ground for assertiveness to blossom.

Consequently, it is essential to educate in assertiveness to construe a diverse and inclusive society collaboratively, exercising the human right to be assertive and cultivating a culture of respect and peace.

Educating in Assertiveness for Exercising the Human Right to be Assertive

Assertiveness involves appropriately expressing ideas, feelings, and boundaries while respecting others' rights, maintaining positive affect in the receiver, and considering potential consequences of the expression. It includes both positive and negative expressions and seeks to achieve personal and instrumental goals. Assertiveness is an essential component of personal and professional interpersonal interactions. It is considered the most constructive communication in interpersonal relationships and a vital component of communication competence (Pfafman, 2020). As such, assertiveness comprises diverse skills, such as solving problems, being non-judgemental, and effectively communicating ideas and information. It also encompasses observing, listening, evaluating, analysing, interpreting, personal autonomy, adaptability (including emotion regulation), stress management, self-awareness, and social awareness. It paves the way for being socially competent, which refers to having sufficient capabilities to speak and act appropriately in context while considering individual rights and the rights of others.

Therefore, the competence of assertiveness means standing up for one's rights calmly and positively while respecting and acknowledging the rights of others and without being aggressive or passively accepting what others consider wrong (Neijmeijer et al., 2020). Furthermore, assertiveness can contribute to achieving the United Nations Sustainable Development Goal 16 by fostering belonging, cultivating a culture of respect, enrichment, and thriving, and promoting diverse, equitable, just, peaceful, and inclusive societies based on intercultural competencies. Consequently, investing in developing people's assertiveness skills and efficient use is necessary.

Individuals are not born assertive; they become assertive through learning. Thus, developing assertiveness skills is a complex process that requires time and practice (Jewell, 2013; Khankeh et al., 2014). The implication, then, is the critical importance of educating in assertiveness for everyone to acquire the assertiveness competencies needed for successfully learning to live together in the modern complexity of a heterogeneous world.

Education is a fundamental resource for harnessing assertiveness as part of learning to live together, which consists of developing an understanding of other people and an appreciation of interdependence—carrying out joint projects and learning to manage conflicts—in a spirit of respect for the values of pluralism, mutual understanding, and peace (Delors, 1996). It is also closely related to the Universal Declaration of Human Rights provisions, which mention that education should promote understanding, tolerance, and friendship among all nations, racial and religious groups. As such, education is the basis for managing relations between individuals and their multiple groups and strengthening respect for human rights and fundamental freedoms.

Educating in assertiveness means teaching people to speak and act appropriately in context, seeking joint construction of meaning (Galanes & Leeds-Hurwitz, 2009). Then, individuals have their perspectives but recognise the views of others, remaining open to learning from them. So, educating in assertiveness teaches comprehension but not necessarily agreement, as human beings agree to listen to and understand multiple perspectives, including those held by groups or individuals with whom they disagree. Based on the Public Dialogue Consortium, the aim of educating in assertiveness would be to establish critical and constructive communication and behaviour that is inclusive rather than exclusive, where the freedom to speak is joined to the right to be heard and the responsibility to listen, where differences are treated as resources rather than barriers, and where conflict is handled collaboratively rather than adversarially and decisions are made creatively instead of defensively. It is a process that comprises an open and respectful exchange of views between individuals and groups with different ethnic, cultural, religious, and linguistic backgrounds and heritage based on mutual understanding and respect, and that includes learning to be flexible and to respect the different varieties of flexibility expected across cultural groups.

Educating in assertiveness provides the skills to maintain a health-promoting lifestyle, develop personal self-affirmation (assertiveness), and improve self-care practices (Jiménez-Bernardino et al., 2017), communication skills, self-confidence, self-esteem, personal and professional growth, and relationships, and cultivate a safer and secure milieu.

One form of education on assertiveness is culturally appropriate assertiveness training (Omura et al., 2019), which is considered one of the interventions that increase the level of personal happiness (Hojjat et al., 2015) and job satisfaction (Yoshinaga et al., 2018), helps individuals to self-actualise without abusing the rights of others, and fosters a better mental health (Golshiri et al., 2023) and quality of life (Ganji et al., 2022). Through assertive training, it is possible to create professionals with high self-worth and self-respect that gain a high level of psychological well-being and an optimal level of organisational citizenship (Abdelaziz et al., 2020). Assertiveness training raises cultural awareness, knowledge, and experience to practise a profession in a culturally competent manner with sensitivity (Kılıç & Sevinç, 2018). It helps individuals build effective social communication, constructively solve conflicts, adapt their behaviour to each situation, and progress in line with their position (Avşar & Ayaz Alkaya, 2017).

Consequently, assertiveness training is pivotal in learning and developing intercultural competencies, interpersonal communication skills, teamwork, problem-solving, planning, and organisation. It can be graded depending on the nature of individuals and their contexts (Hanson et al., 2020) and offered through hybrid education in which face-to-face and online methods are used together, especially when society faces hazardous situations such as the COVID-19 pandemic (Ayhan & Seki Öz, 2021).

Delving Into the Book

This book comprises 12 chapters divided into four sections that address assertiveness from a human rights perspective using a mixed methods approach, particularly in developing and emerging countries.

The first section focuses on assertiveness as a human right and virtue. It consists of Chaps. 1, 2, and 3. The first chapter studies the association of assertiveness with human rights. It addresses how the exercise of assertive rights requires knowledge of human rights. So, educating in assertive rights and their corresponding responsibilities is vital for fully exercising such rights. The second chapter examines how assertiveness as a human right provides the means necessary for empowering individuals and helps them exercise their rights. Exercising such rights highlights the need for education in assertive rights. Likewise, since assertiveness is still not embedded in legislation, the infringement of human rights is promoted. The third chapter explores assertiveness's role in protecting individual rights. It examines how assertiveness helps strengthen human potential and achieve maximum personal fulfilment. Therefore, assertiveness is a virtue for social well-being and personal development.

The second section addresses assertiveness from a social perspective. It comprises Chaps. 4, 5, and 6. The fourth chapter analyses how educating in assertive rights aims for intercultural competence by strengthening respect for human rights and fundamental freedoms and fostering understanding, tolerance, and interpersonal assertiveness among all individuals. It elaborates on how educating in assertive rights is the means that provides individuals and societies with the critical skills and knowledge necessary to become assertive citizens, capable of adapting to change and contributing to their community and culture. Hence, assertive rights are a vital factor for inclusive and intercultural societies. The fifth chapter focuses on how sociology provides the framework to study and assess assertiveness. It considers reflexivity as a crucial factor for a critical comprehension of assertiveness. As a result, sociology is a valuable toolbox for helping establish more assertive societies. The sixth chapter proposes assertiveness as a fundamental factor for peace maintenance, human rights exercise, and conflict prevention. It argues how social work provides the basis for studying, understanding, evaluating, and promoting assertiveness as a human right. It analyses assertiveness as a human right from a humanistic and person-centred approach.

The third section explores assertiveness as the path to building a culture of virtue, peace, and equity. It consists of Chaps. 7, 8, and 9. The seventh chapter analyses how philosophical ethics and psychology provide the foundation for a comprehensive understanding of assertive communication and how assertive communication is a critical factor for making informed decisions. As such, virtue, responsibility, and care are essential elements of assertive communication and for studying assertiveness. The eighth chapter addresses assertiveness as a fundamental factor for establishing peaceful, harmonious societies free of conflict and violence and for diminishing and preventing structural violence. It elaborates on how assertiveness strengthens respect for human rights and fundamental freedoms and promotes activities for maintaining peace, particularly for victims of structural violence. The ninth chapter focuses on how fostering assertiveness in universities promotes human rights, gender equality, and inclusion. It emphasises that assertiveness is a central factor for fostering intercultural competence and that universities are essential for educating in human rights from assertiveness.

The last section analyses the exercise of assertiveness as a right. It comprises Chaps. 10, 11, and 12. The tenth chapter analyses assertiveness as a human right for fostering human dignity and providing the basis for enhancing human dignity in vulnerable people. It states that from a human rights perspective, assertiveness needs to be recognised as a constitutional right by current legislation. The 11th chapter is about sexual assertiveness in homeless female youth. It analyses how sexual assertiveness diminishes sexual violence and fosters sexual health, how sexual education promotes sexual assertiveness and sexual health, and how sexual assertiveness enables the exercise of sexual rights in homeless female youth. The 12th chapter is about how educating in assertiveness is necessary for promoting social justice, equity, and human rights protection. Therefore, assertiveness education is valuable for social change and shared values. Universities offer the ambience needed for educating in assertiveness so that students can harness this skill, become responsible and socially committed citizens, and help improve society.

Therefore, this edited collection explores how assertiveness as a human right promotes human dignity and helps build more just, equitable, peaceful, and inclusive societies, especially in the context of developing and emerging countries. With interdisciplinary contributors working in diverse fields such as psychology, administration, politics, pedagogy, sociology, law, anthropology, philosophy, and social work, the collection brings together theoretical and applied research evidence on assertive rights. The collection examines assertive rights as critical factors for developing assertive behaviour and as a virtue for personal development, empowerment, and thriving. Moreover, this book provides a comprehensive understanding of assertiveness through education and knowledge of human rights, which must be embedded in current legislation to ensure their whole exercise and enjoyment, particularly in developing and emerging countries. The book offers intervention strategies and recommendations for public policy actions. It highlights the importance of assertive rights and their corresponding responsibilities to help establish more peaceful and productive societies. Essentially, this edited collection describes and critically analyses assertiveness as a fundamental human right for fostering intercultural competence, freedom, understanding, and tolerance among all individuals. Its key features are as follows:

- It thoroughly introduces assertive rights for anyone from any subject (e.g., philosophy, pedagogy, sociology, anthropology, social work, psychology, law, and politics).
- It provides a comprehensive analysis and criticism of assertive rights from an interdisciplinary perspective.
- Even though it focuses on the analysis of assertive rights, it offers implications for practice.
- It is attentive to critical stances on human rights and to stultifying privations in the field, particularly among vulnerable groups.

Existing research and books rarely address assertive rights from an interdisciplinary and scientific approach using quantitative and qualitative methodology, particularly in developing and emerging countries. Available books on the market focus on assertive rights as part of building assertive skills through assertiveness training. Seldom do these books focus on assertive rights in the context of philosophy, education, law, sociology, social work, and anthropology. Moreover, this book is consistent with Sustainable Development Goal Number 16 because all chapters provide a solid foundation for developing research-based interventions, programmes, and policy actions that will help foster human rights through assertiveness in individuals, groups, communities, and institutions. The study of assertiveness as a human right is essential for helping establish a culture of respect and peace within individuals, societies, and organisations. Human rights are rarely protected, guaranteed, and exercised in developing and emerging countries. People do not even know all of their human rights. Likewise, in such countries, many interpersonal conflicts associated with harmful and improper communication occur within families, communities, and institutions. For a culture of respect and peace to be established, it is necessary to educate in assertiveness and to promote assertiveness as a human right. How would people exercise their right to be assertive if they are unfamiliar with assertiveness and do not even know they have the right to be assertive? How can a culture of respect and peace be established and promoted when individuals do not behave assertively, are unfamiliar with assertiveness, and do not even know it is their right? How can efficient and sustainable interventions, programmes, and policy actions in assertiveness be developed and conducted without scientific knowledge?

Consequently, this book adds to the growing body of literature on the field, particularly in the context of developing and emerging countries. It provides solid interdisciplinary foundations for studying, analysing, understanding, and assessing assertiveness as a human right across various perspectives and, for example, in vulnerable groups. It also encourages educating in assertiveness as a central factor for fully exercising assertive rights and their corresponding responsibilities, enhancing personal development, and building and forging more just, equitable, and inclusive societies that respect and promote human rights.

Hopefully, this book will pave the way for future research on assertive rights and encourage studies of assertiveness as a human right. The book would appeal to scholars interested in fostering human rights via assertiveness, interpersonal relationships, social well-being, and equitable, just, and inclusive societies.

To sum up, the book addresses assertiveness in the context of human rights, ethics, and classic virtues to promote a culture of respect, justice, and peace within diverse, inclusive, and culturally competent societies under constant collaborative construction and evolution.

References

Abdelaziz, E. M., Diab, I. A., Ouda, M. M. A., Elsharkawy, N. B., & Abdelkader, F. A. (2020). The effectiveness of assertiveness training program on psychological well-being and work engagement among novice psychiatric nurses. *Nursing Forum, 55*(3), 309–319. https://doi.org/10.1111/nuf.12430

Ahmadi, H., Daramadi, P. S., Asadi-Samani, M., Givtaj, H., & Sani, M. R. M. (2017). Effectiveness of group training of assertiveness on social anxiety among deaf and hard of hearing adolescents. *The International Tinnitus Journal, 21*(1), 14–20. https://doi.org/10.5935/0946-5448.20170004

Alberti, R., & Emmons, M. L. (1974). *Your perfect right: A guide to assertive behaviour* (2nd ed.). Impact Press.

Alberti, R. E., & Emmons, M. L. (1970). *Your perfect right: A guide to assertive behaviour*. Impact Publishers.

Allen, A., Kern, M. L., Rozek, C. S., McInereney, D., & Slavich, G. M. (2021). Belonging: A review of conceptual issues, an integrative framework, and directions for future research. *Australian Journal of Psychology, 73*(1), 87. https://doi.org/10.1080/00049530.2021.1883409

Ames, D. R., Lee, A., & Wazlawek, A. S. (2017). Interpersonal assertiveness: Inside the balancing act. *Social and Personality Psychology Compass, 11*(6), 12317–12333. https://doi.org/10.1111/spc3.12317

Ames, D. R., & Wazlawek, A. S. (2014). Pushing in the dark: Causes and consequences of limited self-awareness for interpersonal assertiveness. *Personality & Social Psychology Bulletin, 40*(6), 775–790. https://doi.org/10.1177/0146167214525474

Anim-Sampong, S., Antwi, W. K., Antwi, F. A. A., & Botwe, B. O. (2022). The assertiveness of final year student radiographers during their clinical practice: A study in Ghana. *Journal of Medical Imaging and Radiation Sciences, 53*(4), 605–611. https://doi.org/10.1016/j.jmir.2022.07.010

Aul, K., Ferguson, L., & Russo, B. (2023). Strategy to enhance undergraduate nursing students' assertiveness. *The Journal of Nursing Education, 62*(4), 263–264. https://doi.org/10.3928/01484834-20230208-09

Avşar, F., & Ayaz Alkaya, S. (2017). The effectiveness of assertiveness training for school-aged children on bullying and assertiveness level. *Journal of Pediatric Nursing, 36*, 186–190. https://doi.org/10.1016/j.pedn.2017.06.020

Ayhan, D., & Seki Öz, H. (2021). Effect of assertiveness training on the nursing students' assertiveness and self-esteem levels: Application of hybrid education in COVID-19 pandemic. *Nursing Forum, 56*(4), 807–815. https://doi.org/10.1111/nuf.12610

Bandura, A. (1986). *Social foundations of thought & action: A social cognitive theory.* Prentice-Hall.

Bandura, A. (1989). Human agency in social cognitive theory. *American Psychologist, 44*(9), 1175–1184. https://doi.org/10.1037/0003-066X.44.9.1175

Belmont, J. (2016). *150 more group therapy activities and tips.* PESI Publishing & Media.

Bibic, T. (2020). *HEE assertiveness workbook.* NHS Health Education England. https://london.hee.nhs.uk/sites/default/files/hee_assertiveness_workbook_0.pdf

Cantero-Sánchez, F., León-Rubio, J., Vázquez-Morejón, R., & León-Pérez, J. (2021). Evaluation of an assertiveness training based on the social learning theory for occupational health, safety, and environment practitioners. *Sustainability, 13*(20), 11504. https://doi.org/10.3390/su132011504

Celce-Murcia, M. (2007). Rethinking the role of communicative competence in language teaching. In A. A. Soler & M. P. Safont Jorda (Eds.), *Intercultural language use and language learning* (pp. 41–57). Springer.

Deardorff, D. K. (2011). Promoting understanding and development of intercultural dialogue and peace: A comparative analysis and global perspective of regional studies on intercultural competence. In *Report of the state of the arts and perspectives on intercultural competences and skills*. UNESCO.

Delors, J. (1996). *Learning: The treasure within*. UNESCO.

Eguchi, M., & Hamaguchi, Y. (2015). Causal relationship between assertiveness and adjustment in children: A short-term longitudinal study. *Shinrigaku kenkyu: The Japanese Journal of Psychology, 86*(3), 191–199. https://doi.org/10.4992/jjpsy.86.13079

Eslami, A. A., Rabiei, L., Afzali, S. M., Hamidizadeh, S., & Masoudi, R. (2016). The effectiveness of assertiveness training on the levels of stress, anxiety, and depression of high school students. *Iranian Red Crescent Medical Journal, 18*(1), e21096. https://doi.org/10.5812/ircmj.21096

Fang, L., Hsiao, L. P., Fang, S. H., & Chen, B. C. (2020). Effects of assertiveness and psychosocial work condition on workplace bullying among nurses: A cross-sectional study. *International Journal of Nursing Practice, 26*(6), e12806. https://doi.org/10.1111/ijn.12806

Fantini, A., & Tirmizi, A. (2006). Exploring and assessing intercultural competence. *World Learning Publications. Paper 1*. http://digitalcollections.sit.edu/worldlearning_publications/1F

Francis, R. (2013). *Report of the Mid Staffordshire NHS Foundation Trust public inquiry. Executive summary*. The Stationery Office: Crown. https://assets.publishing.service.gov.uk/government/uploads/system/uploads/attachment_data/file/279124/0947.pdf

Galanes, G., & Leeds-Hurwitz, W. (Eds.). (2009). *Socially constructing communication*. Hampton Press.

Ganji, F., Khani, F., Karimi, Z., & Rabiei, L. (2022). Effect of assertiveness program on the drug use tendency, mental health, and quality of life in clinical students of Shahrekord University of Medical Sciences. *Journal of Education and Health Promotion, 11*, 48. https://doi.org/10.4103/jehp.jehp_107_21

Golshiri, P., Mostofi, A., & Rouzbahani, S. (2023). The effect of problem-solving and assertiveness training on self-esteem and mental health of female adolescents: A randomised clinical trial. *BMC Psychology, 11*(1), 106. https://doi.org/10.1186/s40359-023-01154-x

Hanson, J., Walsh, S., Mason, M., Wadsworth, D., Framp, A., & Watson, K. (2020). 'Speaking up for safety': A graded assertiveness intervention for first year nursing students in preparation for clinical placement: Thematic analysis. *Nurse Education Today, 84*, 104252. https://doi.org/10.1016/j.nedt.2019.104252

Hojjat, S. K., Golmakani, E., Norozi Khalili, M., Shakeri Chenarani, M., Hamidi, M., Akaberi, A., & Rezaei Ardani, A. (2015). The effectiveness of group assertiveness training on happiness in rural adolescent females with substance abusing parents. *Global Journal of Health Science, 8*(2), 156–164. https://doi.org/10.5539/gjhs.v8n2p156

Ibrahim, S. A. (2011). Factors affecting assertiveness among student nurses. *Nurse Education Today, 31*(4), 356–360. https://doi.org/10.1016/j.nedt.2010.07.006

Jewell, A. (2013). Supporting the novice nurse to fly: A literature review. *Nurse Education in Practice, 13*(4), 323–327. https://doi.org/10.1016/j.nepr.2013.04.006

Jiménez-Bernardino, E., Álvarez-Aguirre, A., Reyes-Rocha, B., Casique-Casique, L., Herrera-Paredes, J., & Sánchez-Perales, M. (2017). Health-promoting lifestyle and assertiveness in university workers. *Investigación y Educación en Enfermería, 35*(1), 26–34. https://doi.org/10.17533/udea.iee.v35n1a04

Keyes, C. L. M. (1998). Social well-being. *Social Psychology Quarterly, 61*(2), 121. https://doi.org/10.2307/2787065

Khademi Mofrad, S. H., & Mehrabi, T. (2015). The role of self-efficacy and assertiveness in aggression among high-school students in Isfahan. *Journal of Medicine and Life, 8*(Spec Iss 4), 225–231.

Khankeh, H., Khorasani-Zavareh, D., Hoseini, S. A., Khodai-Ardekandi, M. R., Ekman, S. L., Bohm, K., Nakhaie, M., Ranjbar, M., & Castrén, M. (2014). The journey between ideal and real: Experiences of beginners psychiatric nurses. *Iranian Journal of Nursing and Midwifery Research, 19*(4), 396–403.

Kılıç, S. P., & Sevinç, S. (2018). The relationship between cultural sensitivity and assertiveness in nursing students from Turkey. *Journal of Transcultural Nursing: Official Journal of the Transcultural Nursing Society, 29*(4), 379–386. https://doi.org/10.1177/1043659617716518

Kim, M. (2016). Development and effects of assertiveness training applying Dongsasub Training for nursing students in clinical practice. *Journal of Korean Academy of Nursing, 46*(4), 490–500. https://doi.org/10.4040/jkan.2016.46.4.490

Lee, S., Kim, E., Lee, J., & Morse, B. (2023). Assertiveness educational interventions for nursing students and nurses: A systematic review. *Nurse Education Today, 120*. https://doi.org/10.1016/j.nedt.2022.105655

Leeds-Hurtwitz, W. (2013). *Intercultural competences: Conceptual and operational framework*. UNESCO. https://unesdoc.unesco.org/ark:/48223/pf0000219768

Manesh, R. S., Fallahzadeh, S., Panah, M. S. E., Koochehbiuki, N., Arabi, A., & Sahami, M. A. (2015). The effectiveness of assertiveness training on social anxiety of health volunteers of Yazd. *Psychology, 6*, 782–787. https://doi.org/10.4236/psych.2015.66077

Mitamura, T. (2018). Developing the functional assertiveness scale: Measuring dimensions of objective effectiveness and pragmatic politeness. *Japanese Psychological Research, 60*, 99–110. https://doi.org/10.1111/jpr.12185

Morsink, J. (2009). *Inherent human rights: Philosophical roots of the Universal Declaration*. University of Pennsylvania Press.

Nakamura, Y., Yoshinaga, N., Tanoue, H., Kato, S., Nakamura, S., Aoishi, K., & Shiraishi, Y. (2017). Development and evaluation of a modified brief assertiveness training for nurses in the workplace: A single-group feasibility study. *BMC Nursing, 16*(29). https://doi.org/10.1186/s12912-017-0224-4

Neijmeijer, L., Korzilius, H., Kroon, H., Nijman, H., & Didden, R. (2020). Flexible assertive community treatment for individuals with mild intellectual disability or borderline intellectual functioning: Client variables associated with treatment outcome. *Advances in Mental Health and Intellectual Disabilities, 14*(6), 199–212.

Nickel, J. (2021). Human rights. In E. N. Zalta (Ed.), *The Stanford encyclopedia of philosophy*. https://plato.stanford.edu/archives/fall2021/entries/rights-human/

Niyogi, J., Yesodharan, R., & Dsa, R. J. (2020). Relationship between emotional intelligence, self-esteem, and assertiveness among South Indian youth: A descriptive, cross-sectional study from Karnataka. *Indian Journal of Public Health, 64*(4), 402–404. https://doi.org/10.4103/ijph.IJPH_584_19

Noh, G., & Kim, M. (2021). Effectiveness of assertiveness training, SBAR, and combined SBAR and assertiveness training for nursing students undergoing clinical training: A quasi-experimental study. *Nurse Education Today, 103*. https://doi.org/10.1016/j.nedt.2021.104958

Okbani, R., Batouche, D., Lahmer, M., & Benatta, N. (2019). The self-assertiveness sentiment of hypertensive patients. *Archives of Cardiovascular Diseases Supplements, 11*(3), e374–e375. https://doi.org/10.1016/j.acvdsp.2019.05.105

Omura, M., Levett-Jones, T., & Stone, T. E. (2019). Design and evaluation of an assertiveness communication training programme for nursing students. *Journal of Clinical Nursing, 28*(9–10), 1990–1998. https://doi.org/10.1111/jocn.14813

Omura, M., Maguire, J., Levett-Jones, T., & Stone, T. E. (2016). Effectiveness of assertive communication training programs for health professionals and students: A systematic review protocol. *JBI Database of Systematic Reviews and Implementation Reports, 14*(10), 64–71. https://doi.org/10.11124/JBISRIR-2016-003158

Organization for Economic Cooperation and Development/ Open Society Foundations. (2019). Overview of legal needs surveys and access to justice. In *Legal needs surveys and access to justice*. OECD Publishing. https://doi.org/10.1787/001fafb8-en

Pades Jiménez, A., García-Buades, M. E., & Riquelme, I. (2023). Development of emotional intelligence and assertiveness in physiotherapy students and effects of clinical placements. *Physiotherapy Theory and Practice, 39*(1), 72–79. https://doi.org/10.1080/09593985.2021.2005200

Parray, W. M., & Kumar, S. (2016). Assertiveness among undergraduate students of the university. *The International Journal of Indian Psychology, 4*(1), 203–291. https://doi.org/10.25215/0476.021

Pfafman, T. (2020). Assertiveness. In V. Zeigler-Hill & T. K. Shackelford (Eds.), *Encyclopedia of personality and individual differences.* Springer. https://doi.org/10.1007/978-3-319-24612-3_1044

Pfafman, T. M., & McEwan, B. (2014). Polite women at work: Negotiating professional identity through strategic assertiveness. *Women's Studies in Communication, 37*(2), 202–219. https://doi.org/10.1080/07491409.2014.911231

Phillips, A. (2013). *Developing assertiveness skills for health and social care professionals* (1st ed.). Routledge.

Plantade-Gipch, A., Bruno, J., Strub, L., Bouvard, M., & Martin-Krumm, C. (2023). Emotional regulation, attachment style, and assertiveness as determinants of well-being in emerging adults. *Frontiers in Education, 8.* https://doi.org/10.3389/feduc.2023.1058519

Ramadhan, I., Keliat, B. A., & Wardani, I. Y. (2019). Assertiveness training and family psychoeducational therapies on adolescents' mental resilience in the prevention of drug use in boarding schools. *Enfermería Clínica, 29*(S2), 326–330. https://doi.org/10.1016/j.enfcli.2019.04.040

Royce, A. (2009). A definition of peace. *Peace and Conflict: Journal of Peace Psychology, 10*(2), 101–116. https://doi.org/10.1207/s15327949pac1002_2

Sousa, A. E. d., & Costa, L. F. A. d. (2017). Abordagem Sistêmica Comunitária: Avaliação de um Serviço Socioterapêutico de Saúde Mental em Fortaleza. *Conhecer: Debate Entre O Público E O Privado, 7*(18), 72–90. https://doi.org/10.32335/2238-0426.2017.7.18.324

United Nations Children's Fund. (n.d.). *Mission #9-respect for diversity. Plan 12-Learn to transform.* https://www.unicef.org/lac/en/mission-9-respect-diversity

United Nations Educational, Scientific and Cultural Organization. (2011). *36C/5 Addendum: Draft resolution 2012–2013.* UNESCO. unesdoc.unesco.org/images/0021/002108/210832e.pdf

United Nations Educational, Scientific and Cultural Organization. (2013). *Intercultural competencies: Conceptual and operational framework.* UNESCO.

United Nations Office for Project Services. (2022). *Gender equality and social inclusion mainstreaming in projects strategy 2022–2025.* UNOPS. https://content.unops.org/publications/UNOPS-GESI-Mainstreaming-in-Projects-Strategy_EN.pdf

Vincent, C., Riley, B. B., & Wilkie, D. J. (2015). Developing items to measure theory of planned behaviour constructs for opioid administration for children: Pilot testing. *Pain Management Nursing, 16*(6), 900–909. https://doi.org/10.1016/j.pmn.2015.07.005

Wolpe, J. (1958). *Psychotherapy by reciprocal inhibition*. Stanford University Press.

Yılmaz, F., & Göçen, S. (2013). Sınıf öğretmeni adaylarının kültürlerarası duyarlılık hakkındaki görüşlerinin farklı değişkenlere göre incelenmesi [Investigation of the prospective primary teachers' intercultural sensitivity levels in terms of certain variables]. *Adıyaman Üniversitesi Sosyal Bilimler Enstitüsü Dergisi, 15*, 373–392.

Yoshinaga, N., Nakamura, Y., Tanoue, H., MacLiam, F., Aoishi, K., & Shiraishi, Y. (2018). Is modified brief assertiveness training for nurses effective? A single-group study with long-term follow-up. *Journal of Nursing Management, 26*(1), 59–65. https://doi.org/10.1111/jonm.12521

PART I

Assertiveness as a Human Right and Virtue

Virtue is the health of the soul. It gives a flavour to the smallest leaves of life.
Joseph Joubert

Following the introduction of this edited collection, this first part comprises three chapters thoroughly addressing assertiveness as a human right critical for strengthening human potential and achieving maximum personal fulfilment. It expands on how assertiveness is associated with human rights and is a right. Thus, it traces assertiveness roots from a philosophical perspective, particularly the Aristotelian view, regarding assertiveness as a virtue for social well-being and personal development. It explores how assertiveness as a human right provides the means necessary for empowering individuals and fully exercising their rights. It also states that studying assertive rights and their corresponding responsibilities is essential for effectively exercising the right to be assertive. Exercising these assertive rights requires knowledge of human rights and education in assertive rights. Lastly, it addresses how assertiveness is not embedded in Mexican legislation. Nonetheless, it is partially considered in international treaties.

Therefore, this part provides the foundation for introducing the concept of assertiveness as a virtue based on a human rights perspective.

CHAPTER 2

Assertiveness and Human Rights Origins, Exercise, Education and Duties: How Assertiveness Can Help Us Better Understand Human Rights

Juan Francisco Díez-Spelz

Introduction

This chapter will explore the relationship between human rights and assertiveness to better understand its meaning and practice. The author will compare both concepts to find common connection points. Surprisingly, few studies show the relationship between assertiveness and human rights. Perhaps that is because a culture of human rights privileges only the fact that human beings can claim rights in general and does not analyse what an assertive exercise of rights means in contexts of coexistence. Nevertheless, it is crucial to comprehend why it is fundamental to refer to rights when defining assertiveness.

J. F. Díez-Spelz (✉)
Facultad de Derecho, Universidad Panamericana, Mexico City, Mexico
e-mail: jfdiez@up.edu.mx

S. Castaños-Cervantes, C. Atristain-Suárez (eds.), *Assertiveness in the Context of Human Rights, Ethics, and Classical Virtues*,
https://doi.org/10.1007/978-3-031-60962-6_2

The chapter will analyse some of the connections between these two ideas to prove that, to understand one better, we must pay attention to the other. Therefore, this chapter is divided into four parts: (i) some ideas that connect human rights to the concept of assertiveness are explored; (ii) a reflection on what it means to exercise a right and why it is important to exercise them assertively is stated; (iii) one of the main aspects to find the connection between rights and assertiveness is through education, so in the third part, the author will study the concept of human rights education (HRE) and (iv) finally, the fourth section will present an important idea: to understand human rights through the lenses of assertiveness, we need to also focus in the concept of "human duties".

Some Ideas About Assertiveness and Human Rights

There is no doubt that we live nowadays in a time of rights. As Katherine McNeilly identifies, "human rights are now the primary means to evaluate the past, analyse the present and draw progress towards the future" (McNeilly, 2019, p. 817). The element "rights" in various definitions of assertiveness is one of the main ones. We could say that the exercise of rights in an "assertive" way is essential to the concept of assertiveness and for the idea of human rights. According to the *Great Psychological Dictionary*, "Assertiveness is the ability of a person to defend his rights confidently and gracefully without violating the rights of others. Assertive is a specific, overt behaviour not intended to harm others". *The Concise Oxford Dictionary* defines assertiveness as: "Forthright, positive, insistence on recognising one's rights".

Assertiveness is a concept typically referred to as social and communication skills. It means the ability of human beings to communicate or behave in a way that can bring them to collective objectives easier. Also, the concept of assertiveness is linked to two ideas: on the one hand, the ability to express thoughts and feelings, interests and opinions in a respectful way; on the other hand, it means to treat others with respect and consideration. However, we can also add that it should refer to how we, as human beings, can ask for fair treatment, that is, to claim "rights" towards other human beings, the State or business corporations, to mention just some of them.

As Hearns points out, "assertiveness means standing up for our rights and expressing thoughts, feelings and beliefs directly, honestly and appropriately" (Hearns, 2021, p. 7). In his book *Your Perfect Right*, we find out that assertiveness means "living on an equal footing with other people in your life" (Alberti, 2017, p. 10). Being assertive means expressing oneself in neither an aggressive nor passive way. However, in any case, it is notorious that to evaluate assertive behaviour, we must exercise our rights, considering the rights of others. Hearns claims:

> Assertive self-expression is direct, firm, positive – and, when necessary, persistent – action intended to promote equality in person-to-person relationships. Assertiveness enables us "to act in our own best interests, to stand up for ourselves without undue anxiety, to exercise personal rights without denying the rights of others, and to express our feelings and needs (affection, love, friendship, disappointment, annoyance, anger, regret, sorrow) honestly and comfortably". (Hearns, 2021, p. 17)

Another interesting point is that assertiveness gained popularity precisely because of the civil rights movement. Since its origins, assertiveness has been linked to the study of rights because when we talk about rights, we refer to human relations in which assertive conduct can have an effect. As Peneva and Mavrodiev state:

> [The civil rights movement] highlighted the value and equality of every human being and required the rejection of any benefits in interpersonal relationships associated with social status. In connection with this, several psychologists working in human relationships began to attach importance to "protecting individual rights as a means of self-assertion and as one of the characteristics of assertive behaviour". (Peneva & Mavrodiev, 2013, p. 8)

According to Peneva and Mavrodiev (2013), when the civil rights movement began in the United States, psychologists like Alberti and Emmons or Jakubowski and Lange noted how assertiveness could affect how we protect human rights without affecting the fundamental rights of others. The relationship between human rights and assertive conduct is strong.

For instance, we should refer to Jakubowski and Lange's list of fundamental assertive rights when discussing assertiveness. This list was created by and defined assertiveness as an act of protecting one's human rights without violating the fundamental rights of others. Therefore, to define assertiveness, considering how people exercise their rights or interests, is pivotal. In other words, assertiveness should set the boundaries between one's human rights and the rights of others to maintain the stability of those limits.

The list of the fundamental assertive rights includes, among others, "the right to act in a manner that promoted own dignity and self-respect, as long as this person did not violate the rights of the others with his/her behaviour", "the right to be treated with respect", "the right to take the necessary time to calm down and think", "the right to make mistakes" or "the right to feel good about oneself". As we might see, these rights are strongly related to the exigencies of human dignity (Jakubowski & Lange, 1978).

However, the development of assertiveness relates to more than just the civil rights movement in the United States. However, it can also be found in the International Human Rights Law context. The origins of this field of International Law are connected to situations where a lack of respect for human rights can be identified and circumstances that did not permit an assertive exercise of rights. Paragraph 52 to the Advisory Opinion 26 of the Inter-American Court of Human Rights summarises the origins of IHRL in the years after the Second World War:

> 52. Indeed, the modern development of the international law of treaties accelerated in the aftermath of the Second World War, a historical moment when, faced with the serious, massive and systematic violations committed, the international community considered it necessary to *reaffirm the importance of human dignity and universal, interdependent and indivisible respect for the human rights and fundamental freedoms of all human beings without distinction.* It resulted in the international codification of those rights and freedoms to ensure their practical application, thereby allowing individuals *to claim these at the international level* whenever a State fails in its duty to respect, guarantee and offer integral reparation. The primary instruments of the modern inter-American system proclaim that the rights "based on attributes of the human personality" must be subject to international protection under the American Declaration and the American Convention. It reinforces the catalogue of fundamental rights and, in turn, expands the prospects of access to justice since human rights treaties are endowed with specific oversight mechanisms to safeguard their effective implementation. (CO-26, Inter-American Court of Human Rights, 2020)

Indeed, the development of IHRL has reaffirmed the importance of human dignity and the universal respect of human rights without distinction, which hints at the assertiveness of human behaviour and the actions of governments or other social actors. Also, it is relevant to notice that IHRL allows human beings to claim these rights at an international level when the actions of the State have not been assertive in respecting their rights. In that sense, we can say that "assertiveness" has been an implicit feature of IHRL since its origins and still is today. We could refer to the Universal Declaration of Human Rights (1948) to reinforce this argument. It is one of the first international documents that proclaimed human rights as rights that should be respected by all States, individuals and social groups. The Preamble of the Declaration states:

> Whereas recognition of the inherent dignity and the equal and inalienable rights of all members of the human family is the foundation of freedom, justice and peace in the world.

We can suppose that recognising the foundation of freedom, justice and peace as objectives of rights in a "common and inherent dignity to all members of the human family" brings us to the idea that, to be and behave assertively, we need to live on an equal footing with other human beings. But also, we need to focus on the obligation contained in Article 1 to the UDHR that reads as follows:

> All human beings are born free and equal in dignity and rights. They are endowed with reason and conscience and *should act towards one another in a spirit of brotherhood.*

The reference to the acting necessity under a brotherhood spirit is another connection to how human rights should be exercised in an "assertive" way that enables others' rights recognition. For that to occur, it is also vital for the international community to create the conditions for assertiveness to happen in the context of human rights. In that order of ideas, the Preamble to the International Covenant on Civil and Political Rights states:

> Recognising that, under the Universal Declaration of Human Rights, the ideal of free human beings enjoying civil and political freedom and freedom from fear and want can only be achieved if conditions are created whereby everyone may enjoy his civil and political rights, as well as his economic, social and cultural rights,

The ideas in this paragraph refer to the four freedoms proclaimed by President Roosevelt in his 1941 State to the Union Speech: the freedom of the word, the freedom of religion, the freedom from fear and the freedom of want (Roosevelt, 1941). In this paragraph, there is a hint of interdependence between rights, which is a very relevant aspect to consider their assertive exercise in every context. Because we can infer it is essential to experience adequate living conditions to interact assertively with others. These conditions enable human beings to exercise their rights, not only civil and political rights but also economic, social and cultural ones.

In 1949, UNESCO published *Human Rights: Comments and Interpretations,* a study about the nature of human rights. We should remember that in those years the Human Rights Commission of the United Nations was discussing the Universal Declaration of Human Rights (Glendon, 2011). So, the concept was a controversial one that needed reflection. The study brought different voices from around the world to suggest interpretations of the meaning of human rights. In the chapter "A Fragment of Thoughts Concerning the Nature and the Fulfilment of Human Rights", Professor Arnold J. Lien claimed:

> Since rights exist only in the sphere of the relations of man to man, the occasions for *asserting* them arise when they are threatened, restrained, or suppressed. Bills of rights, therefore, "never have been and probably cannot be complete and definitive catalogues of the rights of man". (Lien, 1948, p. 11)

Therefore, the interest in assertiveness goes hand in hand with the interest in human rights. The human rights movement gained popularity in the second half of the twentieth century and was the first approach to assertive behaviour training in psychology. The connection between the two concepts is, at least, paradoxical. Some psychologists, such as Smith, have "emphasised that the ability to protect own human rights humanely and democratically, without prejudice to the fundamental rights of others, was among the important characteristics of assertive conduct" (Peneva & Mavrodiev, 2013, p. 4). In any case, one of the paradoxes of the link between the two concepts is that of how we, as human beings, exercise those rights.

Assertiveness and Human Rights: An Exercise of a Right

Norberto Bobbio suggests that exercising a right would be very simple because human rights seem attached to a peculiar moral feeling shared by all human beings—nothing genuine in that supposition. "The exercise of any right, particularly human rights, is highly complex" (Bobbio, 2014, p. 38). Moreover, it is complex because of the internal problems of human interaction. Most conflicts of rights happen in the context of interactions. That is why it is not the same to be entitled to a right as to exercise it. Usually, when we only understand rights as "claims", they should be enforced without restriction.

Since the author first started studying human rights, one of his main concerns was the problems we usually face when we understand rights only as claims (Díez, 2014). It seems today that having a right entitles a person to claim an interest in any manner they can, whether it is assertive or aggressive. If the focus of a study of human rights is only the possibility of claiming something from someone in any manner, their practice exercise can turn out to be violent. If we care only about our interests as individuals, we might claim what we think is ours in any way we can, regardless of the legitimacy of the entitlement. We should consider whether exercising a human right aggressively indeed accounts for a human right.

One of the main elements for a human right to authentically be one is how legal subjects exercise them. First, it is a very relevant aspect of assertiveness and rights to consider all human beings as legal persons. Otherwise, an assertive action towards the other could not be possible. Article 16 of the International Covenant on Civil and Political Rights states:

> *Everyone shall have the right to recognition everywhere as a person before the law.*

Being recognised as a person before the law is necessary for the individual to be fully entitled to rights; therefore, it would be difficult to exercise them assertively. However, this brings us to the problem of defining who is a legal person. Tanzil Chowdhury identifies—following Ngaire Naffine—three possibilities:

a. The first one accepts that to be a legal person is subject to legal rights and duties as conferred by legislation. The problem with this aspect is that it operates at a very high level of abstraction. It does not care for metaphysical speculations or concrete scenarios where it would be necessary to encounter "the other" to exercise rights. In that sense, we should only focus on the existence of a given legislation that recognises some entity or individual as a person before the law.

b. The second approach would recognise "any reasonable creature in being". It is a conception that goes back to biological and metaphysical definitions of humanity to sustain that all human beings are subjects before the law for our shared humanity. The theory of human rights generally follows this approach.
c. The third perspective is—in Chowdhury's terms—the most pervasive one. It could be called the "paradigmatic rationalist" or the point of view of the "responsible subject" as an active, autonomous actor who can bear legal duties and assert legal rights. It would be "the ideal legal actor to claim and assert rights properly" (Chowdhury, 2020, pp. 74–75).

In the legal complexity of determining who and why a person is, it is essential to understand what it means to have a right and *assert* it. Samuel Moyn uses an interesting thought experiment to illustrate this point. He refers to Croesus as an individual who owns all the property in each circumstance. Croesus is highly generous and ensures everyone sees his necessities fulfilled (Moyn, 2018). In the context presented by Moyn, the right holders receive their part and, therefore, correctly exercise their rights. However, if only understood as passive agents who claim rights to satisfy their necessities, those persons would not be exercising or asserting their rights but only receiving them. As Jones says, "[t]his fails to capture the sense in which people are agents, active in the world and enabled by secure rights to do things, to engage in activities rather than merely receive benefits" (Jones, 2021, p. 229).

On the other hand, Donnelley talks about three ways in which subjects can exercise rights. He calls how social interaction can happen.

a. *Assertive exercise of a right:* the right is claimed or exercised, and the duty-bearer responds by respecting or violating the right. As a result of this assertive exercise of the right, the right is enjoyed or not in the most vital sense.
b. *Direct enjoyment of a right:* in which the duty-bearer takes a right actively into account in determining how he or she will behave. So,

we can speak of the right being respected or violated and even enjoyed. In this case, there is no claim of the right by the right-holder.

c. *Objective enjoyment of the right:* The right is respected despite no exercise. It should be the norm, in the sense that if everyone recognises the other as a legal subject entitled to some rights, they should be respected without hesitation. (Donnelly, 1989, p. 11).

As we can see, Donnelly refers precisely to an "assertive" exercise of a right as the circumstance in which the right-holder actively claims the right. In contrast, an objective enjoyment of a right might seem passive in some way. It may need two comments. In the first place, it is valid and interesting that the assertion of a right entails dynamic behaviour from the individual. However, as we will see, to be assertive should consist of not only claiming "rights" but also being able to consider "other's rights". In the second place, although an objective enjoyment of a right, in Donnelly's terms, seems like a passive response, it is the ideal situation for human rights assertion. We could guess that assertive attitudes that could be identified in how individuals treat others would make it unnecessary to claim rights or necessities expressly, but that would happen because of our behaviour towards others.

However, this ideal situation is inaccurate because of the endless possibility of human conflict, for the case of people ignoring other's necessities. In this sense, it is interesting to question ourselves about the needs we should consider building an assertive behaviour towards rights. In this sense, there are different approaches. For instance, John Finnis identifies seven basic needs: practical reflection, life, knowledge, play, aesthetic experience, sociability, practical reasonableness and religion (Finnis, 2011). Also, Tony Robbins says there are six core human needs: certainty, variety, significance, love and connection, growth, and contribution (Robbins, n.d., *blog*). These authors agree that the needs we must focus on when clarifying the exercise of rights are not only material but also intellectual and based on the quality of relationships we have towards others.

Therefore, both an assertive or an objective exercise or enjoyment of a human right require a focus on human needs in the sense of recognising the interests and necessities of other persons. Depending on the context, asserting a right by clearly claiming it or behaving in a way that creates the conditions for objectively enjoying a right would be necessary. In the two cases, there could be conditions to observe an assertive exercise of a right. However, while exercising rights, we can also see manifestations of passive or aggressive ways in which persons pretend to satisfy interests or needs. That is why King says, "Assertiveness is not only standing for your rights but doing it calmly, considering others' needs" (King, 2017, p. 7). Moreover, this is important because "assertiveness requires a delicate balance" (King, 2017, p. 15) between passive and aggressive behaviour.

Rob Grace states that norms must know the link between human needs and interests. Legal standards can reflect coherence between both realities and make unnecessary claims to respect them. However, legal norms can also reflect opposition in those aspects. That would make necessary an intervention to formulate laws that help create conditions towards asserting rights. However, the most common situation is compatibility, in which we can observe legal norms that align human needs and interests but still have an essential task to make them defend themselves in everyday situations (Grace, 2022).

However, exercising a human right depends not only on the existence of norms but also on how legal subjects consider their rights and the rights of others. It should consider how legislation treats human beings as legal persons and our human nature and how we interact with others to promote the education of "responsible subjects". There is a possibility towards assertiveness in exercising rights only when human needs and interests align. Furthermore, although legal norms are essential to creating these conditions, they can only authentically be developed through education.

Assertiveness and Human Rights Education

Human rights and assertiveness are also correlated to human rights education. According to some authors, such as Simpkins (2013), the civil rights movement has failed because there has been a lack of human rights education. An education on human rights is mainly related to how people exercise them in real life, coexist with others, and develop a whole human personality. As Article 26 of the UDHR states:

> Education shall be directed to fully develop the human personality and strengthen respect for human rights and fundamental freedoms. It shall promote understanding, tolerance, and friendship among all nations, racial or religious groups and shall further the activities of the United Nations to maintain peace.

Therefore, promoting human rights as a tool for assertive behaviour must be focused on how education can fulfil the necessities of one as a human person and others. In other words, a human rights education needs to promote the mechanisms for an assertive exercise of human rights, capable of creating the conditions for recognising everyone, everywhere and everywhere, as "a person before the law", as stated in Article 16 of the ICCPR.

Education on human rights also means the person should have the tools to behave assertively and stand for her rights in every situation. Article XII of the American Declaration of the Rights and Duties of Man of 1948 states:

> **Article XII.** Every person has the right to an education, which should be based on the principles of liberty, morality, and human solidarity. Likewise, every person has the right to an education that will prepare him to attain a decent life, raise his standard of living, and be a valuable member of society. The right to an education includes the right to equality of opportunity in every case, under natural talents, merit, and the desire to utilise the resources that the State or the community is in a position to provide. Every person has the right to receive, free, at least a primary education.

The position of this chapter is exciting because it hints at the purposes of education and the exercise of rights. On the one hand, the right to education must promote liberty, morality and human solidarity, that is, the capacity to establish assertive relationships with other human beings. Nevertheless, it is also relevant to consider that education on human rights should prepare the person to attain a decent life, raise the standard of living and be a valuable member of society. They do not mean the capacity for claiming and waiting to receive but to stand for oneself based on conditions, merit and other aspects that promote justice and equality. If we understand this together with the necessity of human solidarity, we will have a fascinating point of departure to reflect upon the meaning of asserting rights.

In this sense, the International Covenant on Economic, Social and Cultural Rights (ICESCR) agrees that education shall be directed to the full development of the human person and her dignity. Article 13 of the ICESCR states as follows:

Article 13

1. The States Parties to the present Covenant recognise the right of everyone to education. *They agree that education shall be directed to the full development of the human personality and the sense of its dignity and shall strengthen the respect for human rights and fundamental freedoms.* They further agree that education shall enable all persons to participate effectively in a free society, promote understanding, tolerance, and friendship among all nations and all racial, ethnic or religious groups, and further the activities of the United Nations to maintain peace.

Education on human rights is a means towards assertiveness. As we can see from the wording of Article 13 of the ICESCR, a right to education, in general, must be directed towards the person's full development. If that does not happen, education fails. However, it also requires strengthening respect for others' rights, enabling the person to participate in society. Education on human rights should be focused on convincing persons to train themselves in an assertive exercise of rights in coexistence with others.

According to Felisa Tibbitts, there are three models of human rights education in formal and non-formal realms. Firstly, it should be a means to promote *values and awareness* about the rights and dignity of all human beings. Secondly, it should advance the *accountability* of social actors. Lastly, it should foster social and personal *transformation and change* (Tibbitts, 2017). However, for these three factors to impact reality, they must be linked to an assertive exercise of rights. It does not only mean that people in very different domains will be humanly rights-educated just for knowing the name or even the content of human rights. We must recognise their values and the possible effects of breaching obligations. We also need to imagine how a new society could be created through the assertive practice of human rights.

Nevertheless, for all those purposes, education on human rights needs to be centred on practices that promote universal respect for all human beings' dignity. In this sense, the General Assembly of the United Nations published, in December 2011, a Declaration on Human Rights Education and Training. Article 2 of this document states:

1. Human rights education and training comprise all educational, training, information, awareness-raising and learning activities aimed at *promoting universal respect for and observance of all human rights and fundamental freedoms* and thus contributing, among other things, to the prevention of human rights violations and abuses by *providing persons with knowledge, skills*

> *and understanding and developing their attitudes and behaviours*, to empower them to contribute to the building and promotion of a universal culture of human rights.

Let us analyse some aspects of this definition in an assertiveness key. On the one hand, education on this topic must promote universal respect for human rights and help persons understand their content to develop attitudes and behaviours to build a culture coherent with human rights. In this sense, education on human rights needs promotes the understanding of their content and empowers persons to enjoy or exercise their rights in a way that respects others' rights. It is, precisely, the link between human rights and assertiveness. Education is, therefore, a bridge that connects both concepts. Governments and other actors, such as business corporations or other institutions, are responsible for preventing human rights abuses and influencing the actions of all individuals to transform them to be coherent with the exigencies of human rights (Tibbitts, 2017).

In 2021, the high-level panel discussion on the tenth anniversary of the United Nations Declaration on Human Rights Education and Training: Good Practices, challenges and the way forward reflected upon the challenges of human rights education, especially for the youth, in a global circumstance framed by the pandemic. It was stated that "human rights education was an essential part of the realisation of [all] human rights" and that all sectors of society should participate in understanding those rights better, in theory and practice.

It takes us to the "relational epistemology for human rights education" concept, as Al-Daraweesh and Snauwaert (2014) suggest. One of the main points in this aspiration would be the "relational" one because we usually practise rights concerning others. Therefore, an educational standpoint should help communicate and teach how people should exercise their rights. According to these authors, ideas such as laws, morality, religion or, for this context, "human rights" are a "product of language that should reflect the material structure of society" (Al-Daraweesh & Snauwaert, 2014, p. 53). However, there are different approaches to how society translates the inner meaning of human rights. The latter perceive human rights as assertive claims in the community, in the sense that being assertive demands recognition of human needs and interests (Al-Daraweesh & Snauwaert, 2014). Therefore, through human rights education, assertiveness should promote a fusion of horizons between members of society, including "everything that can be seen from a particular vantage point" (Al-Daraweesh & Snauwaert, 2014, p. 59).

According to Struthers, education on human rights should encompass a commitment to transmit knowledge *about* human rights, but also doing it *through* the exercise of rights and *for* an assertive exercise of these rights. He states, "[t]he three elements of the framework are complementary, and any single one in isolation would need more than one for compliance. Thus, more than just learning about human rights is required. However, building such a culture through education on human rights can only occur with fundamental human rights knowledge" (Struthers, 2014). This framework derives from Article 2.2 of the Declaration on Human Rights Education and Training:

> 2.2. Human rights education and training encompass:
> (a) Education *about* human rights, which includes providing knowledge and understanding of human rights norms and principles, the values that underpin them and the mechanisms for their protection;
> (b) Education *through* human rights, which includes learning and teaching in a way that respects the rights of both educators and learners;
> (c) Education *for* human rights, which includes empowering persons to enjoy and exercise their rights and to respect and uphold the rights of others.

Back in 1949, Arnold Lien stated:

> From the primitive to the contemporary, education (not to be confused with propaganda or indoctrination) has had as its central aim the guidance and training of the individual for the responsible and successful exercise of this right. Nowhere is there "any principle of nature or religion or science or reason which assigns prenatally one man to be master and one to be enslaved, one to be a pauper and one to be the prince (...) these human rights have been wantonly disregarded and suppressed throughout the history of man by all sorts of (...) regimes". (Lien, 1948, p. 12)

In this sense, the cause of forgetting the main objectives of human rights corresponds to a need for authentic education on how all human beings can be responsible and successfully exercise their rights. That is, in an assertive manner. Education is vital because no one can naturally expand all of the potential in the relationships we establish with other human beings. The mere possibility of behaving passively or aggressively when claiming legitimate rights is an invitation to promote education on what it means to be entitled to rights and how they interact with the rights of others.

Assertiveness and "Human Duties"

Finally, speaking of "human duties" is necessary to discuss assertive human rights. If we only understand human rights as claims we are entitled to, we likely exercise them aggressively. According to Jakubowski and Lange (1978), accepting individual rights should be linked to taking greater responsibilities, and it would be necessary to strike a balance between rights and obligations. In the book mentioned above, *Human Rights: Comments and Interpretations*, Mahatma Gandhi stated in a letter to the editor (Julian Huxley) that he apologised for not being able to complete a contribution, for lack of both time and knowledge about the concept and that

> I learnt from my illiterate but wise mother that all rights to be deserved and preserved came from duty well done. Thus, the very right to live accrues to us only when we do the duty of citizenship of the world. From this one fundamental statement, perhaps it is easy to define the duties of Man and Woman and correlate every right to some corresponding duty to be first performed. Every other right can be considered a "usurpation hardly worth fighting for". (Gandhi, 1948, p. 3)

Gandhi's appreciable scepticism about human rights is only understood as rights can be dangerous in enabling the government or other institutions to deny someone the enjoyment of any right under the argument of not having accomplished some duty. Nevertheless, it is true that to understand human rights better, we must think about corresponding responsibilities to be completed by everyone as citizens of the world. It can be related to the fact that, as Hearns states, "[a]ssertiveness reflects genuine converse for everybody's right" (Hearns, 2021, p. 12).

The author accepts the premise that to consider human rights as authentic manifestations of the worth of every human being, we must also consider human beings as "duty bearers", for that would be a better manner to exercise human rights assertively. That is a promotion of anthropology that correlates rights and duties. As Jones suggests:

> Suppose there is a type of individualism to which human rights are committed. In that case, it is a "moral individualism that emphasises the worth and dignity of every individual human being as a holder of civil, political, social, and economic rights while recognising the social nature of persons and the implied commitment to others in accepting duties generated by human rights. (Jones, 2021, p. 223)

Human rights suppose there should be a commitment towards recognising everyone as bearers of human dignity and comprehending persons, governments and institutions as duty-bearers towards others' rights. Human rights, therefore, also generate "human duties", which are means to foster assertive behaviours. If understood from this perspective, which reflects a commitment of all human beings towards the values and transformation encompassed in human rights, it is easier to promote assertiveness in human and social interactions.

This idea is also reflected in some international documents on human rights, which also consider the importance of duties towards others' rights. We can, for instance, recall Article 1 of the UDHR:

> All human beings are born free and equal in dignity and rights. They are endowed with reason and conscience and *should act towards one another in a spirit of brotherhood.*

Also, it is stated in the American Declaration of the Rights and *Duties of Man*, 1948. In this document, the correlation between both concepts is patent. In direct reference to what we can call assertiveness, the following article refers directly to the behaviour of individuals towards others to develop our personality:

> Article XXIX. The individual must conduct himself concerning others so that each person may fully form and develop his personality.

But also, the International Covenant on Civil and Political Rights in its Preamble states:

> Realising that the individual, *having duties to other individuals and to the community* to which he belongs, is under a responsibility to strive for the promotion and observance of the rights recognised in the present Covenant.

The duties we all have as right-bearers are referred not only to other individuals but also to the community or the world in which we live. The American Convention on Human Rights embodies this idea in the following article:

> **Article 32. Relationship between Duties and Rights**
> 1. Every person has responsibilities to their family, community, and humankind.
> 2. The rights of each person are limited by the rights of others, by the security of all, and by the just demands of the general welfare in a democratic society.

The African Charter on Human and Peoples Rights says in its Preamble:

> Considering that the enjoyment of rights and freedoms also implies the performance of duties on the part of everyone.

It is interesting to note that the African Charter also recognises that to exercise rights and duties properly, it is necessary to foster a better understanding of their content through education:

> **Article 25**
> States parties to the present Charter shall have the duty to promote and ensure, through teaching, education and publication, the respect of the rights and freedoms contained in the present Charter and to see to it that these freedoms and rights, as well as corresponding obligations and duties, are understood.

Like the American Convention on Human Rights, the African Charter recognises:

> **Article 27**
> 1. Every individual shall have duties towards their family and society, the State and other legally recognised communities, and the international community.
> 2. The rights and freedoms of everyone shall be exercised with due regard to the rights of others, collective security, morality and common interest.

As for a possible definition of an assertive exercise of rights, this document states:

> **Article 28**
>
> Everyone shall be responsible for respecting and considering their fellow beings without discrimination and maintaining relations to promote, safeguard and reinforce mutual respect and tolerance.

International references to human duties must be considered to foster a better understanding of human rights in the context of assertiveness. If the latter means to stand for our rights, it also signifies the existence of duties towards others, society and the international community.

Conclusions

In this chapter, we have presented some ideas relating to the human rights concept and assertiveness. In this sense, we can conclude that

1. Both the concepts of assertiveness and human rights relate. Not only because the assertiveness definition includes the necessity for the person to stand for her rights but also because the origins of both concepts interact. The beginning of the civil rights movement in the United States and internationally is contemporary, with the first approaches to "assertiveness" in other fields, such as psychology.
2. The exercise of human rights can be passive, aggressive or assertive. Being any of them depends on two aspects: how we understand others and ourselves as legal subjects and how we stand for our rights, whether considering or not the rights of others. The purpose of every exercise of human rights, to be authentic, is to promote assertive behaviours that acknowledge our needs and interests.
3. The author suggests that promoting an assertive exercise of these rights depends mainly on education. This kind of instruction must be focused on better understanding the meaning and contents of human rights and convincing people to internalise the contents of these rights to transform behaviours. It is the education framework about, through and for human rights in contexts of values and awareness, accountability and transformation.
4. The assertive exercise of rights through education shall be based on the idea that we bear rights and responsibilities that we can call

"human duties". To assertively claim a right, we must consider our duties towards other individuals, the family, the country or the international community. This idea is so essential that it is recognised in many international treaties.

5. Finally, the author would like to make a precision for future research. To discuss an assertive exercise of rights, we must reflect upon the nature of the rights we claim. An assertive exercise of rights requires individuals to be entitled to those rights. In other words, if those rights we base our pretension on are authentically human rights that acknowledge the rights of others.

References

Alberti, R. (2017/1974). *Your perfect right: Assertiveness and equality in your life and relationships* (Kindle ed.). Impact.

Al-Daraweesh, F., & Snauwaert, D. T. (2014). *Human rights education beyond universalism and relativism: A relational hermeneutic for global justice*. Palgrave Macmillan.

Bobbio, N. (2014). *L'Etá dei Diritti*. Torino, Giulio Einaudi editore.

Chowdhury, T. (2020). *Time, temporality and legal judgement*. Routledge.

Díez, J. (2014). *El problema de la autenticidad de los derechos humanos. Una aproximación a través del pensamiento ontofenomenológico de Sergio Cotta (The problem of the authenticity of human rights. An approach through the ontophenomenological thinking of Sergio Cotta)*. Universidad Panamericana.

Donnelly, J. (1989). *Universal human rights in theory and practice*. Cornell University Press.

Finnis, J. (2011). *Natural law & natural rights* (2nd ed.). Oxford University Press.

Gandhi, M. (1948). *A letter addressed to the Director General of UNESCO. Human rights: Comments and interpretations*. UNESCO.

Glendon, M. A. (2011). *Un mundo nuevo. Eleanor Roosevelt y la Declaración Universal de Derechos Humanos (A new world. Eleanor Roosevelt and the Universal Declaration of Human Rights)*. Fondo de Cultura Económica-Comisión de Derechos Humanos del Distrito Federal-Universidad Panamericana.

Grace, R. (2022). Incrementalism in international lawmaking: The development of normative frameworks of protection for forcibly displaced persons. In K. P. Van der Ploeg, L. Pasquet, & L. Castellanos-Jankiewicz (Eds.), *International law and time*. Springer Switzerland.

Hearns, A. (2021). *Building assertiveness: How to efficiently transform your life from being passive to being assertive. Build strong relationships with assertive communication*. Kindle Edition.

Inter-American Court of Human Rights Advisory Opinion OC-26/20. (2020, November 9). Requested by the Republic of Colombia. *The obligations on matters of human rights of a state that has denounced the American convention on human rights and the charter of the organization of American States.*

Jakubowski, P., & Lange, A. (1978). *Assertive option: Your rights and responsibilities.* Research Pr Pub.

Jones, C. (2021). Are human rights enough? On human rights and inequality. *Ethics & Global Politics, 14*, 1991138.

King, P. (2017). *The art of everyday assertiveness: Speak up. Say no. Set boundaries. Take back control.* Big Mind LLC.

Lien, A. (1948). *A fragment of thoughts concerning the nature and the fulfilment of human rights.* UNESCO, Human Rights: Comments and Interpretations.

McNeilly, K. (2019). Are rights out of time? International human rights law, temporality, and radical social change. *Social and Legal Studies, 28*(6), 817.

Moyn, S. (2018). *Not enough. Human rights in an unequal world.* Harvard University Press.

Peneva, I., & Mavrodiev, S. (2013). A historical approach to assertiveness. *Psychological Thought, 6*(1), 3–26.

Robbins, T. (n.d.). (*blog*). *Discover the six human needs, Tony Robbin's blog.* https://www.tonyrobbins.com/mind-meaning/do-you-need-to-feel-significant/

Roosevelt, F. (1941). *President Franklin Roosevelt's Annual Message (Four Freedoms) to Congress.* https://www.archives.gov/milestone-documents/president-franklin-roosevelts-annual-message-to-congress

Simpkins, F. (2013). *The unfinished business of the civil rights movement.* RoseDog Books.

Struthers, A. E. C. (2014). Human rights education: Educating about, through and for human rights. *The International Journal of Human Rights, 19*(1), 53–73.

Tibbitts, F. L. (2017). Evolution of human rights education models. In M. Bajaj (Ed.), *Human rights education: Theory, research, praxis.* University of Pennsylvania Press.

UNESCO. (1948). *Human rights: Comments and interpretations.* UNESCO.

Universal Declaration of Human Rights. (1948).

CHAPTER 3

The Right to an Assertive Life: Assertiveness as a Human Right

Martha Frías-Armenta , *Nadia Saraí Corral-Frías* ,
Jennifer Lizeth Espinoza-Romero ,
and Laura Mejías-Rojas

Introduction

Human rights are universal values inherent to all human beings. Each of us seeks the protection of such rights and freedoms that allow individuals to achieve a desirable quality of life (Castilla, 2011). Human rights protect personal dignity and are indispensable for optimal human development

M. Frías-Armenta (✉)
Law Department, Universidad de Sonora, Hermosillo, Mexico
e-mail: martha.frias@unison.mx

N. S. Corral-Frías • L. Mejías-Rojas
Psychology Department, Universidad de Sonora, Hermosillo, Mexico
e-mail: nadia.corral@unison.mx

J. L. Espinoza-Romero
Criminology Department, University Vizcaya de las Américas, Campus Nogales, Nogales, Mexico

S. Castaños Cervantes, C. Atristain-Suárez (eds.), *Assertiveness in the Context of Human Rights, Ethics, and Classical Virtues*,
https://doi.org/10.1007/978-3-031-60962-6_3

(National Human Rights Commission, 2022). Human rights in modern Western societies are typically embodied in constitutions or charters (Zavala & Argüelles, 2018). Globally, they are primarily accrued in international treaties such as the Universal Declaration of Human Rights proclaimed by the United Nations Assembly in 1948 (United Nations, 2022). Assertiveness can be conceived in several ways, from the ability to express feelings, desires, and thoughts to the capacity to defend one's rights and those of others (Naranjo, 2008). It can also be understood as avoiding putting oneself or others through demeaning behaviours. Additionally, it can include the aptitude to recognise and identify one's needs and the capacity to communicate them to others.

Assertiveness as a human right refers to positive assertiveness that empowers people to express their ideas and opinions and optimises social and political relationships (Renger et al., 2019). Assertive people tend to express their views directly and clearly, which may lead to better asserting their rights. Theoretically, respect for the opinions of others is considered an antecedent of assertive behaviour (Renger et al., 2019). Reciprocal respect within a group enables all members to assert their opinions and ideas and requires respect towards others (Renger, 2018). A critical way mutual respect can be achieved is through socialising values and norms.

Members of society acquire values and norms through socialisation within the environment they develop (Cohn & White, 2012). Through this process, people learn to relate to each other by exercising their rights and respecting those of others. The process, often called legal socialisation (LS), is fundamental for establishing personal social and political life. LS encompasses how individuals come into contact with the law and acquire associated values and attitudes (Trinkner & Tyler, 2016). Thus, LS refers to respect and adherence acquired towards laws or legal normativity (Baz-Cores & Fernández-Molina, 2022). The construct also encompasses appropriating norms, values, beliefs, and attitudes towards rules and legal authorities (Trinkner & Cohn, 2014). LS has an essential role in the formation of attitudes and the point of view of people within a society (Nugmanovna, 2022). This type of socialisation (Trinkner & Tyler, 2016) can allow and improve the development of assertiveness, given that through LS people interact with norms, values, attitudes, and competencies and promote an enhanced understanding of social interactions and the law.

LS is a crucial factor needed for the appropriation of rights, given that it is through LS that relevant attitudes and competencies are acquired.

Norms arise and are reinforced by and within the social environment in which people develop, such as school, work, and family (Cohn & White, 2012). Socialisation begins in childhood, and individuals often acquire their own values, beliefs, attitudes, and behavioural and social norms based on familial socialisation. This socialisation helps navigate interactions within the social world. Thus, LS refers to the internalisation of formal and informal rules. Accordingly, the field of LS researches how the law is acquired by individuals and passed on to members of society and how these processes may also affect the law (Trinkner & Reisig, 2021).

The current study used Trinkner and Reisig (2021) as the theoretical basis for LS. The theory proposes four essential elements of LS: fundamentality, reciprocity, ubiquity, and continuity. Fundamentality is premised on the lawyer representing a critical social institution that helps guide human behaviour, especially among strangers (Trinkner & Tyler, 2016). Furthermore, it views law as a vital institution for establishing societal order (Trinkner & Reisig, 2021). Reciprocity reflects the effect of the law on individuals and vice versa. The third element is ubiquity, which relates to the fact that the socialisation process may occur in any context and may be hierarchical in many cases. Historically, these socialising agents have been classified in two ways (Fine & Rooij, 2021): those that do not derive from legal authorities (e.g. parents) and those that do (e.g. the police). The fourth and final element is continuity, which reflects the long-term nature of LS, where it is essential to note that the process should be lifelong (Trinkner & Reisig, 2021). The socialisation of norms helps construct attitudes and values that, in turn, will aid in developing strategies to demand or execute rights, that is, asserting one's rights.

Gregg (2016) argues that human rights must be rethought and reconstructed through the socialisation of assertive individuality (i.e., assertive personhood). Human rights should depend on personal agency (i.e., the capacity to act) and the rationalisation of these within communities. Additionally, the author asserts that promoting human rights should be supported through community socialisation. Thus, to assert one's rights, one must possess certain behaviours and communication skills, including assertiveness. It is essential to highlight that being assertive denotes exercising our rights while respecting those of other people (Ward & Holland, 2018).

Given that norms partly govern human actions, it is reasonable to assume that the appropriation of rights is also based on said norms. The appropriation of norms associated with assertiveness likewise begins during childhood and helps guide the learning of social interaction with the outside world. Once learned, rules are then followed because they are seen as natural, exemplary, or expected (March & Olsen, 2004). Thus, an assertive person possesses the necessary knowledge about their rights that will allow them to effectively demand their fulfilment and sufficient knowledge on how to exercise them properly.

It is important to note that assertiveness is also associated with respect for others, equality for all and human dignity. From a philosophical point of view, recognising the equality of human rights is based on human dignity (Kant, 2016). Fairness is dignified when opinions are mutually respected and considered, where a request, complaint, or concern is distinguished with a response as a sign of respect. Thus, assertive rights provide a basic structure of healthy interpersonal relationships (Naranjo, 2008). There is no formal definition of this concept; however, based on Smith (1985), we define them as declarations that establish the limits of our rights to others, respecting their rights simultaneously. This definition can be established under the presumption that to be assertive, we must believe (or internalise) that we have this right (Ward & Holland, 2018).

Within the previous framework, theoretical work has suggested the presence of 10 assertive rights (Smith, 1985), and, more recently, there has been an expansion to 18 (Riso, 2018). Among these rights are the right to be treated with respect, to be heard and to be considered, to judge one's own needs, to establish priorities and to make decisions. These rights serve as a guide to self-regard of rights and a way to avoid violating the rights of others. It is important to note that self-regard is similar to positive self-esteem within this context and can be defined as an internalised perception of self-worth (Patterson & Joseph, 2006). Thus, an essential factor for acquiring assertiveness is the socialisation and internalisation of these rights. One way we can internalise rights is through self-regard.

The concept of self-regard is related to self-esteem, derived from Honneth's theory of self-recognition, and the positive self-regard theory (Murphy et al., 2020) suggests that people may refer to themselves in three different dimensions: self-competence, self-confidence, and self-respect (Honneth, 1995). Self-respect is the ability to see oneself as an entity with rights and to be treated fairly in the social or legal framework. It includes perceiving oneself with the same dignity and rights that others possess. Self-confidence consists of self-knowledge as an intelligent being who can contribute to the common good within society. A kind, loving, or sympathetic person represents the dimension of self-confidence. Renger

(2018) argues that people with self-respect will feel they can make legitimate claims, reject requirements, or protest injustices. Thus, the perception of unequal treatment may justify inequitable forms of treatment and the lack of the exercise of human rights.

Once values and norms have been socialised and internalised, one can assert their rights. Assertiveness is thus a social competence which aids human coexistence and collaboration (Blynova et al., 2020). It needs to be encouraged to allow for the equitable enjoyment of rights in different social contexts and groups. Thus, the present chapter will provide an interdisciplinary analysis of assertiveness as a human right. Further, it will examine individuals' interpretation and valuation of assertive rights in different contexts. Thus, the objective of this chapter is to analyse the legal, psychological, and sociological interpretation and valuation of assertiveness as a human right.

Method

Research Design: The present study utilised mixed methods. Our theory suggests that exercising assertive rights responds to different conditions linked to the characteristics of legal institutions, individuals, and the social context. Further, the balance between these systems, features, and contexts is what aids in the appropriation and exercise of these rights. Thus, being able to understand and interpret assertiveness as a human right is fundamental to being able to appropriate assertive rights. Three different methods were used to test our hypothesis. Firstly, a qualitative methodology using a hermeneutic approach was used for the legal and philosophical interpretation of assertiveness. This method will attempt to find the meaning of assertiveness within the Mexican legal framework. Secondly, we analysed open-ended questions using content analysis. Finally, we used structural equations models within quantitative methods to examine the association between LS, appropriation of assertive rights, self-regard, and their effect on assertiveness.

Participants: The non-probabilistic sampling consisted of 244 students ($M[SD] = 24.81[12.71]$). Most participants were undergraduates (52.9%), and more than a fifth were graduate students (21.7%), with the remainder representing technical (13.1%) and high school students (12.3%). Most participants identified as female (65.1%, 159 females; 26.2%, 64 males; 1.6%, 4 non-binaries; 6.9%, 17 did not respond or missing data).

Instruments: Socio-demographic questionnaire—it assessed socio-demographic variables (e.g. age, gender, and marital status), knowledge and appropriation of assertive rights, self-regard, LS, and assertiveness. It consisted of three open-ended questions and five Likert-style instruments.

Qualitative Instruments: The assessment of knowledge of rights began with a closed question that asked whether participants were aware of the concept of assertive rights (yes/no). Participants were presented with three open questions to explain their understanding of assertive rights. The first open question asked participants to explain, in their own words, what they knew about assertive rights. The second asked individuals to give their opinion on a hypothetical case they were not previously aware of and to apply their concept of assertive rights. The third question asked participants again to express their understanding of assertive rights (as with the first open question).

Quantitative Instruments: *Appropriation of Assertive Rights* was assessed using a scale constructed explicitly for this study. We used Riso's (2018) list of assertive rights to compose 18 Likert-style questions associated with the ownership of different rights. The scale included items like "I feel that I have the right to have and express my own opinions", "Experiencing and expressing my feelings and being my judge is my right", and "I believe that I can behave according to my interests because it is my right and that I do not have to keep satisfying other people's needs and expectations". The response options ranged from 1, meaning "I do not think they are mine at all", to 7, indicating "completely mine". This scale demonstrated good internal consistency reliability ($\alpha = 0.93$; see Table 3.1), and confirmatory factor analysis revealed acceptable goodness of fit of a four-parcel model.

Legal socialisation was also assessed with a scale specifically constructed for this research. Items were based partly on Trinkner and Reisig (2021) and the four essential elements of LS: fundamentality, reciprocity, ubiquity, and continuity. The scale consisted of 20 items divided into 4 subscales with response options ranging from zero (strongly disagree) to three (strongly agree). The fundamentality subscale included items like "I believe that the law is fundamental to guide interpersonal relationships in society", reciprocity included "I believe that the law includes our values and beliefs", ubiquity included "In school, I learned what the law was", and the continuity subscale included "All my life I have believed that the law must be obeyed". This scale demonstrated good internal consistency

Table 3.1 Descriptive analysis and Alphas of the scales and subscales

Scale	*N*	*Mean*	*SD*	*Alpha*
Self-regard	244	5.97	1.17	0.895
Self-respect	244	5.89	1.25	0.809
Self-confidence	244	5.82	1.12	0.875
Self-capacity	244	5.79	1.02	0.861
Assertive rights	244	6.11	0.84	0.932
Parcel AR1	244	6.13	0.90	0.798
Parcel AR2	244	6.02	0.96	0.786
Parcel AR3	244	6.18	0.92	0.714
Parcel AR4	244	6.11	0.89	0.764
LS	237	3.14	0.45	0.900
Fundamentality	237	3.38	0.54	0.803
Reciprocity	236	3.02	0.53	0.803
Ubiquity	236	3.07	0.55	0.715
Continuity	235	3.24	0.60	0.801
Assertiveness	196	3.23	0.78	0.858
Disagreement	193	2.86	0.96	0.479
Feelings and beliefs	194	3.00	0.91	0.378
Social interactions efficacy	194	3.31	1.00	0.548
Organisational interactions	192	3.26	1.01	0.264
Capacity to express an opinion	192	3.06	1.01	0.289
How to say no	193	3.37	1.02	0.208

Source: Authors' elaboration

and reliability (α = 0.90; see Table 3.1), and confirmatory factor analysis showed acceptable goodness of fit for a four-factor model.

Self-Regard was assessed using a previously validated scale translated into Spanish in-house (Renger, 2018). A total of 12 items were used to evaluate self-respect, self-competence, and self-confidence. All items were back-translated from English to Spanish and then from Spanish to English to verify the translation quality. Items used a scale ranging from one to seven, where one represented "not true at all" and seven signifying "completely true". The self-respect subscale assessed the ability to see oneself as having the same fundamental rights and dignity as others. An example of an item is, "In my daily life, I see myself as a person with equal rights". The original English version (α = 0.91) and our translation (α = 0.91) of the subscale both demonstrated good internal consistency reliability. *Self-competence* evaluates the perception of one's competence or ability. An example of an item is "I feel capable of doing something precious".

Likewise, this subscale's original English version (α = 0.90) and our translation (α = 0.86) demonstrated good internal consistency reliability. The *self-confidence* subscale captured the confidence or self-assurance that people identified in themselves. An example item was, "Most of the time, I see myself as confident". The original English version (α = 0.91) and our translation (α = 0.87) of this subscale demonstrated good internal consistency reliability.

Assertiveness was assessed using a previously validated scale (Rathus, 1973) adapted to Spanish (León & Vargas, 2009). This study included 20 items from 6 subscales out of the original 30 items: demonstrating disagreement, manifesting feelings and beliefs, efficacy in social interactions, interaction with organisations, ability to express thoughts or opinions, and difficulty in saying no. A six-point Likert-type scale is where one represented "very uncharacteristic of me" and six signified "very characteristic of me". The original Spanish validation (α = 0.80) and our (α = 0.85) demonstrated good internal consistency reliability.

Procedure: Students were invited to participate, and were informed about the research objectives before inclusion in the study. Individuals were additionally informed that their participation was voluntary, that they could stop answering the questionnaire at any time, and that all the information would be completely confidential. Once the informed consent was signed, participants were invited to answer the electronic questionnaire via the Qualtrics platform. The estimated response time was approximately 15 minutes.

Data Analysis

Hermeneutics: The study used a hermeneutic method for assertiveness's legal and philosophical interpretation. This method attempts to find the meaning of assertiveness within the Mexican legal framework. The legal hermeneutics analysis consisted of interpreting human rights related to assertive rights. This interpretation was made by studying the legal definitions of these human rights in the jurisprudence issued by the Judiciary Branch of the Federation.

Content Analyses: The open-ended questions were analysed in two different ways. The first consisted of two trained research assistants who independently made categories from the answers to the open-ended questions—the second used Atlas software (*ATLAS.Ti Scientific Software*

Development GmbH [ATLAS.Ti 22 Windows], 2022). First, the general analysis topic was elaborated after a codification system was created by counting and checking categories, such as rights, freedom, and respect. Further, a word count was used to calculate the most repeated words according to the frequency indicator. A system of categories was created.

Additionally, a tendency analysis provided important information regarding word frequency. It allowed the creation of a word cloud for each category and its relationships with the constructs. Afterwards, nominal categories were created by grouping analogies or similarities. This process was accomplished by seeking similarities among answers by simulating that each category was exclusive. Finally, two separate researchers analysed categorisation and codification.

Quantitative Analyses: Quantitative data analyses were performed using the SPSS version 26 statistical package (IBM Corp, 2019) and EQS (Bentler, 2006). Descriptive statistics such as means and standard deviations for continuous variables and frequencies for categorical variables were calculated using SPSS. Likewise, internal consistency reliability, Cronbach's Alpha (α), for each scale and subscale was calculated. Additionally, indexes (mean of all items within each subscale) for each subscale and appropriation of assertive rights parcels were created. Given that some of the scales were specifically constructed or translated for this study, the scales' validity was tested through confirmatory factor analysis. Finally, two models were tested in EQS; first, a confirmatory factor model measured convergent and discriminant validity; second, a structural equation model (Bentler, 2006) was used to test the hypothetical model (see Fig. 3.1). In the structural equations model, the dependent variable, assertiveness, was examined alongside LS, self-regard, and appropriation of assertive rights as independent variables. The model aimed to measure the direct and indirect effects of the independent variables on the dependent variable (assertiveness). Convergent validity was operationalised as significant loading factors with high values. Discriminant validity was tested through low covariation among constructs compared within the factors. Practical and statistical indicators were used to evaluate if the data fit the model. The statistical indicator that assesses the variance between the proposed and saturated model was the chi-square (X^2), its degrees of freedom, and its probability. It is expected to have no significant value (>0.05). The useful indicators included the Comparative Fit Index (CFI) and Bentler-Bonnet Normed Fit Index (NFI), which should have a value higher than 0.90 (Bentler, 2007). Another indicator used was the Root

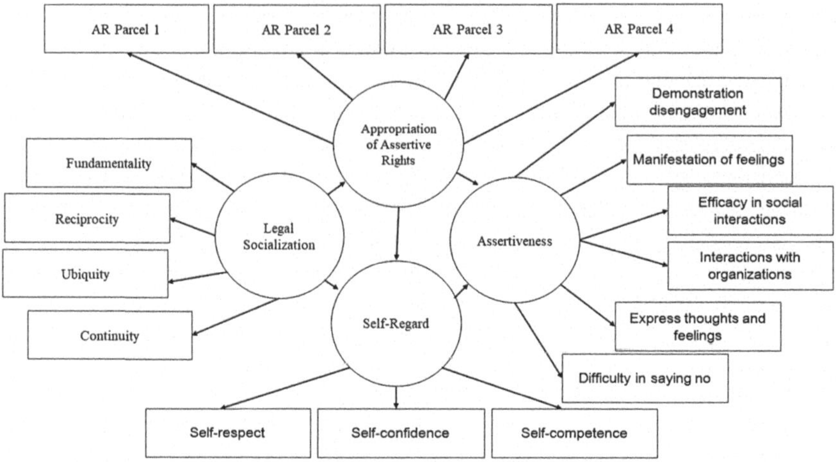

Fig. 3.1 Hypothetical model. Source: Authors' elaboration

Mean Square Error of Approximation (RMSEA), which also measures the fit between the observed and hypothesised variance matrix (values should be ≤0.09) (Browne & Cudeck, 1992).

Results

Hermeneutic Analysis of the Law

Assertiveness as a human right is not established in the United States of Mexico (*Political Constitution of the United States of Mexico*, 2023). However, other rights could be considered part of this concept, such as the right to express an opinion or be heard. The Constitutional reform of 2011 opened the possibility of recognising international human rights norms contemplated in treaties in our country. It is accomplished through a "Control of Conventionality", which allows the application of international laws that best protect the human rights of individuals (González-Pérez, 2011). Likewise, it institutes the hermeneutic principle, which maintains that it is proper to defer to previously established international human rights treaties in interpreting human rights. In addition, the pro persona principle was included, indicating that the most protective norm will always be used, and the interpretation that best guarantees the exercise of the right will be preferred (Castilla, 2011).

From the legal point of view, the concept of human rights goes hand in hand with the idea of legal personality (Rodriguez-Moreno, 2016). Likewise, legal dignity is established as part of these rights, which suggests that people cannot be subject to domination. Dignity implies equality and freedom among people since. It is a prerogative that applies to all in society. Dignity is also manifested in autonomy and the possibility of individual action. As such, the behaviour is not determined by nature but results from personal choice. In this context, freedom is considered self-mastery from the point of view of human rights (Rodriguez-Moreno, 2016). This self-mastery goes hand in hand with dignity and human rights. The process represents the theoretical underpinnings of assertive rights and the exercise of assertiveness in people. In addition to the general concept of human rights, the Political Constitution of the United States of Mexico (*Political Constitution of the United States of Mexico*, 2023) includes freedom of expression and opinion as fundamental rights that could be critical components of assertiveness. Likewise, some resolutions of the Supreme Court of Justice of the Nation (SCJN) define these freedoms and indicate that freedom of expression consists of freely expressing, seeking, transmitting and disseminating ideas, information and opinions (Libertad de Expresión. Dimensión Individual de Este Derecho Fundamental., 2014a). As such, the ability to express one's thoughts must not be undermined (Libertad de Expresión. Dimensiones de Su Contenido, 2007). Furthermore, it is considered a component of human autonomy and a necessary good for the development of personality, freedom of action and personal autonomy (Derecho al Libre Desarrollo de La Personalidad. Su Dimensión Externa e Interna, 2019), as well as the self-expression and self-realisation (Libertad de Expresión. Este Derecho Fundamental Se Relaciona Con Principios Que No Pueden Reducirse a Un Solo Núcleo, 2014b). These concepts of freedom of expression are paired with the exercise of assertiveness; therefore, it can be considered that, in some way, the law protects assertive rights.

Knowledge of Assertive Rights

Most participants responded that they needed to become more familiar with assertive rights (58%). Of those who answered that they knew what assertive rights were, only 4% referred to specific assertive rights, differentiating them from human rights. Most of the respondents identified assertive rights as values and being treated with dignity. In general, they thought of these as rights that we all should have as human beings and are not seen as abilities that can be developed and learned. However, identifying assertive rights as human rights is essential to recognise one's rights and exercise them to protect oneself and others. Figure 3.2 shows word clouds for each of the open-ended questions.

A more detailed description of the categories and examples of answers are shown in Tables 3.2, 3.3, and 3.4; for the first question, participants were prompted to answer, which assessed prior knowledge about assertive rights. The question read, "Could you explain assertive rights?" Our analyses showed that most answers referred to assertive rights as universal or fundamental rights inherent to human beings or people. No categories were explicitly created for these answers; however, most participants assume assertive rights are universal human rights. To a lesser extent, assertive rights were associated with values such as dignity and loyalty, but it was mainly linked to the right to be respected and heard. It is noteworthy among the responses that knowledge of assertive rights was associated with the freedom not to give explanations or not to feel guilty or ashamed. Likewise, participants mention that they can exercise the right to express themselves freely, which does not mean that they do so inappropriately nor make judgements without fear or concern for the consequences they may cause others.

Since many participants needed to learn about assertive rights, we prompted them to speculate what they thought these rights could be. As with the previous question, a category that arose was a lack of knowledge about the topic, suggesting they needed to gain knowledge about the subject. Similar categories emerged, where most mentioned freedom of expression, respect, values and the right to be heard. One new category that arose was autonomy, where participants stated that they thought assertive rights might be associated with making decisions and setting limits.

Finally, given that we hypothesised that many people would not know what assertive rights are, we briefly explained them at the end of the survey and prompted them to give examples of assertive rights. Despite this additional information, the categories mainly stayed the same, although there were some additions to the themes. For instance, participants stated that some examples might be associated with the right to say no and to be able to manage their lives without having to explain it to others.

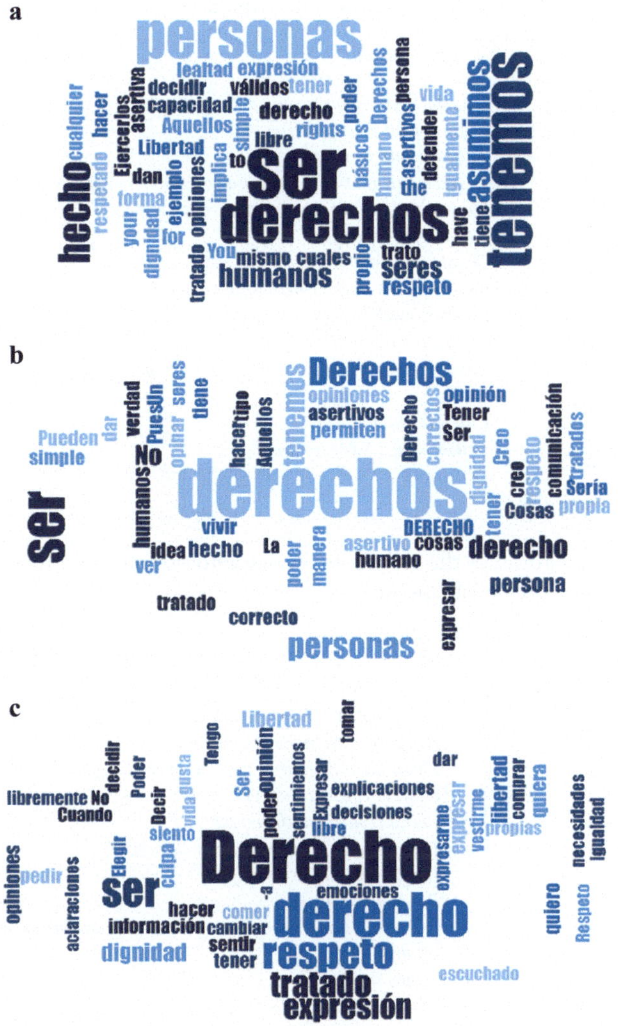

Fig. 3.2 Word clouds for the open-ended questions. *Note.* The open questions were as follows: (**a**) Could you explain to us what assertive rights are? (**b**) If you cannot explain the last question, please give us your opinion of what they might be. (**c**) Now that you know what assertive rights are, write some of these rights that you may know. Source: Authors' elaboration

Table 3.2 Prior knowledge about assertive rights

Category	*Examples response*
Freedom of expression	*"It is the right to have your own opinion".*
	"Respect and free speech".
	"To have your own opinion".
	"To have our own opinions and to be able to express them".
Respect	*"Demand the right to be treated with respect".*
	"Respect for others".
	"Treatment with respect".
Values	*"To be treated with respect and dignity".*
	"Implies loyalty to yourself".
Right to be heard.	*"Rights to be heard".*
	"To express ourselves without meaning that someone might reject us".
Lack of knowledge	*"I do not know".*
	"Truthfully, I have no idea".

Source: Authors' elaboration

Table 3.3 Categories of the conjecture of definition or related topics to assertive rights if these are previously unknown

Category	*Response*
Freedom of expression	*"The rights where you can express yourself".*
	"Respectfully defend my ideas".
	"Right to have my own opinion".
Respect	*"Demand the right to be treated with respect".*
	"Respect towards others".
	"Being treated with respect".
Values	*"Loyalty to one-self and towards others".*
	"Implies loyalty to oneself".
Right to be heard	*"Right to be heard".*
Universal rights	*"Express without it, meaning that someone might reject".*
	"Right to water".
	"Right to food".
Lack of knowledge	*"I would not be able to explain to be truthful".*
Autonomy	*"I do not know".*
	"The right to think and make decisions by myself".
	"Change".
	"Capacity to give limits".

Source: Authors' elaboration

Table 3.4 Categories of examples of assertive rights

Category	*Example response*
Freedom of expression	*"Participation in politics".* *"Not having to keep quiet".* *"Right to have my own opinion.* *"To be able to express myself freely without having anyone give their opinion".* *"To express my opinions".*
Respect	*"Right to be treated with respect and dignity".*
Values	*"Respect, equality, expression, dignity".* *"Loyalty to myself".*
Right to be heard	*"Demand to be heard".*
Universal rights	*"To express ourselves without fearing that someone may reject us".* *"The right to freedom, to dress myself, to speak".*
Lack of knowledge	*"I would not be able to explain to be truthful".*
Autonomy	*"I really do not know".* *"Right to say no".* *"Not having to prove anything to anyone and what I am capable of".* *"Ask for information".* *"To decide what to do with my life, time, relationships and work".*

Source: Authors' elaboration

These results generally suggest that students need more knowledge about the definition of assertive rights and possible examples. Although some made conjectures, most were associated with values or universal rights. Some could give examples once a definition was given, but many maintained a vision of universal human rights instead of assertive rights.

Structural Equations Models

Confirmatory factor analysis results demonstrated strong factor loadings between the constructs and their indicators and low inter-correlations among factors. The LS factor was comprised of the four proposed dimensions represented in four indices fundamentality (λ = 0.59), reciprocity (λ = 0.79), ubiquity (λ = 0.82) and continuity (λ = 0.75). The Self-Regard factor consisted of the three proposed factors: Self-respect (λ = 0.57), Self-competence (λ = 0.81) and Self-confidence (λ = 0.86). The Assertiveness scale was composed of seven subscales: demonstration of dissent (λ = 0.70), the manifestation of feelings and beliefs (λ = 0.69), efficacy in social interactions (λ = 60), interaction with organisations (λ = 0.54), ability to speak thoughts or opinions (λ = 0.77) and difficulty in saying no (λ = 0.64). The Assertive Rights factor comprised of four parcels: (AR1: λ = 0.92, AR2: λ = 0.93, AR3: λ = 0.89, AR4 λ = 0.87). The covariance between LS and Assertiveness as well as Assertiveness and Assertive Rights were not significant. On the other hand, Assertiveness and Self-Regard (0.24), Self-Regard and Assertive Rights (0.66), LS and Self-Regard (0.32), and LS and Assertive Rights (0.32) were low to moderate and significant. The statistical goodness-of-fit indicators suggested good fit ($\chi^2_{(113)}$ = 211, p < 0.0001, BBNFI = 0.88, BBNNFI = 0.93, CFI = 0.94, and RMSEA = 0.06).

The structural equation model, shown in Fig. 3.3, suggests a relationship between LS, Assertive Rights, Self-Regard and Assertiveness factors. LS was directly and positively related to Assertive Rights (*structural coefficient* = 0.29), Assertive Rights to Self-Regard (*structural coefficient* = 0.57) and Self-Regard to Assertiveness (*structural coefficient* = 0.28). The statistical goodness-of-fit indicators suggested good fit of the model ($\chi^2_{(61)}$ = 166, p < 0.0001, BBNFI = 0.87, BBNNFI = 0.93, CFI = 0.94, the RMSEA = 0.05 and the R^2 of the model was R^2 = 0.06).

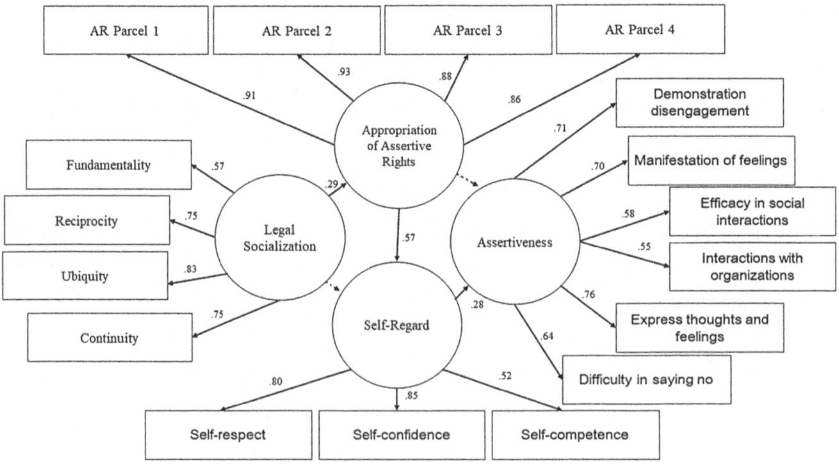

Fig. 3.3 Structural model of the relationship between LS, Assertive Rights, Self-Regard and Assertiveness. Source: Authors' elaboration

Discussion

The present study used three distinct methods to explore assertive rights in Mexican students. The hermeneutic analysis demonstrated that although no specific law is associated with assertive rights, it can be within national and international conventions. In line with this lack of laws within Mexico, knowledge about assertive rights is low within our sample. Finally, the SEM suggests, in partial agreeance with our hypothesis, that to assert one's rights one needs to know about them, which can occur through socialisation, but, most importantly, through internalisation of these rights. Thus, this study suggests that students must start by acquiring knowledge of their assertive rights. It encourages acquiring competencies that will allow adequate respect for their rights.

Our analyses of the law suggested that freedom of expression in the legal context and assertiveness coincide in exercising autonomy and self-expression, the ability to fully manifest oneself, and freedom of action. It can be considered that, in a certain way, the law protects assertive rights and the exercise of assertiveness in human beings since the Mexican Constitution protects freedom of expression, opinion and all human rights. It represents the protection of human dignity and the development of personality in all human beings.

Within our qualitative analyses, we found one of the most significant results of this study. Our results suggest that most participants do not know they are legally guaranteed assertive rights and cannot describe them effectively. Within the legal environment, they related assertive rights to fundamental human rights everyone enjoys, such as freedom of expression and the right to be heard. However, assertive rights were recognised as part of universal human rights and not specifically those associated with asserting one's ideas and will. To the authors' knowledge, this phenomenon has yet to be examined, specifically in students. However, there are some studies regarding self-advocacy in students with disabilities (Test et al., 2005) and a call for more studies (Schena et al., 2022) suggesting a great need for more research. In congruence with previous calls, possible intervention initiatives aimed at improving knowledge of and fostering assertive rights (Schena et al., 2022). Our results, thus, provide a foundation for the underlying issues surrounding this phenomenon and motivation for future studies.

Confirmatory factor analyses showed convergent and discriminant validity for the scales used in the present study. The measures used were good approximations for the constructs we sought to assess. The indicators were related to the proposed constructs, and the constructs discriminated against each other. Thus, the instruments also showed construct validity. The analyses also supported the factor structure of the LS scale that was created for this study based on the Trinkner and Reisig theory (2021).

The structural model suggested that LS and assertive rights indirectly affected assertiveness through self-regard. As hypothesised, LS directly affected the appropriation of assertive rights, which could be interpreted as LS creating a context for people to take ownership of their rights (Trinkner & Tyler, 2016). In this sense, people will feel that they can internalise their rights if, while growing up, some resources and norms reinforce the belief (Cohn & White, 2012). The appropriation of rights or the feeling that one possesses them helps individuals feel respected, safe and able to exercise their rights (Renger, 2018). Congruent with previous research, our data suggest that high self-regard helps people to be more assertive. Results indicate that believing in one's ability and security, equality and self-respect are the most direct predictors of assertiveness (Renger, 2018). LS and the appropriation of assertive rights also play an important indirect role, serving as the context for developing such self-regard. Thus, the present results suggest that being assertive helps to grow up in an environment that respects the rights of individuals and socialises norms. It appears to aid in the development of self-regard (self-capacity, self-security and self-respect), which may lead to the development of assertive behaviour. Finally, although we expected a relationship between LS and self-regard, this relationship was insignificant in our model. One explanation could be that LS may be more directly associated with acquiring values, attitudes and attachment to norms (Baz-Cores & Fernández-Molina, 2022), and self-regard is more connected to self-worth or self-esteem. Our model provides a possible mechanism through which LS can have an indirect association with assertiveness.

Like most studies, the present has limitations. Firstly, this study was conducted with a small student sample. The sample was also primarily female participants. It is thus imperative to replicate this study in other populations and include larger samples for the results to be more robust. Additionally, the proposed model only explained 6% of the variance. We must seek further factors associated with assertiveness.

Conclusions and Recommendations

This study suggests that a series of individual, social, and legal conditions combined are needed to be assertive. The development of LS encourages people to take ownership of their rights, which means they recognise that they can be holders of rights and that other people also have them. It gives rise to an awareness of self-regard, which would help people be more assertive. Although the different contexts do not work at the same level, they are all necessary (legal, social and individual) where social and legal contexts aid in the development of the individual, that is, competencies that give rise to assertiveness in people (Blynova et al., 2020).

It is important to consider education in human rights, human dignity, assertiveness and self-respect to empower people to exercise and demand their rights and respect for human dignity. In this sense, Regilme. (2019) proposes that human rights based on dignity, self-worth and self-recognition should be incorporated into the school curriculum from primary education. Similarly, Gregg (2016) proposes empowering communities in the exercise of their rights. Our results suggest that students do not know their assertive rights. Although more than the requirement of increasing knowledge of rights, training people further to exercise their rights, especially assertive rights discussed in the present chapter, is crucial.

References

ATLAS.ti Scientific Software Development GmbH [ATLAS.ti 22 Windows]. (2022). https://atlasti.com

Baz-Cores, O., & Fernández-Molina, E. (2022). An empirical approach to the study of legal socialisation in adolescence. *European Journal of Criminology, 19*(2), 237–258. https://doi.org/10.1177/1477370819896212

Bentler, P. M. (2006). *EQS, structural equations program manual*. Multivariate Statistical Software, Inc.

Bentler, P. M. (2007). On tests and indices for evaluating structural models. *Personality and Individual Differences, 42*(5), 825–829. https://doi.org/10.1016/j.paid.2006.09.024

Blynova, O., Moiseienko, V., Los, O., Burlakova, I., Yevdokimova, O., Toba, M., & Popovych, I. (2020). Assertiveness as a factor of students' choice of behavior strategies in social interaction. *Revista Inclusiones, 7*(4), 259–272.

Browne, M. W., & Cudeck, R. (1992). Alternative ways of assessing model fit. *Sociological Methods & Research, 21*(2), 230–258. https://doi.org/10.1177/0049124192021002005

Castilla, K. (2011). Un nuevo panorama constitucional para el derecho internacional de los derechos humanos en México (A new constitutional panorama for international human rights law in Mexico). *Estudios Constitucionales, 9*(2), 123–164.

Cohn, E. S., & White, S. O. (2012). *Legal socialisation: A study of norms and rules.* Springer Science & Business Media.

Derecho al libre desarrollo de la personalidad. (2019). Su dimensión externa e interna, 2019357, Suprema corte de justicia de la Nación, Tomo I (Its external and internal dimension, 2019357, Supreme Court of Justice of the Nation, Volume I). *Gaceta del Semanario Judicial de la Federación, Libro, 63*, 491. https://sjf2.scjn.gob.mx/detalle/tesis/2019357

Fine, A. D., & Rooij, B. (2021). Legal socialisation: Understanding the obligation to obey the law. *Journal of Social Issues, 77*(2), 367–391. https://doi.org/10.1111/josi.12440

González-Pérez, L. R. (2011). El sistema no-jurisdiccional de protección de los derechos humanos en México. IUS (The non-jurisdictional system of protection of human rights in Mexico). Revista Del Instituto de Ciencias Jurídicas de Puebla, México.

Gregg, B. (2016). *The human rights state: Justice within and beyond sovereign nations.* University of Pennsylvania Press.

Honneth, A. (1995). *The struggle for recognition.* Polity Press.

IBM Corp. (2019). *IBM SPSS statistics for Windows, version 26.0.* IBM Corp.

Kant, M. (2016). *Fundamentacion De La Metafisica De Las Costumbres (Groundwork of the metaphysics of morals).* Editorial Porrúa.

León, M., & Vargas, T. (2009). Validación y estandarización de la escala de asertividad de Rathus (R.A.S.) en una muestra de adultos costarricenses (Validation and standardization of the Rathus Assertiveness Scale (R.A.S.) in a sample of Costa Rican adults). *Revista Costarricense de Psicología, 28*(41/42), 169/185.

Libertad de expresión. (2007). Dimensiones de su contenido, 172479, Suprema Corte de Justicia de la Nación, pleno, P./J. 25/2007, Tomo XXV (Dimensions of its content, 172479, Supreme Court of Justice of the Nation, plenary session, P./J. 25/2007, Volume XXV). *Semanario Judicial de la Federación y su Gaceta, 1520.* https://sjf2.scjn.gob.mx/detalle/tesis/172479

Libertad de expresión. (2014a). Dimensión individual de este derecho fundamental., 2008100, Suprema Corte de Justicia de la Nación, Primera sala, Tomo 1 (Individual dimension of this fundamental right., 2008100, Supreme Court of Justice of the Nation, First room, Volume 1). *Gaceta del Semanario Judicial de la Federación, Libro 13*, 233. https://sjf2.scjn.gob.mx/detalle/tesis/2008100

Libertad de expresión. (2014b). Este derecho fundamental se relaciona con principios que no pueden reducirse a un solo núcleo, 2008104, Suprema Corte de Justicia de la Nación, Primera Sala, CDXVIII/2014 (10a.)., Tomo 1 (This fundamental right is related to principles that cannot be reduced to a single nucleus, 2008104, Supreme Court of Justice of the Nation, First Chamber, CDXVIII/2014 (10th)., Volume 1). *Gaceta del Semanario Judicial de la Federación, 236*. https://sjf2.scjn.gob.mx/detalle/tesis/2008104

March, J. G., & Olsen, J. P. (2004). *The logic of appropriateness*. ARENA working paper 04/09. University of Oslo.

Murphy, D., Joseph, S., Demetriou, E., & Karimi Mofrad, P. (2020). Unconditional positive self-regard, intrinsic aspirations and authenticity: Pathways to psychological well-being. *Journal of Humanistic Psychology, 60*(2), 258–279. https://doi.org/10.1177/0022167816688314

Naranjo, P. (2008). Relaciones interpersonales adecuadas mediante una Comunicación y conducta asertivas (Appropriate interpersonal relationships through assertive communication and behaviour). *Actualidades Investigativas En Educación, 8*(1), 1–27.

National Human Rights Commission. (2022). *¿Qué son los derechos humanos? (What are human rights?)*. https://www.cndh.org.mx/derechos-humanos/que-son-los-derechos-humanos

Nugmanovna, M. A. (2022). Legal socialisation of the individual and legal culture in modern civil society: (Socio-philosophical analysis). *Thematics Journal of Social Sciences, 8*(2).

Patterson, T. G., & Joseph, S. (2006). Development of a self-report measure of unconditional positive self-regard. *Psychology and Psychotherapy: Theory, Research and Practice, 79*(4), 557–570. https://doi.org/10.1348/147608305X89414

Political Constitution of the United States of Mexico. (2023). (testimony of Congreso de la Unión Mexico). https://www.diputados.gob.mx/LeyesBiblio/pdf/CPEUM.pdf

Rathus, S. A. (1973). A 30-item schedule for assessing assertive behaviour. *Behaviour Therapy, 4*(3), 398–406. https://doi.org/10.1016/S0005-7894(73)80120-0

Regilme, S. S. F. (2019). The global politics of human rights: From human rights to human dignity? *International Political Science Review, 40*(2), 279–290.

Renger, D. (2018). Believing in one's equal rights: Self-respect as a predictor of assertiveness. *Self and Identity, 17*(1), 1–21. https://doi.org/10.1080/15298868.2017.1313307

Renger, D., Mommert, A., Renger, S., Miché, M., & Simon, B. (2019). Voicing one's ideas: Intragroup respect as an antecedent of assertive behavior. *Basic and Applied Social Psychology, 41*(1), 34–47. https://doi.org/10.1080/01973533.2018.1542306

Riso, W. (2018). *El derecho a decir no. Aprenda a decir no y gane siendo asertivo* (*The right to say no. Learn to say no and win by being assertive*). Editorial Planeta Mexicana, S.A. de C.V.

Rodriguez-Moreno, A. (2016). *Algunos conceptos fundamentales para el nacimiento de los derechos humanos: Fernando Vázquez de Menchaca (Some fundamental concepts for the birth of human rights: Fernando Vázquez de Menchaca)*. Comisión Nacional de Derechos.

Schena, D., Rosales, R., & Rowe, E. (2022). Teaching self-advocacy skills: A review and call for research. *Journal of Behavioral Education*. https://doi.org/10.1007/s10864-022-09472-7

Smith, M. J. (1985). *When I say no, I feel guilty*. Bantam Books.

Test, D. W., Fowler, C. H., Wood, W. M., Brewer, D. M., & Eddy, S. (2005). A conceptual framework of self-advocacy for students with disabilities. *Remedial and Special Education, 26*(1), 43–54. https://doi.org/10.1177/07419325050260010601

Trinkner, R., & Cohn, E. S. (2014). Putting the "social" back in legal socialisation: Procedural justice, legitimacy, and cynicism in legal and nonlegal authorities. *Law and Human Behavior, 38*(6), 602–617. https://doi.org/10.1037/lhb0000107

Trinkner, R., & Reisig, M. D. (2021). Celebrating 50 years of legal socialisation. *Journal of Social Issues, 77*(2), 281–290.

Trinkner, R., & Tyler, T. R. (2016). Legal socialisation: Coercion versus consent in an era of mistrust. *Annual Review of Law and Social Science, 12*, 417–439.

United Nations. (2022). *Declaración Universal de derechos humanos (Universal declaration of human rights)*. https://www.un.org/es/about-us/universal-declaration-of-human-rights

Ward, C., & Holland, S. (2018). *Assertiveness: A practical approach*. Routledge.

Zavala, J. J. A., & Argüelles, J. J. I. (2018). Derechos Humanos y Dignidad Humana (Human rights and human dignity). Iustitia Socialis. *Revista Arbitrada de Ciencias Jurídicas y Criminalísticas, 3*(4), 8–23.

CHAPTER 4

Tracing Classical Roots of Assertiveness: The Aristotelian Virtue

Enrique Siqueiros-Fernández

Introduction

Following Aristotle's method of inquiry, this chapter begins by acknowledging assertiveness's ordinary and technical meaning. The Online Cambridge Dictionary defines assertiveness as the "quality of being confident and not frightened to say what you want or believe" (Cambridge University Press, 2023). It comes from the Latin *assero* (*-sertum*), meaning "declare", "defend" or "claimed" (VOX, 2009, p. 44). Now, synthesising Peneva and Mavrodiev's historical analysis of the technical term, we can define assertiveness as a social competence of "advocating for yourself to achieve your objectives and overcome difficulties" (Peneva & Mavrodiev, 2013, p. 3) by being able to spontaneously express one's feelings, ideas, needs or rights without getting worked up, being aggressive or violating other people's rights. Such a complex definition carried several assumptions about mental health, political rights, rhetoric skills and life purpose.

E. Siqueiros-Fernández (✉)
Universidad Panamericana, Mexico City, Mexico
e-mail: jesiqueiros@up.edu.mx

S. Castaños-Cervantes, C. Atristain-Suárez (eds.), *Assertiveness in the Context of Human Rights, Ethics, and Classical Virtues*,
https://doi.org/10.1007/978-3-031-60962-6_4

Along with scholars like Carlos Llano-Cifuentes (2000), Héctor Zagal and Llano-Cifuentes (2001) or Matthias P. Hühn and Marcel Meyer (2023),[1] the author returned to Aristotle's teachings to bring light to current business ethics and management because the Greek philosopher shares fundamental contemporary psychological and political assumptions. Unlike modern psychologists narrowed by specialisation, Aristotle could offer comprehensive and coherent explanations of complex phenomena based on three underlying principles: *arête* (excellence or virtue), *phronesis* (practical wisdom) and *eudaimonia* (happiness or flourishing) (Hursthouse & Pettigrove, 2022). These principles contemplate a broader scope of topics that matter for assertiveness, such as "virtues and vices, motives and moral character, moral education, moral wisdom or discernment, friendship and family relationships, a deep concept of happiness, the role of the emotions in our moral life and the fundamentally important questions of what sorts of persons we should be and how we should live" (Hursthouse & Pettigrove, 2022, p. 1).

The chapter faces three conceptual challenges in drawing bridges between two historical bodies of knowledge: (1) there is no exact translation of assertiveness in the *Corpus Aristotelicum*; (2) conciliating diverse disciplines, authors and worldviews; (3) understanding the evolution of the expression assertiveness.

First, although Aristotle does not have an explicit theory of assertiveness or a word to describe it, there is a strong match between his work and the behavioural therapy assumptions regarding human psychology, mental disorders and citizen rights and duties. In addition, his efforts to describe a coherent human nature ecosystem allow us to understand assertiveness in its full context: from a physics notion of the present moment or instant (*exaiphnês*) for judging spontaneous behaviours or the psychological analysis of human action to the necessity of rhetoric skills and its political role. More important, he has a pedagogical purpose: "In the practical sciences [Ethics], the end is not to attain a theoretic knowledge of the various subjects, but rather to carry out our theories in action [...] to become good" (Aristotle, 1926, 1179b1).

[1] "In the leadership literature of the past 100 years, rhetoric has been a topic for a long time, and ethics was introduced some 30 years ago. However, the three topics, leadership, rhetoric, and ethics, have not been connected. [...] For Aristotle, leadership, ethics, and rhetoric were inseparable: without ethics, there could neither be good nor rhetoric, and rhetoric was the bridge between leader and follower and back" (Hühn & Meyer, 2023, abstract).

Second, despite the evident gulf between current scientific and political frameworks and those of the fourth century BC (for instance, Universal Human Rights vs aristocratic Greek citizenship or the developments of Endocrinology vs Hippocratic humours), fundamental gnoseological (scientific and political) principles remain: a biological, societal, self-centred and rhetorical approach to mental health and disorders. First, by considering humans as "political animals" (*zoon politicon*) (Aristotle, 1995a, 1253a6), Aristotle shares a clinical psychology starting point: humans are animals. For example, the disciple of Ivan Pavlov and the first modern researcher on assertiveness, Andrew Salter, stated that "once we realise that humans are nothing but animals, everything becomes crystal clear. The world makes sense for the first time" (Salter, 2002, p. 92). Second, starting from an intrinsic social nature, Aristotle would agree with DSM-5's fundamental mental disorder criteria: the inability to function in society. "A mental disorder is […] usually associated with significant distress or disability in social, occupational, or other important activities" (APA, DSM-5, 2013). In Aristotle's words: "[…] a man who is incapable of entering into a partnership, or who is so self-sufficing […] must be either a lower animal or a god" (Aristotle, 1995a, 1253a29). Third, as "speaking animals" (*zoon logon*) (Aristotle, 1995a, 1253a10), Aristotle assigned the same importance to our communication ability as leading assertiveness experts: "For the effectiveness of interpersonal relationships, the absorption of a few skills was necessary and the most important of which was the ability to speak openly about own feelings and desires" (Lazarus, 1973; Salter, 2002; Wolpe, 1990, as referred to in Peneva & Mavrodiev, 2013, p. 7). Finally, like contemporary psychology and Western citizenship, Aristotle's worldview rests primarily on individual flourishing: to live a good and happy life.

Third, assertiveness evolved into slightly different modern historical meanings and uses: from a psychiatric criterion of mental health and a public speaking skill to a geopolitical behaviour in international affairs, "a confident and direct way to defend one country's rights or claims" (Chen et al., 2013, p. 177). Such diversity of disciplines asks for a transdisciplinary approach. Luckily, Aristotle's philosophy of human affairs or "political science is developed in the three works on Ethics, the book of Politics, Rhetoric and, maybe, in the book of Poetics" (my translation of Zagal, 2013, p. 94). Now, we will introduce Aristotle's theoretical framework:

> The author claims that Aristotle sets a robust intellectual framework to understand, communicate and develop assertiveness. It is by articulating a comprehensive and common-sense theory of human nature as rational-social animality (*zoon logon-politikon*). Aristotle's Nicomachean Ethics aims to demonstrate how we might attain a good and happy life (*eudaimonia*) through virtuous action (*arete*) led by rational life-long choices (*prohairesis*). That is, how to acquire practical wisdom or prudence (*phronesis*).

Once we have settled Aristotle's ethics framework and vocabulary, we can trace the origins of assertiveness' conceptual evolution described by Ivelina Peneva and Stoil Mavrodiev in their *Historical Approach to Assertiveness* (2013).

Reducing Uncertainty: Assertiveness as a Method to Control Mental Weakness

This section discusses how Aristotle's philosophy of education and the clinical psychology therapy share a similar method to address mental disorders, and both aim to reduce uncertainty by developing assertive skills. "The beginning of the experimental study of assertiveness commenced in the middle of last century, and it was related to clinical practice [...]: These clinical psychologists accepted uncertainty (non-assertiveness) as a reason for some mental illnesses [such as] insecurity, loneliness and deficiency in communication" (Peneva & Mavrodiev, 2013, p. 3). Although using different language, Aristotle can find strong similarities between his study of virtuous behaviour or assertiveness as evidence of a healthy mental condition: the ability to choose and pursue a happy life. If, for Aristotle, the end of human life is *eudaimonia* (happiness), and a requisite for happiness is *eupraxis* (acting and reacting well), assertiveness is a requirement for happiness. *Eupraxia* or doing well means to judge, act and react appropriately, that is, following the principle of the right measure or golden mean. In this sense, wrongdoing means going against one's interest, evidence of mental weakness.

Facing the complexity of defining mental health and a good life, both Aristotle's and contemporary approaches to assertiveness analyzed mental disruptions instead of just successful assertive conducts and characters: "From the perspective of clinical psychology, assertiveness has been viewed mainly concerning the occurrence of some psychological disorders" (Romek, 2003, pp. 8–9 as referred in Peneva & Mavrodiev, 2013, p. 3).

In 1949, Andrew Salter worked with depressed clients "unable to openly and spontaneously express their feelings, desires and needs […] limited in their self-realisation and consequently experienced difficulties in contact with other people" (Peneva & Mavrodiev, 2013, p. 4). Salter's "self-realisation" is Aristotle's rational lifelong choice (*prohairesis*), a self-commitment with your future self: how you want to live to become what you want.

So, to understand and treat mental illnesses in social-speaking animals, they consider the opposite: antisocial behaviours and evident disorders, that is, communication challenges and actions against one's interests or commitments. The following research summary about causes of mental disorders in clinical psychology fields maps closely with Aristotle's classification of weak or flawed moral characters: "the sources of uncertainty (non-assertiveness) may be conditionally divided into three groups – conative (behavioural), cognitive and emotional" (Romek, 2003, pp. 8–9 as referred in Peneva & Mavrodiev, 2013, p. 7). Likewise, in the fourth century BC, Aristotle classified three immoral characters somehow mirroring the three non-assertive groups: "the states of moral character to be avoided are of three kinds – vice, incontinence and bestiality" (Aristotle, 1926, 1145a1): (A) The conative or behavioural source fits the vicious character (*kakos*) because vice is a habit, that is, a persistent spontaneous incorrect behaviour, like repeatedly failing "to speak openly about your feelings and desires" (Peneva & Mavrodiev, 2013, p. 7) or the other extreme: speaking too often and opening about them. (B) The emotional cause matches incontinence (*akratic*) or a weak-willed character when he or she, according to Aristotle "acts by passion, not with commitment (*prohairoumenos*)" (Aristotle, 1926, 1111b13), that is, knowing the correct behaviour but giving in once pained by the struggle or the deprivation of pleasure. Like avoiding speaking up due to social fear: "Clinical psychologists define social fear as one of the main causes of uncertainty, and in particular the fear of rejection, mocked or shamed in some way" (Peneva & Mavrodiev, 2013, p. 8). And, finally, (C) an extreme cognitive disorder can relate to Aristotle's bestiality because "in a bestial man […] the intellect is not corrupted […] but entirely lacking" (Aristotle, 1926, 1150a1). A more moderate case is when irrationality of belief may lead to misconceptions about the world and yourself (Peneva & Mavrodiev, 2013), like "the profligate (*akolastos*) yields to his appetites from choice, considering it right always to pursue pleasure" (Aristotle, 1926, 1146b20).

Once identified sources of mental illnesses and weak moral characters are present, it is easier to define assertive casualties. Salter identified characteristics of solid and assertive personalities: emotionality and expressiveness of speech, ability to oppose and counter others' opinions, using the personal pronoun "I", accepting praises as self-respect and adequate assessment of one's own strengths and abilities; impulsiveness in own actions and refusal of planning as a manifestation of own improvisational inclinations (Salter, 2002, pp. 57–59). Also, Aristotle describes strong characters in contrast with the weak ones (vicious, incontinent and bestiality). The contraries of two of these are evident: one we call virtue, the other continence; to brutishness, it would be most fitting to oppose superhuman virtue, a heroic and divine kind of virtue, as Homer has represented Priam saying of Hector that he was outstanding. After understanding sources of uncertainty and weak characters and describing solid assertive skills and personalities, one can approach their methods to control mental illnesses.

While clinical psychologists offer therapy for correcting non-assertiveness or uncertainty, Aristotle offers a virtuous education for preventing it. There is a variety of therapies and ongoing discussion about non-assertiveness treatments. Salter developed the "conditioned reflex therapy [...] for full and spontaneous expression of personal feelings, desires and needs as a condition for the expansion of the opportunities for self-realisation and personal development". But "The American psychologist Steven Stein also did not consider appropriate proclamation of all emotions. [...] but also enough power over personal impulses, so that they could be expressed in an appropriate form and with appropriate force" (Stein & Book, 2006, pp. 73–93 as referred to in Peneva & Mavrodiev, 2013, p. 5). Later, Lazarus identified four groups of habits possessed by assertive personalities, conditions for a fulfilling life: to talk about one's own desires and needs openly; to say "No"; to openly talk about one's own positive and negative feelings; to establish contacts, to begin, maintain and end a conversation. According to the author, "these abilities were not only an expression of the behavioural side of the personality but also included cognitive elements such as propulsion, life philosophy and personal assessments" (Lazarus, 1971, pp. 1–7, as referred to in Peneva & Mavrodiev, 2013, p. 6).

On the other hand, Aristotle offers a way to prevent the lack of assertiveness: virtuous education. His philosophy of education is illustrated with the most potent assertiveness analogy introduced at the beginning of the Nichomaquean ethics: *kathaper toxotai*, to be "like archers": aiming at the knowledge of the good and hitting the mean. With good aim, people are at some point protected from harmful or good fortune, that is, from uncertainty. The most famous example of a non-assertive character subject to uncertainty is the tragic hero, who fails to hit the mark (*hamartia*): "This is the sort of man who is not pre-eminently virtuous and just, and yet it is through no badness or villainy of his own that he falls into the fortune, but rather through some flaw in him, he being one of those who are in high station and good fortune, like Oedipus and Thyestes" (Aristotle, 1932, 1453a). Oedipus met his fate because of a *hamartia* or tragic mistake originated by incontinence or depravity of his character. He lacked self-knowledge and self-assessment and was subject to the tragic hero's *hybrus* or disproportion. *Hybrus* is wanton violence arising from the pride of strength or passion, insolence (Liddell & Scott, 1968). So, if Oedipus had not thought magnanimously about himself, he would probably have been able to ask nicely for the right to cross the street or manage his rage during the argument, and he would not have killed his father.

Moreover, if he had known himself, he would have known he was the prince and the queen's son. And so on. Unlike young Plato, who expelled the poets from the imaginary Republic (597e) for the risk of corrupting the citizens, Aristotle saw tragedies as didactic tools: contemplating your life and behaviour in a tragic hero's shoes. To pity him and fear his destiny so that you purify your emotions (catharsis) and abstain from specific paths or try to shield yourself from fortune by acquiring virtue: moderation and self-assessment.

Aristotle's philosophy of education aims to prevent citizens from falling victim to fate. Furthermore, the responsibilities of education are not only family and school but also the state.[2] The education content follows cognitive diversity: education for reasons, emotions and dispositions. The aim is to develop virtuous behaviour to be assertive. The following passage summarises his notion of virtue:

> one can be frightened or bold, feel desire or anger or pity, and experience pleasure and pain in general, either too much or too little, and in both cases

[2] "And it is difficult to obtain a right education in virtue from youth up without being brought up under right laws; for to live temperately and hardily is not pleasant to most men, especially when young; hence the nurture and exercises of the young should be regulated by law since temperance, and hardiness will not be painful when they have become habitual" (NE, 1179b20).

> wrongly; whereas to feel these feelings at the right time, on the right occasion, towards the right people, for the right purpose and in the right manner, is to feel the best amount of them, which is the mean amount—and the best amount is, of course, the mark of virtue. (Aristotle, 1926, 1106b20)

Finally, there is the question for Aristotle's curriculum inspired in the famous *paideia*, Greek pedagogic ideal. According to the philosopher, there must be "three canons to guide education: moderation, possibility and suitability". Here is a summary of the different subjects recommended for different ages: For domestic education, he recommends movement exercises, resistance to challenging weather, reading tales and adult life roleplays, among others (Aristotle, 1995a, 1336b1–1336b20). For the education of the youth, he shared the standard practices and insisted on music: "reading and writing, gymnastics, music, and fourth, with some people, drawing" (Aristotle, 1995a, 1337b25). For the Lyceum, besides intellectual knowledge like logic, metaphysics and biology, his school focused on practical knowledge: rhetoric, ethics and politics.

Aristotle's account of education had a political end, harmony between individual and collective well-being: "The virtue of the state is, of course, caused by the citizens who share in its government being virtuous, and in our state, all the citizens share in the government" (Aristotle, 1995a, 1332a35).

Ruling and Being Ruled: Protecting Our Rights Without Violating Others' Rights

It seems that the political use of assertiveness "as a means of protecting individual rights" (Peneva & Mavrodiev, 2013, p. 13) is far from Aristotle's worldview since there were no human rights in Periclean Athens but a very narrow citizen membership (Aristotle, 1995a, 1275a). Nevertheless, his work has three features that enlighten current political assertiveness discussions: First feature is a strong sense of citizenship as a condition of the possibility of a good city and a happy life. Second feature is an account of rights and responsibilities that anticipates the discussion of contemporary approaches to political assertiveness: while protecting rights means protecting them in different circumstances (Smith, 2006, as referred in Peneva & Mavrodiev, 2013, p. 11), it also means honouring your responsibilities (Bishop, 2010; Jakubowski & Lange, 1976; Smith, 1985, as referred in

Peneva & Mavrodiev, 2013, p. 13). The third and final feature is a complete rhetoric theory behind citizen membership.

First, about the strong sense of citizenship (harmony between individual rights and collective well-being), psychologist Manuel John Smith (1985) states that "assertive training and compliance with assertive rights were important not only for the specific person but for the society as a whole, as they would help to harmonise the social and labour relations" (Smith, 2006, referred in Peneva & Mavrodiev, 2013, p. 11). In that sense, Aristotle's views on harmonious citizenship rest on two radical premodern assumptions: humans as political animals and good cities because of good citizens. Unlike modern anthropologies behind contractual theories such as Hobbes'[3] or Rousseau's[4] (Bennett, 2017), for the Greek philosopher, humans are not atomic individuals but intrinsic social mammals: "political animals" (*Zoon Politikon*) (Aristotle, 1995a, 1253a6). Moreover, unlike Machiavelli's,[5] in Hobbes' aetiology of well-ordered societies, Aristotle believed that a good city depends on virtuous (assertive) citizens (Aristotle, 1995a, 1332a35), not just on good laws.

Second is the problem of not only protecting rights but also respecting responsibilities. "Some psychologists have emphasised the danger of people with less experience in human relationships interpreting" the principles of political assertiveness literally.[6] They emphasise that "your rights may produce an inadequate increase of self-evaluation and individualism"

[3] Hobbesian anthropological atomism is clearly expressed in his hypothetical state of nature, prior to sociability, a war of all against all: *Bellum omnium contra omnes* (Hobbes, Preface).

[4] "Each individual, who on his own is a complete and solitary whole…" (Rousseau in Bennett, 2017, pp. 2, 7).

[5] "They who lay the foundations of a State and furnish it with laws must […] assume that all men are bad, and will always, when they have a free field, give loose to their evil inclinations […] men never behave well unless compelled, and that whenever they are free to act as they please, and are under no restraint everything falls at once into confusion and disorder. It has been said that poverty and hunger are needed to make men industrious, so laws are needed to make them good" (Machiavelli, 1883, pp. 1, 3).

[6] "1. The right to judge your own behaviour, thoughts, and emotions and to take responsibility for their initiation and consequences upon yourself. 2. The right to offer no reasons or excuses for justifying one's behaviour. 3. The right to judge if you were responsible for solving other people's problems. 4. The right to change your mind. 5. The right to make mistakes and be responsible for them. 6. The right to say, 'I do not know'. 7. The right to be independent of the goodwill of others before coping with them. 8. The right to be illogical in making decisions. 9. The right to say, 'I do not understand'. 10. The right to say, 'I do not care'" (Smith, 1985, pp. 47–72).

(Stepanov, 2006, pp. 81–85, referred to in Peneva & Mavrodiev, 2013, p. 12). In this regard, it was noted that everyone had responsibilities in addition to rights (Bishop, 2010; Jakubowski & Lange, 1976; Smith, 1985, referred to in Peneva & Mavrodiev, 2013). Aristotle's account rests on that assumption: virtuous citizens, that is, people who protect their rights and honour their responsibilities, are a condition of the possibility of a good city (Aristotle, 1995a, 1332a35). Here lies the relevance of demanding rights and knowing obligations. He states the recognition of rights and responsibilities with his famous formulation of the ruling cycle: "All must share alike in ruling and being ruled in turn. For equality means for persons who are similar to identity of status" (Aristotle, 1995a, 1332b15). "In a sense, therefore, we must say that the rulers and ruled are the same, and in a sense different" (Aristotle, 1995a, 1332b).

Finally, there is a discussion in the last section about rhetoric, the ability to express yourself and protect your rights in different circumstances, that is, the art of persuasion (Aristotle, 1995b, 1356a). For Aristotle, the political ability to persuade, a particular form of assertiveness, is "a bridge between private and public, individual interest and the common good, and equity and law" (Nichols, 1987, p. 1).

At this point, the author has made a case for Aristotelian virtue as a method to prevent mental illness and a political principle to help citizens demand their rights while respecting the rights of others. Although using different language, the philosopher can find strong similarities between his study of virtuous behaviour and assertiveness as defining and pursuing a happy life.

Practical Wisdom: Self-improvement and Self-fulfilment

The stronger case for research on assertiveness's roots in Aristotle's work is the idea of self-fulfilment. In the 60s, "self-improvement and self-actualisation" (Peneva & Mavrodiev, 2013, p. 3), and again in the 80s and 90s, the focus on strengthening the human potential and achieving maximum personal fulfilment (Peneva & Mavrodiev, 2013, p. 3) is rooted directly in the Aristotelian "practical wisdom" (*phronesis*) and lifelong rational choices (*prohairesis*) (Aristotle, 1995a). It needs assertive or prudent decisions to achieve self-fulfilment. In the philosopher's words: "There are two things in which the welfare of all men consists: one of these is the correct establishment of the aim and end of their actions, the other the ascertainment of the actions leading to that end" (Aristotle, 1995a, 1331b). He continues:

> a prudent man can deliberate well about what is good and advantageous for himself, not in some one department, for instance, what is good for his health or strength, but what is advantageous to the good life in general. It is proved by the fact that we also speak of people as prudent or wise in something when they calculate well intending to attain some end of value (other than those ends which are the object of art so that the prudent man, in general, will be the man who is good at deliberating in general. (Aristotle, 1926, 1140a20)

The Aristotelian scholar Hector Zagal gives us some examples: "[prudence] is about the intellectual exploration around the means […] the quest for health as a component of a good life. Drinking water becomes *práxis* when the agent chooses it, aiming for his final cause: happiness" (my translation of Zagal, 2013, p. 107). Choosing health over wealth is a good life goal. And then drinking water daily instead of soda or beer is an example of practical wisdom. Maybe the most evident example is sacrificing present pleasures to save money for retirement, as PR Massingham (2019) explained in *An Aristotelian Interpretation of Practical Wisdom: The Case of Retirees.* Aristotle can say that the morally excellent man, the *spoudaios*, is characterised by acting according to *prohairesis* (Chamberlain, 1984). Furthermore, doing it so often does not mean extra effort, like developing the habit of saving for retirement.

If, for our philosopher, the end of human life is happiness (*eudaimonia*), and a requisite for happiness is prudence (*phronesis*), good life choices (*prohairesis*) and acting and reacting well (*eupraxis*), assertiveness is a requirement for happiness. Assertiveness is good judgement and performance. In this sense, wrongdoing means going against your own interests, evidence of some degree of mental illness (see first section) and an obstacle to your personal development. *Eupraxia*, or doing well, means to judge, act and react adequately, following the principle of the proper measure: a complete account of assertiveness. The end of *eupraxia* is to flourish and live the best life possible.

Furthermore, for Aristotle, a good life is fundamentally a social life (Aristotle, 1995a, 1253a28–1253a30), and human sociability rests in our speaking ability. So, the key to being sociable is mastering social skills, especially public speaking abilities (Aristotle, 1995a, 1253a10): "The most important [skill for interpersonal relationships is] the ability to speak openly about own feelings and desires" (Lazarus, 1973; Salter, 2002; Wolpe, 1990, as referred to in Peneva & Mavrodiev, 2013, p. 7).

The Art of Persuasion: Social Skills in Various Communication Fields

This last section (1) stresses that assertive communication and the art of persuasion are the same things: "express their desires and feelings openly, positively, and directly so that others will respond to them in more satisfying ways" (Matsumoto, 2009, p. 53), (2) traces the roots of assertive communication into ancient Greek thought, (3) describes virtuous characteristics as a condition of the possibility of virtuous communications, (4) analyses the elements of persuasive art and (5) address the critical problem of persuasion and assertive communication: timing and spontaneity.

Due to a better understanding of assertiveness during the twenty-first century, the research decreased. The therapy increased as "skills in various spheres of public life", for instance in the realm of education, family relationships, women's rights, sexual relationships, management and human resources, as well as for entrepreneurs, nurses and athletes, and in politics, religion or tourism (Peneva & Mavrodiev, 2013, p. 16). Even though there are few attributions to Aristotle, it is almost certain that therapy is rooted in or, at least, can benefit from his ancient art of rhetoric (Aristotle, 1995b, 1356a).

Before Aristotle, Plato already knew that social and communication skills facilitate social and professional success:

> I call it the ability to persuade with speeches either judges in the law courts or statesmen in the council-chamber of the commons in the Assembly or an audience at any other meeting that may be held on public affairs. Moreover, I tell you that under this power, you will have the doctor as your slave and the trainer as your slave; your money-getter will turn out to be making money not for himself but for another—in fact, for you who can speak and persuade the multitude. (Plato, 1967, 452e)

Aiming to trace this conceptual relationship, especially in public speaking, we will discuss Aristotle's three primary rhetorical elements: *logos*, *pathos* and *ethos* (Aristotle, 1995b, 1356a1–1356a4). Those elements survived the rhetoric tradition into current cultural expressions. Today, you find them in Barack Obama's exemplary speeches or McKinsey and Co.'s onboarding manuals.

One can trace the intimate relationship between assertiveness and persuasion to the famous cosmogonical tale in Plato's *Timaeus*: Plato's god or demiurge did not create the world at his will, out of nothing, but persuaded (*peitho*) a chaotic matter to arrange a well-ordered universe. "Reason was controlling Necessity by persuading her to conduct to the best end most of the things coming into existence" (Plato, 1925, 48a). The demiurge performed with Aristotelian virtue: he did not force matter nor give up in his ruling efforts but persuaded her/it to behave. That is assertive communication: "Assertive behaviour is a middle point of two opposites. At the deficit end of the pole is passivity, whereas at the excess end is aggression" (Immanuel, 2020, p. 2). However, the Greek experts in rhetoric, infamous enemies of Plato, were the sophists, "merchants of knowledge" able to "persuade with speeches either judges in the law courts or statesmen in the council-chamber of the commons in the Assembly or an audience at any other meeting that may be held on public affairs" (Plato, 1967, 452e–453a). Moreover, their hero was the *polytropos* (resourceful) Ulysses, a "man of many ways".

Aristotle systematised these 4x4 social-speaking skills into the art of rhetoric: "the faculty of discovering in any particular case all of the available means of persuasion" (Aristotle, 1995b, 1356a). It is saying the right thing at the right time, in the right way. Going back to the twenty-first century, the ancient art of persuasion is our assertive speaking: "To be assertive, a human being not only ought to know his/her rights but also should be able to apply them in different situations and under different circumstances" (Smith, 2006 in Peneva & Mavrodiev, 2013, p. 11). The criterion is the same: the proportionality principle or golden mean, at the foundation of the Aristotelian virtue notion.

Assertive communication requires virtuous speakers. Neither passive nor aggressive. Neither too self-controlled nor too loose. Both extremes were studied as evidence of mental illness. Salter called "inhibitory" individuals to the first case due to their lack of "expressiveness of speech" and "impulsiveness in own actions" (Salter, 2002, pp. 57–59 in Peneva & Mavrodiev, 2013, p. 5). On the other extreme is the lack of self-control: "According to Stepanov, communication was more effective and comprehensive not during spontaneous expression of feelings, but when they were deliberately controlled by the situation (Stepanov, 2006, pp. 23–25 in Peneva & Mavrodiev, 2013). Also, Steven Stein "did not consider appropriate proclamation of all emotions. He believed that an assertive personality possessed not only capable of emotional self-analysis [...] but also enough power over personal impulses so that they could be expressed in the appropriate form and with appropriate force" (Stein & Book, 2006, pp. 73–93 in Peneva & Mavrodiev, 2013, p. 5). Aristotle gives several examples of virtuous (mid-point) behaviour in communication, from good mood (wit) and truthfulness dosage (honesty) to anger management (gentleness). In NE, he describes the virtue of wit:

> one form of relaxation is playful conversation. Here, too, we feel that there is a certain standard of good taste in social behaviour and a certain propriety in the sort of things we say and in our manner of saying them, and also in the sort of things we allow to be said to us [...] And it is clear that in these matters too it is possible either to exceed or to fall short of the mean. (Aristotle, 1926, 1128a1)

Then truthful:

> as generally understood then, the boaster is a man who pretends to creditable qualities that he does not possess, or possesses in a lesser degree than he makes out, while conversely the self-depreciator disclaims or disparages good qualities that he does possess; midway between them is the straightforward sort of man who [...] admits the truth about his own qualifications without either exaggeration or understatement. (Aristotle, 1926, 1127a20)

And finally, a gentle people's anger management:

> both states of character [the harsh and the slavish man] are wrong, it is clear that the state midway between them is right, for it is neither too hasty nor too slow-tempered, nor does it get angry with the people with whom it ought not nor fail to get angry with those with whom it ought. The gentleman would be midway between the harsh and slavish man. (Aristotle, 1981, 1231b25)

Once shown virtuous characters in communication, let us understand good communication itself: its goal or final cause. Rhetoric is the art of persuasion, and persuasion is rooted in three elements: *ethos* (credibility), *pathos* (emotions) and *logos* (reasons), "The first depends upon the moral character of the speaker, the second upon putting the hearer into a certain frame of mind, the third upon the speech itself, in so far as it proves or seems to prove" (Aristotle, 1995b, 1356a1–1356a4). The arrangement of the three elements depends on the right measure principle. Because the right measure or "proportion (*kairos*) is best in all things" (Hesiod, 1914, p. 694); in other words, they depend on the Aristotelian virtue: a purposive disposition (self-interest choice), lying in a mean (between passive and aggressive) and determined by the right reason (prudence). Even Though they analyse different phenomena, it is remarkable that the psychological sources of non-assertiveness, "conative (behavioural), cognitive and emotional" fit the categories of our rhetoric elements: *ethos* (behaviour), *logos* (cognitive) and *pathos* (emotional). Both descriptions come from a functional analysis of human psychology and behaviour.

One last but radical problem is timing. Persuasion and assertiveness are time-sensitive; usually, they perform, receive feedback and see results in a given instant. That means that one cannot calculate but act and react spontaneously. As we just read, failing to do that is evidence of a lack of mental health and speaking skills. Salter and Wolpe "accepted that the main characteristic of assertive personalities was the ability of open and spontaneous expression of feelings and [Wolpe] defined assertiveness as "socially justified motor or verbal expression of feelings" (Salter, 2002, pp. 57–59; Wolpe, 1990 in Peneva & Mavrodiev, 2013). Now, both Aristotle and contemporary psychology address the problem of spontaneity in assertiveness: for Aristotle, "this skill consists on the apprehension of the middle term without resorting to demonstration. *Anchínoia* is possessed by those who grasp the middle term in a non-discursive and immediate way: 'Acumen (*anchínoia*) consists of getting the middle right, in an imperceptible time'" (Zagal, 2018, p. 138) This sharp-wittedness is spontaneous, in other words, comes naturally. Can it be learned? The foundation of Aristotle's ethics and rhetoric is the idea of an acquired or second nature that allows spontaneous behaviour resulting from the development of habits: "Habit is hard to change just because it is like nature" (Aristotle, 1926, 1152a29–1152a33). The common expression "it comes naturally" refers to the development of an ability to do something without effort and calculation. Public speaking comes naturally for some people; through study and repetition, it became second nature for others. In contemporary psychology, a habit "…is a more or less fixed way of thinking, willing, or feeling acquired through previous repetition of a mental experience" (Andrews, 1903, p. 121). The behavioural economist and Nobel Award winner Daniel Kahneman offered a narrative to address this issue: he distinguished between two mental systems: system 1 for fast spontaneous thinking and system 2 for slow discursive thinking, one for intuition and the other for calculation (Kahneman, 2011). Repeating an action enough times makes it familiar, and it flows without resorting to system 2: you do it spontaneously with system 1. The goal of social and speaking skills is to express and moderate yourself spontaneously. The ultimate example is Aristotle's famous remark on anger management:

> anybody can become angry—that is easy [...] but to be angry [...] to the right person, and the right amount, and at the right time, and for the right purpose, and in the right way—this is not within everybody's power and is not easy; so that to do these things properly is rare, praiseworthy, and noble. (Aristotle, 1926, 1109a25–1109a30)

Conclusions

The study and development of assertiveness in clinical psychology, human rights advocacy, lifelong coaching, and rhetoric training aim to reduce uncertainty by developing assertive skills. It is the final goal of Aristotle's ethics and philosophy of education. While Aristotle's approach seeks to prevent a lack of assertiveness, contemporary guidelines aim to correct it. An Aristotelian framework, that is, a comprehensive approach to human nature, helps us understand what it means to be assertive (reduce and deal with uncertainty), what the preconditions of it: to know yourself (wants, needs and rights of your present and future self), to harmonise your behaviour with correct judgements, feelings and decisions, that is, to be prudent and make good lifelong choices and to unlock your mind and body by refining your thinking and speaking skills (to be persuasive).

Resorting to ancient wisdom allows us to develop a narrative of the root causes, purposes and mechanisms of assertiveness. Aristotle's theory of virtue explains the conditions of possibility of the evolving term "assertiveness": (1) To correctly control and express and reduce uncertainty by hitting the mid-point between submission and aggressiveness, that is, being virtuous (Aristotle, 1926, 1097b–1098a). (2) To advocate for ourselves and ask for our rights without violating other people's rights through education to rule and be ruled (Aristotle, 1926, 1181b13). (3) To fulfil ourselves by choosing the proper ends and means with practical wisdom. (4) To express ourselves adequately and be persuasive with rhetoric (Aristotle, 1995b, 1356a).

References

American Psychiatric Association. (2013). *Diagnostic and statistical manual of mental disorders* (5th ed.). American Psychiatric Association.

Andrews, B. R. (1903). Habit. *The American Journal of Psychology, 14*(2), 121–149. https://doi.org/10.2307/1412711. ISSN 0002-9556. JSTOR 141271.

Aristotle. (1926). *Nicomachean Ethics* (NE). (H. Rackham, Trans.). Loeb Classical Library 73. Harvard University Press.

Aristotle. (1932). *Poetics.* (W.H. Fyfe, Trans.). Harvard University Press and William Heinemann Ltd.

Aristotle. (1981). *Eudemian Ethics* (EE). *Aristotle in 23 Volumes*, Vol. 20 (H. Rackham, Trans.). Harvard University Press and William Heinemann Ltd.

Aristotle. (1995a). Politics. In J. Barnes (Ed.), *The complete works of Aristotle Princeton.* Princeton University Press.

Aristotle. (1995b). Rhetoric. In J. Barnes (Ed.), *The complete works of Aristotle Princeton.* Princeton University Press.

Bennett, J. (2017). *The social contract* (1762) *of Jean-Jacques Rousseau.* https://www.earlymoderntexts.com/assets/pdfs/rousseau1762.pdf

Chamberlain, C. (1984). The meaning of prohairesis in Aristotle's Ethics. In *Transactions of the American Philological Association (1974–2014)* (Vol. 114, pp. 147–157). The Johns Hopkins University Press.

Chen, D., Pu, X., & Johnston, A. (2013). Debating China's assertiveness. *Quarterly Journal: International Security, 38*(3), 176–183.

Diccionario Ilustrado Latín: Latino Español- Español Latín (Illustrated Latin Dictionary: Latin Spanish- Spanish Latin). (2009). Vox.

Hesiod. (1914). *Works and days, the Homeric hymns and Homerica with an English Translation by Hugh G. Evelyn-White.* Harvard University Press and William Heinemann Ltd.

Hühn, M. P., & Meyer, M. (2023). Sophistry or wisdom in words: Aristotle on rhetoric and leadership. *Business Ethics, the Environment & Responsibility.* https://doi.org/10.1111/beer.12516

Hursthouse, R., & Pettigrove, G. (2022). Virtue ethics. In E. Zalta & U. Nodelmand (Eds.), *The Stanford encyclopedia of philosophy.* https://plato.stanford.edu/archives/win2022/entries/ethics-virtue/

Immanuel, E. U. (2020). Initial development of assertive behaviour inventory. *Practicum Psychologia, 9*(2) https://journals.aphriapub.com/index.php/PP/article/view/1069

Kahneman, D. (2011). *Thinking fast and slow.* Penguin Books.

Lazarus, A. A. (1973). On assertive behaviour: A brief note. *Behaviour Therapy, 4*(5), 697–699. https://doi.org/10.1016/S0005-7894(73)80161-3

Liddell, H. G., & Scott, R. (1968). *A Greek-English lexicon.* Clarendon Press.

Llano-Cifuentes, C. (2000). *La amistad en la empresa (Friendship in organizations)*. Fondo de Cultura Económica.

Machiavelli, N. (1883). *Discourses on the first decade of Titus Livius*. London Kegel Paul, Trench & Co., Paternoster Square.

Massingham, P. (2019). An Aristotelian interpretation of practical wisdom: The case of retirees. *Springer Nature; Palgrave Communications, 5*(1), 123.

Matsumoto, D. (Ed.). (2009). *The Cambridge dictionary of psychology*. Cambridge University Press.

Nichols, M. P. (1987). Aristotle's defense of rhetoric. *The Journal of Politics, 49*(3), 657–677.

Online Cambridge Dictionary. (2023). *Definition of assertiveness*. Cambridge University Press. https://dictionary.cambridge.org/us/dictionary/english/assertiveness

Peneva, I., & Mavrodiev, S. (2013). A historical approach to assertiveness. *Psychological Thought, 6*(1), 3–26.

Plato. (1925). *Plato in twelve volumes*. Vol. 9 (W. R. M. Lamb, Trans.). Harvard University Press and William Heinemann Ltd.

Plato. (1967). *Plato in twelve volumes*. Vol. 3 (W. R. M. Lamb, Trans.). Harvard University Press and William Heinemann Ltd.

Romek, V. G. (2003). Trening uverennosti v mezhlichnostnyh otnosheniyah [Training of Confidence in Interpersonal Relations], *Saint -Petersburg, Russia: Rech (rus)*., https://www.klex.ru/809

Salter, A. (2002). *Conditioned reflex therapy: The classic book on assertiveness that began behaviour therapy*. Wellness Institute.

Smith, M. J. (2006). Trening uverennosti v sebe: kompleks upražnenij dlâ razvitiâ uverennosti [Training of self-confidence: A set of exercises to develop confidence]., Retrieved from http://www.orator.biz/library/books/traning_uverennosti_v_sebe/

Stein, S., & Book, H. (2006). The EQ edge: Emotional intelligence and your success, *Toronto, Ontario: Jossey-Bass.*, 978-0-470-68161-9

Wolpe, J. (1990). *The practice of behaviour therapy* (4th ed.). Pergamon Press.

Zagal, H. (2013). Right appetite, prudence and practical truth. The guidelines of the Eupraxía in the Nicomachean. *Metafísica y Persona, 9*, 91–101.

Zagal, H. (2018). Sýnesis, euphyía y anchínoia en Aristóteles. Algunas habilidades para el conocimiento del singular (Sýnesis, euphyía and anchínoia in Aristotle. Some skills for knowledge of the singular). *Anuario Filosófico, 32*(1), 129–145. https://doi.org/10.15581/009.32.29599

Zagal, H., & Llano-Cifuentes, C. (2001). *El rescate ético de la empresa y el mercado (The ethical rescue of the company and the market)*. Trillas.

PART II

Assertiveness from a Social Perspective

A healthy social life is found only when, in the mirror of each soul, the whole community finds its reflection, and when, in the whole community, the virtue of each one is living.
Rudolf Steiner

After a comprehensive understanding of assertiveness and assertiveness as a human right and virtue, the second part consists of three chapters examining assertiveness from a social perspective. It addresses assertiveness as a critical factor for peace maintenance, human rights exercise, and conflict prevention. Therefore, assertive rights are essential for promoting peace, justice, equity, inclusion, and intercultural competence. It highlights education's central role in building assertiveness since it targets intercultural competence by strengthening respect for human rights and fundamental freedoms, fostering understanding, tolerance, and interpersonal assertiveness among all individuals. Likewise, educating in assertive rights is the means that provides individuals and societies with the critical skills and knowledge necessary to become assertive citizens, capable of adapting to change and contributing to their community and culture.

Furthermore, it explores how Sociology provides the framework needed for the study and assessment of assertiveness and how it is a valuable tool for building more assertive societies. It delves into Reflexivity to offer a critical, comprehensive understanding of assertiveness.

Finally, it uses Social Work as the foundation for the study, comprehension, assessment, and promotion of assertiveness as a human right, which also requires a humanistic and person-centred approach.

Consequently, this part sets the basis for a comprehensive understanding of assertiveness from a social perspective.

CHAPTER 5

The Importance of Assertiveness in Social Anthropology

Francisco José Argüello-Zepeda

Introduction

Assertiveness, a social skill or communication style, is essential in human relations. Since the twentieth century, in the framework of globalisation, cultural contact has had an enormous expansion related to cultural diversity (Surpell, 1981), partly due to the development of communication and migratory processes, which require learning new social skills to communicate with other people from other cultures and within one's own culture. These processes are relevant today given the fact that people and social groups constantly interact in different national and international spaces.

The following chapter examines the essential components of assertiveness from psychology and communication to apply them to social anthropology, particularly in the dimensions of culture, otherness, interculturality, and its conditions. It is about relating assertiveness to the cultural context and intercultural competencies based on documentary research of

F. J. Argüello-Zepeda (✉)
Centro de Investigación Multidisciplinaria en Educación,
Universidad Autónoma del Estado de México, Toluca, Mexico

S. Castaños-Cervantes, C. Atristain-Suárez (eds.), *Assertiveness in the Context of Human Rights, Ethics, and Classical Virtues*,
https://doi.org/10.1007/978-3-031-60962-6_5

bibliohemerographic sources. It would make it possible to understand and prevent conflicts between social groups of different cultures, mestizo-indigenous or within indigenous cultures.

Basic Aspects of Assertiveness

Assertiveness has been considered a pendulum behaviour, oscillating between passive and aggressive attitude and a communication style (De la Plaza, 2012). It is also considered a skill related to self-esteem and respect for oneself and others (Castanyer, 2021).

In this regard, Alberti and Emmons (1999, p. 7) point out:

> Assertive behaviour promotes equality in human relationships, allowing us to act according to our interests, defend our opinions without feeling guilty, express our feelings honestly and comfortably, and exercise our rights without violating others.

Assertiveness encompasses various components: For their part, Bach and Forés (2010) define it as a meta-skill and an attitude or resource to communicate respectfully and in a timely and adequate manner. They privilege empathy and consideration for the other or a more compassionate encounter with others. All of this is intended to promote the common good. It is also vital for these authors to consider the context, culture, and country.

- Security and self-confidence; mutual respect in relationships; exercising our rights and opinions; freely expressing our feelings; congruent use of verbal and non-verbal language (Alberti & Emmons, 1999).
- Non-violence and the ability to assert oneself peacefully (Parent, 2006, quoted by Vargas, 2012).
- Respect for the rights of others, active listening, empathy, and development of social skills—the ability to talk and solve problems and manners (Shapiro, 1997).
- Non-verbal components—look, facial expression, body language, gestures (Castanyer, 2021).
- Paralinguistic components—volume, fluency, clarity, and speed (Castanyer, 2021).
- Verbal components—speech duration, feedback, questions (Castanyer, 2021).

This ability has been considered a middle ground between shyness and aggression (Vargas, 2012) while promoting self-esteem (Alberti & Emmons, 1999; Castanyer, 2021). The latter is a positive feeling derived from a positive evaluation of oneself, even acknowledging personal defects. It is close to security.

Field of Study of Social Anthropology and Learning Skills

As Harris (2001) points out, anthropology studies the human being in the past, present, and future, biologically and culturally. One of its branches, social anthropology, "consists of the description and analysis of cultures – socially learned traditions – of the past and present" (Harris, 2001, p. 14) and focuses on the origin and development of civilisations and their forms of behaviour (González, 2001).

A central concept in anthropology is that of culture, which has a holistic character and is therefore defined as the totality of learned behaviour (Salzmann, 1991) or as a system of signs and symbols (Geertz, 2005). It is also interpreted as the social heritage of a human community and the integrated set of traditions (Ribeiro, 1990). As the representatives of cultural relativism refer, each culture is unique and has forms of socialisation or enculturation, as shown by Margaret Mead's studies on the Pacific islands in the 1920s. Each culture has a specific scale of values and traditions.

> Human beings are humanised by integrating into these sets of traditions. At the same time, they are simultaneously incorporated into a specific ethnic entity by learning its language, being trained to do things according to its logic, behaving according to the norms that it consecrates, and, finally, living according to their uses and customs. (Ribeiro, 1990, p. 23)

It is essential to distinguish the difference between the concepts of enculturation or enculturation from the concept of acculturation:

> Enculturation or endoculturation involves learning norms, social skills, and values (Harris, 2001). This socialising process occurs within each culture; conversely, acculturation, understood as cultural loans, occurs between cultures according some authors as Melville Herskovits and Robert Redfield.

In this regard, Aguirre Beltrán (1957) perceives it as synonymous with cultural contact and, more specifically, as "the study of cultural transmission in process" (p. 208) while taking up a definition from another author:

> Acculturation is the process of change that emerges from the contact of groups that participate in different cultures. It is characterised by the continued development of a forced conflict between life forms of opposite senses that tend to their total identification. It manifests objectively at different levels of contradiction. (Gortari, 1956, p. 49)

In this regard, the cultural framework must be considered to understand how traditions and social skills are learned. Within these skills, it is interesting to highlight assertiveness, which is, along with empathy, a means to promote the common good. Assertiveness implies a training process that must begin with self-assessment, setting realistic goals, carrying out real-life tests, and re-evaluating the results. However, a cultural context will only sometimes favour assertive behaviour (Alberti & Emmons, 1999). In this regard, Castanyer (2021) states that it is necessary to identify the problem behaviour in its cognitive, motor and emotional dimensions and accurately identify the specific conditions that incite fear among people.

Regarding empathy, it is the ability to understand the feelings and emotions of others based on the recognition of the other as similar (López et al., 2014), which depends on individual and sociocultural factors. Similarly, Rogers interprets empathy as "the intimate understanding of the other, of the internal world of the other, as he is living it, even if he does not know how he is living it". It is also defined as the ability to read and feel the emotions and thoughts of others because it is a quality not only possessed by human beings but also by animals (Vargas, 2004). Authors like Rifkin (2010, p. 146) refer to empathic consciousness to explain human evolution, and as he mentions: "Suppose we live in a participatory world; our bodily experience is continuous interaction with others. In that case, empathy becomes how we enter the lives of others. It is also how we understand and form our everyday reality".

Interculturality, Multiculturality, and Otherness

Today, within multicultural societies, there are countless conflicts and misunderstandings between different social groups. According to Valencia et al. (2015), conflicts are inherent to human nature and can give rise to situations of violence or be regulated peacefully. Nevertheless, in the context of globalisation they tend to expand. As Rehaag (2006) points out, it is necessary to learn intercultural skills, which in turn encompass various linguistic sub-competences of the geographical area at a social and individual level, including empathy and understanding of the other, as well as "the ability to reflect on one's own culture and the acceptance of cultural relativism" (p. 7).

The author mentioned above distinguishes between multiculturalism and interculturality. The first implies parallel lives between different cultures. In contrast, the second suggests an interaction process between various cultures, which would embody the challenge to lean towards the cultural appreciation of the one and recognition of the "other", as the assertive attitude claims. For his part, Nivón (2012), picking up on García Canclini, states, "Both terms imply two modes of social production: multiculturalism suggests acceptance of the heterogeneous; interculturality implies that different parties are what they are in negotiation, conflict and reciprocal basis relationships".

Another interpretation of inter- and multiculturalism is offered by Dietz (2017), who points out that the multicultural approach considers the internal composition of society and its segmentation into different groups, while the intercultural perspective emphasises the type and quality of intergroup relations. According to Dietz and Mateos (2011), discourses on intercultural education are influenced by multiculturalism, which, according to Kymlicka (1996), encompasses different manifestations of cultural pluralism.

On the other hand, the issue of otherness is essential not only from a philosophical perspective (Lévinas, Ricoeur) but also from anthropology, as Harris (2001) has stated in the emic–etic relationship (outlook of the informant and the researcher, respectively), as well as in Krotz (quoted by Cansino, 2002), who understands it as a special kind of difference related to the experience of strangeness. It simultaneously constitutes a utopian thought, which would make it possible to build a bridge between anthropology and utopia. "In the alterity category, the other—in a sense described by Krotz—is not considered as such with its characteristics and even less with its natural ones, but as a community member, as a culture bearer" (Cansino, 2002, p. 134).

For Alegre and Guglielmi (2006), the meaning of the other has been changing according to the historical context and the predominant anthropological current, so that in the nineteenth-century evolutionism framework, "the other" has an inferiority connotation, as opposed to the functionalism of the first half of the twentieth century, where "the other" is related to a diverse and alien concept. Nonetheless, after World War II, another vision of otherness was developing as a counterpart to the hegemonic culture, with the influence of neo-Marxist positions.

Construction Process of Assertive Cultural Dialogue

Global economic, technological, and cultural interdependence requires developing intercultural communication considering globalisation. As Huntington (2015) points out, the world has undergone three phases: wars between kingdoms, conflicts over ideologies, and a clash of cultures today.

In this regard, it is imperative to promote an intercultural dialogue on a global scale (García, 2018), defined as "communication developed from cultures, so it cannot be restrained to a definition deprived of historical context" (García, 2012, p. 289). The author above considers the concept of culture, which she perceives as "the space-time we inhabit", essential to identify what is valuable in each culture (tradition, language, skin colour).

Other authors understand culture as a stage (Brockman, 2012) or as a whole (quoted by Harris, 2001; Salzmann, 1991). The latter states that culture includes various economic, political, social, and symbolic aspects and considers its specificity and the fact that it does not remain static but changes. At the same time, it suggests the need to promote a dialogical culture recognising the vulnerability of human beings. Also, it warns of the risks of monoculturalism (a closed society) and multiculturalism (a fragmented society).

For his part, Dussel (2010) captures the existing tensions within the culture and emphasises the asymmetry of different cultures, as well as the need to conduct a self-criticism of our own culture to carry out a genuine intercultural dialogue. Meanwhile, Fornet-Betancourt (2006), from a Latin American philosophy angle, interprets culture as an open process that requires the need for appropriation. In the first of his 11 theses on interculturality, he mentions, "Interculturality suggests diversity and difference, dialogue and contrast, which in turn implies a process of openness, lack of definition and even contradiction" (p. 29). It, therefore, suggests an action plan to achieve intercultural dialogue, which is ideal for him to build a global culture, representing a fair dialogue between "North" and "South".

Picking up on García, "interculturality is the opportunity to learn from each other" (2012, p. 298) while also emphasising the ethos, which "conveys the space-time relationship of human beings, it is a continuous habitual way of behaving, of being in time" (2018, p. 91). Hence, he references the intercultural ethos, which implies that both cultures value and respect their own and that of others.

Interculturality from a Historical Perspective

Since pre-Hispanic times, there have been various schools for the training of the Mexicas—as warriors, priests, or artists—who spoke Nahuatl, a language learned by the missionaries who arrived in the New World in the sixteenth century and reflected in catechisms. In the eighteenth century, an effort was made by the indigenous communities for the development of education. In the nineteenth century, with the liberal equality policy, the indigenous were assumed to be citizens, and the Castilian language was promoted; amid economic limitations, itinerant teachers emerged. At the end of this century, cultural diversity was seen as a burden and limiting economic development. In the twentieth century, in the 1920s, the cultural missions of José Vasconcelos and Moisés Sáenz, both educators who held managerial positions in the Ministry of Public Education (SEP), were promoted in 1921.

Anthropologists (Gamio, Sáenz and de la Fuente) contributed to developing a cultural policy of an indigenous nature from 1920 to 1940, creating the town's houses, the home of the indigenous student, and the bilingual primers (Escalante, 2023). Bilingual and bicultural education was supported at this time by Moisés Sáenz, who between 1932 and 1933 directed the educational and indigenous project "Estación Experimental de Carapan", a Purépecha community in the state of Michoacán, and later by Gonzalo Aguirre Beltrán, who was in charge of the National Indigenous Institute (INI) at the national level and proposed a theory of acculturation and cultural change (1957). From Gamio and Sáenz to Aguirre Beltrán, the indigenous position was based on the idea of integrating indigenous groups into Mexican society with a humanistic sense and based on bilingual and bicultural education.

Later, the idea of integration and assimilation was changed by developing a multicultural project proposed by Bonfil (1992) in which the indigenous peoples' culture was respected. From here, an intercultural policy based on intercultural education was promoted, first at the primary level and, later, in the new millennium, at the level of higher education, where the presence of Silvia Schmelkes stands out, who considers the strategic relationship between interculturality and biological and cultural diversity. For her, the foundations of intercultural education are the philosophy of otherness and democracy. The primary education curriculum of 2004 is intercultural.

Intercultural education at the higher level has as its antecedent the creation of the Autonomous Indigenous University of Mexico (UIEM) in 2001, located in Sinaloa. Years later, the first intercultural university emerged in San Felipe del Progreso, State of Mexico. The UIEM appeared in 2004 with the support of Dr Silvia Schmelkes, who has collaborated on intercultural policy in Mexico at the SEP. The first rector of the Intercultural University of the State of Mexico was Dr Felipe González Ortiz, who was responsible for building the UIEM building, which is circular, a copy of the pyramid of Ehécatl, the Mexica god of wind.

At the UIEM, academic mobility programmes allow students to do academic stays in North and Central America. Since its creation, enrollment has included both indigenous and mestizo populations. Recently, new offices have been created in Tepetlixpa and Xonacatlán, State of Mexico, where undergraduate programmes in intercultural health, sustainable development, and nursing are taught. According to González (2017, p. 140), the intercultural education system has as its goal: "the training of professionals committed to their communities of origin in whose actions scientific knowledge (Western) and ancestral knowledge (non-Western) are articulated".

Another of the purposes of these intercultural spaces is the consolidation of intercultural pedagogy. It has been possible to incorporate cultural aspects and the indigenous worldview in intercultural universities, but greater student participation in the curriculum is needed, as Sandoval (2018) points out. As various anthropologists (Felipe González, Saúl Alejandro) point out, the essence of interculturality implies the recognition of cultural diversity. The interculturality project benefits society in general, as well as the original peoples.

Interculturality implies considering the encounter between cultures, which has occurred since ancient times. In colonial times, cultural contact between the old and new world took place in a framework of asymmetrical intercultural relations, which caused different types of negative impacts on the indigenous population of Latin America. On this point, Fábregas (1992) outlines the case of the Choles of Chiapas, an ethnic group from the Mexican southeast that maintained exchange relations with other indigenous cultures, such as the Tzeltales and Zoques in pre-colonial times. Upon the Spanish conqueror's arrival, the disease's transmission affected their living and health conditions, which was unknown to the population.

As for the English colonisation, there was a Massachusetts Indian extermination in the current region of Massachusetts, in the United States, contrary to the colonisation in Latin America by the Spanish. Even though it began with physical violence, it later favoured miscegenation, using the indigenous population as cheap labour on farms and in mines. That is why the conquerors did not annihilate them, as Paz (2008) points out. Another example of negative impacts within intercultural relations between mestizos and indigenous people occurs in the Yoreme Mayo region, as described by Sandoval (2013, p. 196):

> In this ethnic region, we can hardly mention social and cultural homogeneity or a structural and functional unity in the society that has inhabited it. Integrating the Yoreme Mayo ethnic group into the mestizo ethnic group was presumed to be forced and juxtaposed in many ways. However, in general, it has been interpreted as a product of the continuous colonisation in which the agony of their culture is immersed.

Intercultural relations can be positive or negative, depending on the historical and cultural context, and are subject to a negotiation process. It is worth mentioning that there may also be disagreements and conflicts within indigenous cultures due to territorial issues and the appropriation of products emanating from land, as in the case discussed above (Sandoval, 2013). In some cases, indigenous peoples are expelled from their lands for having different religious beliefs, as in the central region of Chiapas or the name of "environmental conservation".

Case Analysis

In both cases introduced below, asymmetric intercultural relations and violence prevail, the latter defined as any intentional act that inflicts harm on others (Delgadillo, 2010) and, more specifically, a type of direct and cultural violence following Galtung's (1995) typology. These relationships changed as a result of ethnic and religious conflicts in the Balkans at the end of the twentieth century, giving rise to manifestations of direct and cultural violence that mainly affected women who had played an active and caring role in military groups and peacekeeping operations (Slapsak, 2001; Valencia et al., 2015) (case 1) or else in the experience of intercultural education in Mexico, which display cases of cultural violence about students from diverse indigenous cultures (case 2).

Case 1. The Breakup of Yugoslavia in the 1990s

As Hobsbawm (1998) mentions, Yugoslavia was formed in the early twentieth century (1918) and disintegrated (starting in 1991) in the historical context of the end of World War I and the fall of socialism, respectively. The first emerging nations were Serbia and Slovenia; afterwards, Croatia, Montenegro, Bosnia, Herzegovina, and Macedonia were annexed.

Before the ethnic and religious conflict occurred in 1991, which led to an intermittent civil war in the former Yugoslavia (Brom, 2007), there were positive and healthy intercultural relations between its inhabitants. Sarajevo, the capital of Bosnia and Herzegovina, was a multicultural city where Muslims, Orthodox, and Catholics lived side by side. According to Otero (2002), in this Balkan region, there was ethnic and religious diversity, and a factor of unity was the defence against external threats due to the historical control that the Austro-Hungarian Empire had exercised. According to Rodríguez (2014), another element that united them was the Serbian-Croatian or Croatian-Serbian language, "But the only firm and identifiable difference between Serbs and Croats is a religious one: Croats are Catholic, and Serbs are members of the Serbian Orthodox Church. Muslims by 'nationality'... are descendants of Muslims" (p. 55).

The conflict began in 1991, in the context of the disintegration of the socialist bloc, as Cela and Parras point out:

> After the fall of the Berlin Wall in 1989, the socialist States were also dissolving. However, there was still a case to be solved in Yugoslavia held together

> by Josip Broz "Tito", a Federal Republic made up of 6 Republics: Serbia, Croatia, Slovenia, Bosnia and Herzegovina, Montenegro, and Macedonia. (p. 85)

In addition to these six south Slavic peoples, there were some minorities within the multinational state, such as Albanians, Hungarians, Gypsies, and Turks, who later renamed them "nationalities" or "narodnost" (Garde, 1993).

Upon the death of "Tito" in 1980 and due to an economic and political crisis, the emancipation process of the Republics mentioned above hastened, favouring the beginning of a war that would cause the death of almost 200 thousand people and more than 2 million displaced people. "When [Croatia's] independence was effective and recognised by the EU and the US, in April 1992, Serbian paramilitary forces began bombing Sarajevo, thus initiating one of the bloodiest wars of ethnic cleansing of the 20th Century".

According to the authors mentioned above, three years later, the massacre of 7500 Muslims by the Serbs in Srebrenica occurred due to the Western power's passivity and the intervention lack from the UN and the media. All of this has remained in the people's collective memory, so, today, there is prolonged grief among people who lost relatives. For the worse, the conflict remains latent.

Once again, history repeats itself—as Marx said in the 18th Brumaire of Luis Bonaparte—we are still unable to learn from past mistakes. The case mentioned above, considered genocide, was a severe attack on human rights on the threshold of the new millennium. It is also worrisome that the demands for peace by many people of different ethnic compositions were not heard—at a rally held in the conflict zone in 1992, which was repressed, thus preventing an assertive dialogue between the parties in confrontation.

In case 1, a historical matter, Serbia's hegemony over other nations is observed, not only territorially but also due to its military power. "Greater Serbia" justifies its policy of ethnic cleansing due to the situation it experienced in the World War II, where it was allegedly discriminated against. It serves as a justification for leaders and guards to exercise physical, psychological, and gender violence against Albanians, Croats, and Bosnians. As Rodríguez (2014) points out, Serbia builds a myth that it was discriminated against in the previous conflict, which justifies the atrocities committed. On the UN side, reference has been made to its generally passive attitude towards the ethnic conflict. In this sense, the human rights of the "other" were not respected, and the behaviours were far from reality.

Case 2. Intercultural Education Experiences in Mexico

Mention should be made of the experiences throughout indigenous education in Mexico, which began in the wake of the Mexican Revolution to promote bilingual education in rural areas as part of an indigenous policy that sought the integration of indigenous people into the nation. It is worth mentioning the work of anthropologist and pedagogue Moisés Sáenz, who participated in the project "Experimental stay for the integration of Indigenous people" developed in Carapan, Michoacán, while promoting the bilingual indigenous school. However, in this transition stage of learning Spanish for the new generations, the indigenous language was undermined concerning the national language, partly due to the negative influence of some teachers and parents on the indigenous children, downplaying the importance of their mother tongue (Morales & Vázquez, 2007).

Discourse on intercultural education has been influenced by multiculturalism (Dietz & Mateos, 2011). Subsequently, multicultural policies have been enforced formally in Mexico and other countries, where legislation on cultural diversity and the rights of minorities has been passed in the new millennium. However, the exclusion towards rural and urban areas persists in practice. Intercultural education in Mexico, as such, arose in the wake of neoliberal governments at the beginning of the millennium, where an official interculturality of an assimilative nature was promoted (Sandoval, 2013). Unfortunately, it has not managed to overcome the acculturation policy surfacing in the middle of the twentieth century, which intended to integrate the indigenous people into the national society (Fábregas, 2013).

Intercultural education arises first in basic education (primary and secondary). It was subsequently extended to the level of higher education, creating 13 intercultural universities, all dependent on the Ministry of Public Education (SEP) and some Intercultural Normal Schools, which are intended to promote careers consistent with the indigenous culture and language. Nevertheless, the adequacy of knowledge between different cultures and the development of a horizontal pedagogy is needed in these experiences of intercultural education in Mexico to build a critical interculturality. For his part, Fábregas (2013) notes the existing tensions in intercultural universities between the old scheme of acculturation and assimilation of indigenous politics and the new intercultural projects.

There is a gap between discourse and reality (Dietz & Mateos, 2011; Sandoval, 2013). As Sandoval (2018, p. 24) points out, "Intercultural education was the response of the State to the indigenous movement and in particular to the demand for education of the Zapatista indigenous people in the Mexican southeast". On this matter, it is worth mentioning the 1994 indigenous insurrection of the EZLN in the state of Chiapas, where the Mexican State acknowledged a negotiation process with the leaders of the indigenous movement. It led to a dialogue between both parties, recognising the indigenous rights in the San Andrés Agreement, social and cultural rights they previously did not have. However, these rights were not embodied in the Mexican constitution, which was an act of legal violence on the part of the Mexican government; after that, the EZLN left the negotiating table.

The Intercultural University of the State of Mexico case is worth mentioning, built in the Mazahua region in San Felipe del Progreso. The enrollment comprises 70% of students from different indigenous cultures, and the remaining 30% are mestizos, with one international student. The career options range from sustainability, indigenous language, and intercultural communication to nursing. However, it has yet to reach the status of other higher education institutions, such as the public university, due to its reduced budget, negatively impacting teachers' working conditions.

To understand the official discourse in the educational field (see Table 5.1), it is worth mentioning the New Mexican Education, which constitutes a pedagogical proposal of the SEP in the framework of the

Table 5.1 Comparison of the official discourse in the Mexican educational field versus reality

Category	*Official speech*	*Reality*
Cultural diversity	Inclusion Culture of peace	Discrimination Violence
Citizen responsibility	Democratic culture Critical thinking Environmental care	Simulation
Educational quality	Financing	No resources

Source: Author's elaboration, based on the conference of the SEP University and Intercultural General Director, given at the Faculty of Behavioural Sciences of the UAEM (01/30/2023)

current government administration. It aims to promote an integral formation, articulate the different educational levels of the Mexican education system, and promote the following guiding principles, which unfortunately contrast with reality.

Even though there is a certain coherence in the official discourse, the actual conditions still need to be met to carry out this proposal in some HEIs, especially regarding institutions with limited budgets, such as those in the Mexican southeast, intercultural universities, or intercultural normal schools. In short, it can be affirmed that intercultural dialogue remains a political-ideological discourse in the cases described. Further work is needed to build positive, horizontal, intercultural relations to promote a culture of peace, as Sandoval (2018) points out.

Conclusions

The topic of assertiveness has been analysed from a psychological perspective (as balanced behaviour and regarding self-esteem) and in Communication Sciences (as a communication style). Nevertheless, it must also be addressed from the point of view of other disciplines, such as anthropology, particularly in the social anthropology subdiscipline, given its impact on generating consistent behaviours that strengthen people's self-esteem and social groups, as well as the respect and recognition of the "other", all of this allowing to prevent and resolve multicultural conflicts simultaneously.

Intercultural relations have existed since ancient times, and asymmetrical relations, based on domination and exclusion, as Sandoval (2013) has pointed out, where one ethnic group is subject to another (mestizos, hegemonic society), prevail. However, there may also be intercultural relations of negotiation and reciprocal basis, which need to be empowered.

As per the cases described, more than the existence of intercultural discourse and its institutions is required. The discourse mentioned above is also insufficient when it fails to establish consensus agreements. Hence, it is crucial to promote intercultural dialogue, which implies recognising the rights of the "other" and understanding this as a process that implies certain risks and personal, institutional, and contextual restraints to achieve an assertive intercultural dialogue satisfactorily. As has been seen throughout the text, the essence of interculturality is recognition of cultural diversity and respect for otherness, which requires an assertive ethos, which must be built.

References

Aguirre Beltrán, G. (1957). *El proceso de aculturación y el cambio socio-cultural (The process of acculturation and socio-cultural change)*. Fondo de Cultura Económica.

Alberti, E., & Emmons, M. (1999). *Viviendo con autoestima (Living with self-esteem)*. Editorial Pax Mexico.

Alegre, J., & Guglielmi, F. (2006). Exploración de la otredad en la filosofía contemporánea (Exploration of otherness in contemporary philosophy). *Nuevo itinerario Revista digital de filosofía, 2*, 1–17.

Bach, E., & Forés, A. (2010). *La asertividad: Para gente extraordinaria (Assertiveness: For extraordinary people)*. Plataforma editorial.

Bonfil, G. (1992). *Pensar nuestra cultura: Ensayos (Thinking our culture: Essays)*. Alianza editorial.

Brockman, J. (2012). Introducción (Introduction). In J. Brockman (Ed.), *Cultura (Culture)*. Crítica.

Brom, J. (2007). *Esbozo de historia universal (Outline of universal history)*. Grijalbo.

Cansino, C. (2002). *Esteban Krotz, La otredad cultural. Entre utopía y ciencia. Un estudio sobre el origen, el desarrollo y la orientación de la antropología (Esteban Krotz, Cultural otherness. Between utopia and science. A study on the origin, development, and orientation of anthropology)*. Fondo de Cultura Económica and Universidad Autónoma Metropolitana-Iztapalapa.

Castanyer, O. (2021). *Asertividad, sana autoestima (Assertiveness, A healthy self-esteem)*. Desclée Brouwer.

De la Plaza, J. (2012). *La inteligencia asertiva: Cómo, cuándo y dónde expresar lo que piensas (Assertiveness intelligence: How, when and wher to express your thoughts)*. V & R. Editoras.

Delgadillo, L. (2010). *Violencia laboral, Una realidad incómoda: Estudios de caso desde una perspectiva de género (Work violence, an uncomfortable reality: Case studies from a gender-based approach)*. Universidad Autónoma del Estado de México.

Dietz, G. (2017). Interculturalidad, una aproximación antropológica (Interculturality, an anthropological approach). *Perfiles educativos, XXXIX*(156), 192–207.

Dietz, G., & Mateos, L. (2011). *Interculturalidad y educación intercultural en México, Un análisis de los discursos nacionales e internacionales en su impacto en los modelos educativos mexicanos (Interculturality and intercultural education in Mexico, An analysis of national and international discourses in their impact on Mexican educational models)*. Secretaría de Educación Pública.

Dussel, E. (2010). Transmodernidad e interculturalidad (Interpretación desde la filosofía de la liberación) (Transmodernity and interculturality [Interpretation from the philosophy of liberation]. In A. Mondragón & F. Monroy (Eds.),

Interculturalidad, historia, experiencias y utopías (Interculturality, history, experiences and utopias). Plaza y Valdés.

Escalante, C. (2023, March 23). Historiografía de la educación indígena en México (Historiography of indigenous education in Mexico) [Conference]. Jornada de educación indígena, Toluca, Mexico.

Fábregas, A. (1992). *Pueblos y culturas de Chiapas (Towns and cultures of Chiapas)*. Miguel Ángel Porrúa, Librero Editor.

Fábregas, A. (2013). La educación superior como vehículo para la articulación intercultural en América Latina (Higher education as a vehicle for the intercultural articulation in Latin America). *Punto norte, 2*, 139–150.

Fornet-Betancourt, R. (2006). Interculturalidad o barbarie, 11 tesis provisionales para el mejoramiento de la teorías y prácticas de la interculturalidad como alternativa de otra humanidad (Interculturality or barbarism, 11 provisional theses for the improvement of the theories and practices of interculturality as an alternative to another humanity). *Comunicación, 4*, 27–49.

Galtung, J. (1995). *Violencia, paz e investigación sobre la paz, Investigaciones teóricas, sociedad y cultura contemporánea (Violence, peace and peace research, Theoretical research, contemporary society and culture*). Tecnos.

García, C. (2012). El diálogo intercultural, una necesidad insoslayable (Intercultural dialogue, an unavoidable need). In M. H. Fernández (Ed.), *Ciencias sociales, humanidades y salud, Metodología y análisis (Social sciences, humanities and health, Methodology and análisis)* (pp. 289–299). ECICUSXXI, Editorial Centro de Investigación campus Universitario Siglo XXI; Centro de Investigación de Investigación de Estudios Comparados de América Latina, CIECAL; Instituto de Estudios Históricos y Económicos de la Universidad Complutense de Madrid.

García, C. (2018). *Hacia la construcción de un ethos intercultural (Towards building an intercultural ethos)*. Editorial Torres Asociados.

Garde, P. (1993). La ex Yugoslavia: una trampa (The former Yugoslavia: A trap). In *El correo de la UNESCO* (pp. 39–42). UNESCO.

Geertz, C. (2005). *La interpretación de las culturas (Interpretation of cultures)*. Gedisa.

González, A. (2001). Las estructuras elementales de la antropología social: la caja negra, en ¡¿Antropología?¡ ¿Y eso qué es? (The elementary structures of social anthropology: The black box, in Anthropology? And what is that?). *Revista Diario de Campo*, Suplemento 16, noviembre, INAH / CONACULTA.

González, F. (2017). Orientalismo e interculturalidad en el marco de la emergencia del intelectual originario de América (Orientalism and interculturality in the framework of the emergence of the intellectual originating from America). In F. González et al. (Eds.), *Horizontes: Interculturalidad, estudios poscoloniales e indianidad (Horizons: Interculturality, postcolonial studies and Indianness)*. Universidad Autónoma del Estado de México.

Gortari, E. (1956). *Introducción a la lógica dialéctica (Introduction to dialectical logic)*. Fondo de Cultura Económica.

Harris, M. (2001). *Antropología Cultural (Cultural anthropology)*. Alianza editorial.

Hobsbawm, E. (1998). *Historia del siglo XX (History of 20th century)*. Crítica. http://uiem.edomex.gob.mx/planteles

Huntington, S. (2015). *El choque de civilizaciones: y la reconfiguración del orden mundial (The clash of civilizations: and the reconfiguration of the world order)*. Paidós.

Kymlicka, W. (1996). *Ciudadanía multicultural, Una teoría liberal de los derechos de las minorías (Multicultural citizenship, A liberal theory of minority rights)*. Paidós.

López, M., Arán, V., & Richaud, M. (2014). Empatía: Desde la percepción automática hasta los procesos controlados (Empathy: From automatic perception to controlled processes.). *Avances en psicología latinoamericana, 32*(1), 37–51.

Morales, R., & Vázquez, N. (2007). *Inequidad en la educación indígena; El proceso de enseñanza-aprendizaje (Inequity in indigenous education; The teaching-learning process)* [Bachelor's Thesis]. Universidad Autónoma del Estado de México.

Nivón, E. (2012). Néstor García Canclini y las políticas culturales (Néstor García Canclini and cultural policies). In E. Nivón (Ed.), *Voces híbridas, Reflexiones en torno a la obra de García Canclini (Hybrid voices, Reflections on the work of García Canclini)* (pp. 31–47). Universidad Autónoma Metropolitana and Siglo veintiuno editores.

Otero, M. (2002). Reseña de La desintegración de Yugoslavia de Carlos Taibo (Review of The Disintegration of Yugoslavia by Carlos Taibo). *Aldea mundo, 7*(3), 111–114.

Parent, J. (2006). Fenomenología de la no violencia (Phenomenology of nonviolence). *Tiempo de educar, 7*(13), 9–29.

Paz, O. (2008). *El laberinto de la soledad (The Labyrinth of Solitude)*. Cátedra.

Rehaag, I. (2006). Reflexiones acerca de la interculturalidad (Reflections on interculturality). *CPU-e Revista de investigación educativa, 2*, 1–9.

Ribeiro, D. (1990). Cultura y enajenación (Culture and alienation). In H. Zemelman (Coord.), *Cultura y política en América Latina (Culture and politics in Latin America)*. Siglo veintiuno editores & Editorial de la Universidad de las Naciones Unidas.

Rifkin, J. (2010). *La civilización empática, La carrera hacia una conciencia global en un mundo en crisis (Empathic civilization, The race towards global consciousness in a world in crisis)*. Paidós Estado y Sociedad.

Rodríguez, I. (2014). El esencialismo racial y el genocidio. El caso de Yugoslavia (Bosnia-Hersegovina) (Racial essentialism and genocide. The case of Yugoslavia [Bosnia-Hersegovin]). *Cuicuilco, 21*(60), 45–66.

Salzmann, Z. (1991). *Antropología; Panorama general (Anthropology: General overview)*. Editorial Patria.

Sandoval, E. (2013). *Educaciones interculturales en México (Intercultural education in Mexico)*. Estudios Sociológicos.

Sandoval, E. (2018). *Etnografía e investigación acción intercultural para los conflictos y la paz: metodologías descolonizadoras (Ethnography and intercultural action research for conflict and peace: decolonizing methodologies)*. Editorial Alfonso Arena.

Shapiro, L. (1997). *La inteligencia emocional de los niños (Emotional intelligence in children)*. Vergara Editor S.A.

Slapsak, S. (2001). The use of women and the role of women in the Yugoslav War. In I. Skjelsbaek & D. Smith (Eds.), *Gender, peace & conflict* (pp. 161–183). SAGE Publications, Ltd.

Surpell, R. (1981). *Influencia de la cultura en el comportamiento (Influence of culture on behavior)*. Ediciones CEAC.

Valencia, P., Jiménez, J., & Muñoz, F. (2015). Complejidad, conflictividad y paz, Una perspectiva global (Complexity, conflict and peace, A global perspective). In P. Valencia, F. Muñoz, & C. Flores (Eds.), *Conflictos y paces (Conflicts and peace)* (pp. 13–49). Editorial Universidad de Granada.

Vargas, G. (2004). *Comunícate, cautiva y convence (Communicate, captivate and convince)*. Aguilar.

Vargas, H. (2012). "Ahimsa y Satyagraha: Principios de actuación que buscan la justicia basada en la fuerza de un corazón compasivo y osado" ("Ahimsa and Satyagraha: Principles of action that seek justice based on the strength of a compassionate and daring heart"). In M. H. Fernández (Ed.), *Ciencias sociales, humanidades y salud, Metodología y análisis (Social sciences, humanities and health, Methodology and análisis)* (pp. 279–288). ECICUSXXI, Editorial Centro de Investigación campus Universitario Siglo XXI; Centro de Investigación de Investigación de Estudios Comparados de América Latina, CIECAL; Instituto de Estudios Históricos y Económicos de la Universidad Complutense de Madrid.

CHAPTER 6

Assertiveness: A View from the Perspective of Reflexivity

Ramón C. Rocha-Manilla

Introduction

During its development, assertiveness has been detached from the sociological approach, even though it corresponds to a problem of study in this discipline. The difficulty in the management of assertiveness (in social actors who direct public policies, who have managerial functions, or who play roles of power in health or education) has been the origin of most of the representation of various collective phenomena such as social movements, social disorganisation, symbolic violence or other types of manifestations of community nonconformity.[1] Nevertheless, in another exploitation, due to the lack of way, subjects dominated by traditional structures reproduce relations of subjection and objectification of

[1] It is essential to not confuse assertiveness with "aggressiveness", confused with belligerence, obscenity and lousy faith (Caballo, 1983, p. 53).

R. C. Rocha-Manilla (✉)
Benemérita Universidad Autónoma de Puebla BUAP, Puebla, México

Universidad de la Salud UNISA CDMX, CDMX, México

S. Castaños Cervantes, C. Atristain-Suárez (eds.), *Assertiveness in the Context of Human Rights, Ethics, and Classical Virtues*,
https://doi.org/10.1007/978-3-031-60962-6_6

assertiveness to the personal and community *habitus*, generating this, among other problems, the lack of assertiveness in the development of health. In this context, the general objective of this essay is to seek an approach to the study of assertiveness from sociology through reflexivity, taking as empirical elements some personal data from experience as a surgeon. This approach is relevant; assertiveness is a phenomenon whose contrast (non-assertive behaviour) entails risky social interactions. This approach to the study of sociology can contribute to its better understanding, application and *praxis* in this field of knowledge, in addition to collaborating with other scientific disciplines also interested in this topic.

In Sociology, Reflexivity and Assertiveness

Assertiveness, its etymological origin in Latin, is composed of the suffix *dad* (meaning quality) on the word assertive. Therefore, "assertive" contains the suffix *ivo*, which means passive or active relation to the word *assert*, and *assertus*, which means to affirm that something is true.[2] In the second half of the twentieth century, assertiveness was discussed concretely. During the previous centuries, especially during the Middle Ages, assertive behaviours were unthinkable even in the Western world, given the dominance of dogmatic thinking based on the impossibility of *asserting ("asertivar" in Spanish and proposed as a new neologism)*[3] against the behaviour determined by theocentric paradigms. Later, with the Renaissance, from the fifteenth century onwards, thinkers sought to question the dominant dogmatism and from countries where the apparatus of the Holy Inquisition did not interfere. From rationalism and empiricism they launched incentives to rethink the behaviour, approaching assertiveness. However, this could be in doubt when considering the reason that questions the medieval and Renaissance dogma since this was only sectorised. According to Bourdieu (1999a), "the development of reason is inseparable from the progressive autonomization of social microcosms based on privilege, in which modes of thought and action are theoretically universal but, in practice, monopolised by some, have been gradually invented". Thus, the possible assertiveness in these centuries would not be

[2] http://etimologias.dechile.net/?asertividad#:~:text=This%20word%20comes%20from%20lat%20C3%ADn,intertwine%2C%20link%2C%20link%2C%20draw.

[3] *Assertivate ("asertivar" in Spanish)*, this concept is proposed for the present essay to cite it as the assertive practice in social interaction to distinguish it from assertive behaviour.

universal. Any therapist for assertive behaviour would have been burned alive at the stake of the Holy Inquisition for trying to *assertivise* his patients. We would have to continue exploring whether ideological movements, such as rationalism, empiricism, liberalism (that of the seventeenth century), historical materialism and other dispositions in the last 500 years, have been concrete processes that contributed to achieving *assertiveness in* populations that were gradually freeing themselves from dogmatic behaviours that prevented them from the freedom to decide.

Assertiveness is a topic that began to be discussed more frequently in the seventies of the twentieth century (Caballo, 1983). As a concept, assertiveness refers to the self-assertion of the personality, self-confidence, self-esteem, poise, confidence and efficient communication (Rodríguez & Serralde, 1991). Assertive practice is a healthy behaviour described as an appropriate action, alien to the anxiety between individuals (Wolpe, 1993). In a cognitive view, assertive practice consists of expressing what one believes, feels and desires directly and honestly, asserting one's rights and respecting the rights of others (Gaeta González & Galvanovskis Kasparane, 2009).

Assertiveness is a behaviour and social practice based on recognition, truthfulness, affirmation, dignity, courage and honesty. Its first approach has been from psychology, which has been in charge of studying it and generating options for its study through the so-called assertiveness training, mainly used to decondition maladaptive habits of anxiety response to other people's behaviour, exploring the appropriate expression of other emotions that these people evoke (Wolpe, 1993).

Without going into further detail, assertiveness in psychology is a behaviour (for sociology, it is a *praxis*) which can be divided into four specific and distinct response patterns: the first is the ability to say "no", the second is the ability to ask for favours and make demands, the third is the ability to express positive and negative feelings and the fourth is the ability to initiate, continue and end general conversations (Lazarus, 1973, cited by Flores Galaz, 2002).

As a behaviour, assertiveness is a personality trait that seeks to establish functional relationships that seek positive results. This personality trait is not isolated but social since it acts within specific socio-cultural contexts; hence, its concept is not universal, so it must be adapted to the needs and the culture (Castaños-Cervantes, 2008). In a sociological view, assertiveness is not a behaviour but a *praxis* or social practice; it is proposed to refer to it in this essay with the neologism *assertivate ("asertivar" in Spanish)*, this being a practice dependent on the social field where the subjects interact and the cultural reproduction in which it lives, where sociology operates.

Sociology is a science that can study assertiveness, not as behaviour but as social interaction and practice, as we propose when referring to *assertiveness.* If we want to conceptualise it, for the usefulness of this article, we can resort to Simmel's contributions (Ritzer, 2001) to refer to sociology as *the science of social interaction.* However, going further and sustaining the construction of this operational definition for this manuscript in the reflexive stance, we start from Pierre Bourdieu's contributions that sociology is a critical science which produces fear because it lifts the veil of hidden, even repressed things (Bourdieu, 2000); consequently, sociology is a discipline that explores by questioning. Consequently, sociology is *the critical science of social interaction.* Moreover, what does sociology criticise? It criticises the reason for social interaction.

In this way, social interaction is responsible for the entire field of study of sociology: everyday life such as school, labour and domestic social reproduction, to mention other more specific ones such as the process of health-disease-care, social movements, social disorganisation, power relations, cultural copy, reproduction of violence, class struggle, inequality, among other senses. These practices, in a *negative way* for the exercise of their dignity and human rights, can be developed without assertiveness, without *asserting*; that is, their social actors say and act without being able to say "no" or saying "no" when it is not what they want, or they want it because there is a *doxa* that conditions them; their actors act with passivity or aggressiveness, but not in a middle, neutral, focused, conscious or reflexive plane.

Reflexivity constitutes the origin of the processes of *detraditionalisation* characteristic of contemporary societies—that is, the methods of relativisation and questioning of cultural traditions (Murguía Lores, 2002). The *detraditionalisation* intensifies the reflexive process of the construction of individual and collective identities, which can then be cemented from the confluence of cultural elements and social relations that have very diverse origins: from the routine ones that result from daily interaction to those that make possible the processes of *unanchoring*[4] that separate the

[4] De-anchoring is a term proposed by Giddens stating that there is a distancing between event, time and space in the present age. According to him, this is the basis of the increasingly dynamic nature of modernity, which is stimulated by electronic technologies.

physical circumstance from the social situation, embodying one of the most critical consequences of modernity (Giddens, 1995, cited by Murguía Lores, 2002). Bourdieu proposes a reflexive sociology that reveals the researcher's prejudices, values and social position vis-à-vis the object, categories, procedures and analysis methods. He calls this procedure the *objectification of the objectifying subject* (Bourdieu, 1997), which is oriented towards a self-socio analysis to make the research more rigorous. Under Bourdieusian epistemology, considering his view of social phenomena, assertiveness for sociology does not refer to a way of using it to understand reality, but assertiveness should be taken as an instrument to know the construction of this reality.

The dominant paradigms, or *doxas*, are cultural structures that can contravene an assertive practice; that is to say, the *doxa* can repress *assertiveness*, it has put it in crisis, for denial bows to the hegemonic medical model, patriarchal norms, power relations or social rules. So, reflexivity in Bourdieu shows that the most disinterested or most audacious decisions can be understood starting from the logic that moves the agents to the social field and from the strategies to increase and conserve capital (Giglia, 2003) to increase the accumulated economic, social, cultural or symbolic work, in the form of money.

Reflexivity is shown as an effort to *objectify the subject of objectification*. It requires this to be fully realised with a disenchanted reflection on the principles and conditions of functioning of social science as a whole. An essential part of the work of objectifying the subject of objectification consists of considering assertive exercise (as is done with other practices, such as health, education or scientific work) as a habitus, a body or set of dispositions that become automatic, incorporated, of which we are not aware unless we perform an explicit act of objectification (Giglia, 2003). One can only think of assertiveness as a practice of making a science of the scientific field, call it "sociology of sociology or science of science" (Bourdieu, 2001). As such, a sociological approach from reflexivity to assertiveness, that is, to the field of assertive social practices, requires using the tools provided by reflexivity to objectify the subject in his assertive exercise.

Formation of an Assertive *Habitus*: *To Assertivate* (*"Asertivar"* in Spanish)

From sociology, assertiveness, as a social practice, is inserted into the *habitus, i.e., assertiveness* is incorporated into the *habitus*. The conditionings associated with a particular class produce *habitus*, which "is a system of durable and transferable dispositions, structured structures predisposed to function as structuring structures, that is, as generating and organising principles of practices and representations that can be objectively adapted to their goal without supposing the conscious purpose of certain ends, nor the express mastery of the operations necessary to reach them, objectively 'regulated' and 'regular' without being at all the product of obedience to certain rules, and, for all that, collectively orchestrated without being the product of the organising action of an orchestra conductor" (Bourdieu, 1972, p. 178). The *habitus* is individual to the subjects, although constructed communally, and is incorporated into their bodies through accumulated experiences; with this, they carry out systems of schemes of perception, appreciation and action-to-act strategies adapted and renewed incessantly but framed within the impositional and structural limits of which they are the product, and which define them (Bourdieu, 1999a).

In other words, as Alicia Gutiérrez (2005, p. 68) refers, it can be explained that "habitus refers to those dispositions to act, perceive, value, feel and think in a certain way rather than another, dispositions that the individual has internalised in the course of his history. The habitus is, then, a history-made body".

The concept of *habitus* denotes that individuals' actions are understood not only by the present situation but also by the situations lived in the past. These past experiences give us endless ways of feeling, perceiving, thinking and acting. Depending on these internalised schemes, persons will act in one way or another in each situation (Martín-Criado, 2022). Therefore, the *habitus* is shaped with the characteristics of three elements. The first is that it has a systematic character, in which numerous schemes are presented that are applied in various fields, where the subject learns them by moving in a structured social world, where the logic of "yes" or "no" assertiveness would be present. However, at the same time, it would produce a set of systematic choices in multiple domains to generate new novel practices from those principles, hence the starting point of school or family training and its reproduction in the construction of assertiveness in childhood. The second, the *habitus*, is incorporated from childhood, where these basic schemes are learned with the *body in the body*, in a process that does not pass through consciousness; consequently, the subject reproduces these schemes in his practices involuntarily and not consciously. The third is the persistent *habitus*, which is very resistant to change due to its deep rooting in the bodies and because, from them, the subject selects the areas and information more in line with his *habitus*, being difficult to modify (Martín-Criado, 2022).

Consequently, assertiveness can be structured in the *habitus* of the people by the actions of education or promotion of mental health, and these actions can contribute to de-structuring the *habitus* of people who tend not to *assert*; this is done by psychology through therapies and training for the acquisition of assertive skills, intervening psychologically in the de-structuring of the *habitus*. It is not a matter of psychologising sociology but instead of identifying which public policies, cultural practices or power relations can contribute to an assertiveness approach in the *habitus*.

The *habitus* can be restructured according to social influence, as does public opinion; in itself, this opinion internalises the impact of the life of the subjects; public opinion constantly reaffirms the structuring of the *habitus*. It can be associated with the proposal referred to in the *teoría del Espiral del Silencio (theory of the Spiral of Silence)*, formulated by Elizabeth Noëlle Neumann in the 1970s. According to this theory, public opinion results from individuals' interaction with their environment. Public opinion stimulates the possibility for individuals not to isolate themselves socially, "in order not to find themselves isolated, an individual can renounce his judgment. And this is the condition of life in a human society; otherwise, integration would not be possible" (Noëlle-Neumann, 1995, p. 200). Public opinion is an expression of *doxa* based on a reflexive approach. The *doxa* is what *people unknowingly accept* (Bourdieu & Eagleton, 2003), which embodies dominant ideas that are adhered to in the form of practices for the unconscious manipulation of the body (Bernal et al., 2018), as in the case of the worker who does not refuse to do a favour requested by the employer, because of the beliefs that the systems of domination have imposed on the mind. *Doxa* is "beliefs or opinions that are presented as natural and unquestionable and that imply practical knowledge" (Bourdieu, 2001, p. 9); in other words, *doxa* is an everyday, unreflective, naturalised practice that is constituted as a central element in the formation of ideas (Bernal et al., 2018). *Doxa* works subtly "through language, through the body, through attitudes towards things, which are below the level of consciousness" (Bourdieu & Eagleton, 2003, p. 299).

Thus, *doxa*, whether expressed in public opinion, in the media, in the dialogues of everyday life, in the religious sermon, or in political discourse, is part of the structures of daily life that is seen as natural, and, therefore, it is not questioned; the worker does not question that the boss asks him for an extra favour at work because the power structures allow it, but the worker does not dare to ask the boss for a favour, because the *doxa* makes him distrust his security, makes him shy, fearful, makes him not be assertive. In an interview between Bourdieu and Eagleton (2003, p. 299), it is stated that *doxa* is something people accept without knowing. The authors exemplified this: "When you ask a sample of individuals what the main factors of success in school are, the lower they are on the social scale, the more they will believe in natural talent or gifts, the more they will believe that those who are successful are better endowed with intellectual capacities granted by nature. Furthermore, the more they accept their own exclusion, the more they believe they are stupid, and the more they affirm, 'Yes, I wasn't good at English, I wasn't good at French, I wasn't good at mathematics'. This is not to say that dominated individuals tolerate anything, but they accept much more than we think and much more than they are aware of". Identifying assertiveness in the previous example, we can see that the *doxa* contributes to preventing subjects from considering themselves unfit and refusing because they think they cannot or should not, that is, subjects of lower social scale or who share lesser attributes associated with success by the dominant *doxa*, their *assertiveness* will be limited, framed according to the *doxa*.

Following Bourdieu's example and thinking more about Latin American daily life, we can see the *doxa in the* case of a patient I remember, who, when explaining the cost of her treatment,[5] said that she had neither money nor time to rest and, therefore, she would have to endure her pain because she is indebted to a department store that offers products on credit but with shameless interest. This store provides a particular type of prestige or fashion in its purchase, showing in its promotion models or famous people with phenotypes of Western beauty prototypes. The patient consumes these products and is put into debt. However, in addition, she has committed herself because a neighbouring family visited her to invite her to be the godmother of her daughter's fifteenth birthday, and even knowing about her debts, the patient accepted, committing to buy the teenager's dress, which will have a high cost. The patient did not know

[5] The cost was stipulated in the medication purchase and the rest of the time I had to take.

how to say "no" in the face of the *doxa,* has become poorer and postpones her medical care. This is the situation of many people and families in Mexico.

This doxa contributes to constructing and maintaining a form of language, a way of speaking. The speech comes from a power structure or institution that says what to talk about and determines the discourse that the physician pronounces in front of his patient, to the point of being able to scold, forbid or threaten him. After the first consultation, many patients are known who tell the doctor, "I thought he was going to scold me". According to Bourdieu (1985, p. 69), "the use of language, which implies both the manner and the matter of discourse, depends on the social position of the speaker, a position that governs the access he/she may have to the language of the institution, to the official, orthodox, legitimate word". Patients prepare their language before entering the doctor's field of power; they reproduce a process of self-censorship that fights over assertiveness because, institutionally, they must say *yes* to everything the doctor tells them; we doctors get to point out our patient's overweight or obesity, when it would be unlikely that the patient would do the same towards us; And if he does so, he would be out of his position according to the institutional structure, and would be seen as disrespectful; "the authorised spokesperson can only act by words on other agents and, through his work, on things themselves to the extent that his word concentrates the symbolic capital accumulated by the group that he has given that mandate and with whose power he is invested" (Idem). Hence, the physician who reproduces the forms of language learning in the *hidden curriculum*[6] of his training and updating accumulates that symbolic capital that makes him maintain his power. The patient, who recognises that he needs medical intervention, is subject to that power by reproducing the conditioned, non-assertive language on a medical *doxa* that intervenes in his *habitus* as a patient.

The *habitus* in the subjects confronts public opinion and fights the symbolic structures represented in its ideas. Suppose these are in the minority of public opinion. In that case, it represses the expression of those ideas that make up its cultural capital, and in order not to remain isolated, it adheres to its social behaviour to that of the dominators in public opinion; we can describe public opinion as "the dominant tendency that imposes a

[6] These are learning processes reproduced by the academic *habitus* and incorporated by students, even though these aspects do not appear in the official curriculum.

posture and behaviour of submission, while threatening the rebellious individual with isolation and, for the politician, with a loss of popular support" (Noëlle-Neumann, 1995, p. 201). The doxa then is a collective habitus that does not generate reflection in the subjects; so, the doxa can stimulate that the assertive practice is not expressed, giving difficulties when asserting; the doxa contributes to forming the capitals that will build the habitus.

Public opinion generates oppression. According to cultural activist Augusto Boal (1931–2009), "oppression is when the monologue of another dominates one person and has no opportunity to respond" (quoted by Bertrand von, 2023). Oppression is generated by a narrative of domination, where it is not that the majority has the voice of domination but that some are the ones who have it because they possess the means to dominate and are positioned in the part of the structure that allows them to dominate. This dominant narrative is driven by people with more voice and power, while others are silenced (von Bertrand, 2023); that is public opinion.

Public opinion seeks to condition the *habitus*, individual or collective, which can contradict *assertiveness*. If the subjects put their assertiveness at risk in the face of public opinion, they could adopt two possibilities: submission not to be rejected or empowerment by encouraging their assertiveness. However, this could label them antagonists to the supposedly established positive order.

Nonetheless, the hegemony of public opinion media has had disadvantages since liquid modernity with the globalisation of social networks. The *habitus* struggles to build the identity of the subjects who face the community and the doxa; according to Bauman (2001), "identity is invented when the community collapses". The *doxa* struggles to manage the identity of its subjects in its way, and of course, *asserting* collapses the *doxa*. As a result, identity becomes a way of rethinking the community through more flexible schemes to interpret the sense of connection with the rest of the subjects, which do not necessarily have to do with the identity that creates the community through the regular engagement one has in how the public opinion of common issues is treated and discussed (Cirera Bianco, 2018).

There is an illusion in social networks and their digital media that makes people believe that what is manifested in them is accurate or assertive, generating a more homogeneous approach to public opinion, and where individualisation has been encouraged by the lack of identification due to the growing increase of social networks as symbolic channels of interaction (Cirera Bianco, 2018). Nevertheless, in the explosion of these networks, as procurers in the formation of public policies, a struggle has been generated to consciously or unconsciously make a culture of assertiveness, emerging new agents in media that reach great popularity and have been driven by their unity, or by the tools that electronic systems have to get more people, such as algorithms, or the manipulation of electronic penetration formats, as we have seen in the pandemic caused by the massive infection of SARS CoV2 (COVID-19), where prophets, specialists, agents of opinion and other subjects that have oriented or disoriented an assertiveness towards the disease emerged. There are numerous examples like this one, and new ones are published daily.

Social networks can disrupt assertiveness, generating nonconformity and settling democracies. There is nonconformity in some governments' actions for not improving the quality and efficiency of politics, in addition to corruption, lack of transparency and a low quality of life (Downs, 1973). Inequality has been motivated by the competition offered by the capitalist system, where the social networks push away the assertiveness of the subjects, structuring consumerist and dissatisfied *habitus*; on the other hand, we see it in some consolidated democracies, primarily its population not subject to the imposition of public opinion, explaining how different, in unconsolidated democracies, the low level of participation and the spiral of silence does not question the *doxa* and weakens assertiveness.

In practice, subjects recognise in the *doxa* the public or private actors that influence the structuring of their *habitus*; they recognise them and position them as agents that will constantly feed the box of ideas of each person; they set them to such a degree that they consider that these subjects of opinion are not wrong, and therefore they dispose of them as a necessity of consumption. Consequently, *doxa* and its agents of view accumulate in the cultural capitals of the subjects that, without assertive criteria, structure the *habitus* of those they dominate, as the hegemonic medical model does to its patients, and this is achieved by keeping critical thinking disengaged in them, making subjects or communities without *assertivating*.

It can be seen in the health phenomenon when one once attended to a patient with a small child with a neurological disability. Upon reviewing her case, it turned out that the child had difficulty breathing at birth, leading to the neuronal death of a part of the brain, which made her doctor and the private hospital treating her request a monthly CT scan to monitor the brain, an unnecessary situation since a single study is sufficient to assess the brain atrophy generated, which is irreversible. The mother accepted the economic burden of covering the studies month after month, and although some family members questioned the monthly repetition of this auxiliary diagnosis from their non-medical knowledge, the mother did not ask for it; she accepted it until she could not pay any more. After seeing her, she was told that the study was unnecessary, and she agreed not to do it anymore; that is, the power of another doctor decided for her. In the process that referred her to no longer do the tomography, she argued that it was necessary because her previous physician had indicated it; there was no *assertiveness* until it was decided to explain to her the physiological reason why the study should not be repeated, and that this reply, more than ignorance of the treating physician, could be due to a business, it is here when is considered that she *asserted*, especially when she said that she would no longer believe so quickly in physicians; perhaps this experience touched her *habitus*.

On another occasion, a patient in consultation, when asked why he thought his type 2 diabetes mellitus originated, said that it was his fault. When questioned, he said that this was what the doctor diagnosed, and "*…he was right; he drank a lot of soft drinks, and I did not pay attention* (sic)". This case, like many others, reproduces responsibilities in patients and subjects them to follow the indications of their doctors, many of whom tell their patients that if they ignore them, they will die. The subordinates do not question the form of administration; they even make themselves responsible for it (Mager Hois, 2010). So, under this reference, *unassertive* subjects reproduce models of domination based on exploitation.

Assertiveness does not depend on the individual but on the subject's perception system in which he has grown up. When agents do not have a horizon, they do not develop it, so they do not have to say no; they do not have other options because these are unthinkable.[7]

The medical system generates public opinion from consulting rooms, radio and television programs, journalistic publications and political discourse, legitimising the official medical action. In this way, the public opinion that contributes to the *doxa* creates in the subjects a collective *habitus*, which is not difficult to question due to the established structure of domination. These structures of domination construct symbolic violence; domination tends to take the form of a much more effective and, in

[7] Personal communication with Dr. Sergio Lorenzo Sandoval Aragón, March 14th, 2023.

this sense, more brutal means of oppression. Therefore, in contemporary societies, violence has become soft and invisible (Bourdieu & Eagleton, 2003).

These structures of domination, of reproduction of symbolic violence, try to maintain the structured *doxa*, directing the social dynamics: the patriarchal model maintains the *doxa* for the control of the feminine; the political model maintains the *doxa* for the subjugation of the population; the mercantile model maintains the *doxa* for consumption; the idea, intentional or not, is to prevent the woman from not saying "no" to the primary care of the children; the idea is that the citizen does not say "no" to an unjust regulation; the idea is that the consumer does not refuse before the offer of a usurious credit. The idea is to avoid the assertiveness of the woman, the citizen and the consumer, to avoid using *Episteme*.

Episteme comes from the Greek Latin etymological root, meaning science or knowledge. *As an intellectual expression, Episteme* is a philosophical process that generates science. Practically in philosophy (and it is the debate in sociology), the *Episteme* seeks to discriminate between *doxa* and scientific knowledge; the theoretical practice aims to determine, from a conception of knowledge understood as a "subject-object" relationship, the objectivity of the subject's representations and the reality of the presentations given to the subject from the object, in order to be able to establish the conditions of truth of a knowledge understood as a "proposition" (Benedito Casanova, 2022, p. 166). The *Episteme* subdues the *doxa,* but this subjection is to leave without communication channels levels of the configuration of social knowledge that is being composed as a map of diverse regions; it is not an easy task to determine the structure of not knowing of people using only the words of those who know (Elias, 1990). That is why the *Episteme* must complexify its action before the *doxa* since this can cause the individuals not to *assertivate ("asertivar" in Spanish)*; we could thus consider that to *assertivate ("asertivar" in Spanish)* is an *episteme.* It is impossible to separate or antagonise *assertivation* with the social field, the *doxa* that submits it. Suppose we insist that assertivation is not a category but a tool to understand reality and that assertivation is not configured as the antagonist of doxa. In that case, we contribute to the idea that the *Episteme* constructs together with *doxa the* words and the form that is lacking to say "no" when the structure prevents or hinders saying it.

The social field represents the world constructed under principles of differentiation or distribution and by the set of active properties within the social universe capable of conferring strength and power to its holder. The agents and their groups are hence defined (recognised) by their relative position in this space. Each in its position, without occupying two opposite regions. The properties selected in this space being active, they can also be described as a field of forces, as a set of objective relations of forces that are imposed on all those who enter the field and that is irreducible to the interactions of individual agents, or their interactions (Bourdieu, 1989). According to Bourdieu (1999b), just as the scientific field is a space of struggle, where there are interests at stake, where the various agents and institutions occupy different positions according to the specific capital they possess and elaborate different strategies to defend their capital (Bourdieu, 1999b), the common field of subjects who do not reflect to say "no", or to ask for favours and make demands, or to express positive and negative feelings, or to initiate, continue and end general conversations, is subject to the *doxa* reproduced as a process of symbolic violence that structures a *habitus* that is not very assertive.

Conclusions

Developing assertiveness as a social practice could help as a tool that sociology has of such a phenomenon, not as a behaviour, but as a social practice. The development of an applied, practical, reflexive sociology would be focused on the sociology of education, proposing school processes that will motivate the conformation of an assertive habitus from childhood, or in medical sociology, especially in Primary Health Care, proposing elements for a health promotion that achieves educational processes in the subjects to stimulate them to be more assertive in the prevention of diseases. Similarly, the approach from assertiveness as a search in social interaction can be developed in political sociology, sociology of culture, sociology of communication, gender, work, human rights, religions and more branches of the study and practice of this social science, primarily, by making reflexivity in how the doxa is structured, and that stimulates symbolic violence, sociologically, it is the meeting point for the reproduction of the lack of assertiveness in social life. With these approaches, we can understand sociology's field of action to link social interaction in assertive planes.

Interdisciplinary approaches to this phenomenon can be visualised, thinking of a collaboration with psychology, communication, philosophy, anthropology, medicine and others, who, in an articulated way, build diagnostic and action ways to improve the conditions of assertiveness, both individual and collective.

It remains to reflect on the *assertiveness*, in addition to the practice of the subject, the practice of the institution or government that asks the citizens and they answer "no"; to reflect on the response of these power structures to the denial of a population that, for whatever circumstances, says "no" to them.

Perhaps this initiatory world to study assertiveness from sociology could contribute to maturing *assertiveness* as a social practice so that its results contribute to achieving societies less impoverished by the inability to say "no"; voters more empowered to say "no" so that they elect better rulers; or social movements of more excellent resolute health. Undoubtedly, the world in the study of *habitus* and *doxa*, from sociology, will produce more answers and practices in the study of assertiveness.

References

Bauman, Z. (2001). *Community. In search of security in a hostile world.* Siglo XXI.

Benedito Casanova, A. (2022). The Bourdieu effect: A sociology of education practised as epistemological critique. *Revista de Sociologia de la Educacion - RASE, 15*(2), 161–183. https://doi.org/10.7203/RASE.15.2.24221

Bernal, A., Lub, J., Quintero Camacho, L. (2018). *The world of doxa as an obstacle to the formation of thought in school. The social and armed conflict and the Colombian peace agreements as an illustration.* Universidad Pedagógica Nacional. https://repository.cinde.org.co/bitstream/handle/20.500.11907/2579/MUNDODOXA.pdf?sequence=1&isAllowed=y

Bourdieu, P. (1972). *Esquisse d'une théorie de la pratique, précédé de Trois études d'ethnologie kabyle.* Droz.

Bourdieu, P. (1985). *What does it mean to speak?* Editorial Aka SA. https://imaginariosyrepresentaciones.files.wordpress.com/2014/08/que-significa-hablar-bourdieu.pdf

Bourdieu, P. (1989). Social space and the genesis of "classes". *Estudios sobre las Culturas Contemporáneas, 3*(7), 27–55. https://www.redalyc.org/pdf/316/31630703.pdf

Bourdieu, P. (1997). *Things said.* Editorial Gedisa.

Bourdieu, P. (1999a). *Meditaciones Pascalianas (Pascalian Meditations).* Anagrama.

Bourdieu, P. (1999b). *Intelectuales, política y poder (Intellectuals, politics, and power).* Eudeba.

Bourdieu, P. (2000). Interview with Pierre Bourdieu: "Sociology, is it a science?". *La Recherche, 331*. https://sociologiacritica.es/2010/02/06/entrevista-con-pierre-bourdieu-la-sociologia-es-una-ciencia/

Bourdieu, P. (2001). *Science de la science et reflexivité*. Raisons d'agir.

Bourdieu, P., & Eagleton, T. (2003). *Doxa and daily life*. In S. Zizek (Ed.), *Ideology: A map of the question* (pp. 295–308). Fund of Economic Culture. https://desarmandolacultura.files.wordpress.com/2018/04/zizek-slavoj-ideologia-un-mapa-de-la-cuestion.pdf

Caballo, V. (1983). Assertiveness: Definitions and dimensions. *Estudios de Psicología, 13*. https://dialnet.unirioja.es/descarga/articulo/65876.pdf

Castaños-Cervantes, S. (2008). *Standardisation of the Gambrill and Richell II assertiveness inventory* [Bachelor's thesis, Universidad Nacional Autónoma de México]. Universidad Nacional Autónoma de México. http://132.248.9.195/ptd2009/enero/0638252/0638252_A1.pdf

Cirera Bianco, J. (2018). The comfort zone in Zygmunt Bauman: The trap of the new digital media. *Sapienza Organizacional, 5*(9), 55–80. https://www.redalyc.org/journal/5530/553056570004/html/

Downs, A. (1973). *Teoría económica de la democracia (Economic theory of democracy)*. Aguilar.

Elias, N. (1990). *Compromiso y distanciamientos (Commitment and distancing)*. Península.

Flores Galaz, M. (2002). *Assertiveness: A necessary social skill in today's world*. https://www.revistauniversitaria.uady.mx/pdf/221/ru2214.pdf

Gaeta González, L., & Galvanovskis Kasparane, A. (2009). Assertiveness: A theoretical-empirical analysis. *Enseñanza e Investigación en Psicología, 14*(2), 403–425. https://www.redalyc.org/articulo.oa?id=29211992013

Giddens, A. (1995). *Modernidad e identidad del yo (Modernity and identity of the self)*. Península.

Giglia, Á. (2003). Pierre Bourdieu and the reflexive perspective in the social sciences. *Desacatos, 11*, 149–160. https://www.scielo.org.mx/pdf/desacatos/n11/n11a10.pdf

Gutiérrez, A. (2005). *Las prácticas sociales: una introducción a Pierre Bourdieu (Social practices: An introduction to Pierre Bourdieu)*. Ferreyra editor. Córdoba, Argentina. http://www.fhycs.unam.edu.ar/carreras/wp-content/uploads/2017/03/Alicia-B.-Gutierrez-Las-practicas-sociale-s-una-introduccion-a-Pierre-Bourdieu..pdf

Mager Hois, E. (2010). Ideology and power. *Multidiscipline, 5*(5). https://www.revistas.unam.mx/index.php/multidisciplina/article/view/27770

Martín-Criado, M. (2022). *Uses and abuses of the habitus concept. Tla-melaua – revista de ciencias sociales, Special Issue of summer*, 38–55. http://www.apps.buap.mx/ojs3/index.php/tlamelaua/article/view/2165/pdf

Murguía Lores, A. (2002). Durkheim and culture. Una lectura contemporánea (A contemporary lecture). *Sociológica, 17*(50), 83–102. http://www.redalyc.org/articulo.oa?id=305026563004

Noëlle-Neumann, E. (1995). *The spiral of silence*. Paidós.

Ritzer, G. (2001). *Classic sociological theory*. McGraw Hill. https://significanteotro.files.wordpress.com/2017/02/47832383-teoria-sociologica-clasica-george-ritzer.pdf

Rodríguez, E. & Serralde, M. (1991). *Asertividad para negociar (Assertiveness to negotiate)*. McGraw-Hill. https://www.academia.edu/39781355/Asertividad_para_negociar_Mauro_Rodr%C3%ADguez_Estrada_Martha_Serralde

von Bertrand, E. (2023). *Silences in the academy*. Footnote. https://piedepagina.mx/silencio-en-la-academia/

Wolpe, J. (1993). *Practice of behavior therapy*. Trillas.

CHAPTER 7

Assertive Rights and Intervention in Social Work

Sandra Rubí Amador-Corral, Luz Alejandra Escalera-Silva, and Elio Francisco Vázquez-Luna

Introduction

The word 'assertiveness' comes from the Latin *assertus*, which means 'to affirm' or 'to claim'; in this sense, here it refers to the act of affirming personality, confidence, self-esteem, the defence of one self's rights without impacting or violating the rights of anyone else. Assertiveness implies expressing tastes, interests, opinions or feelings without fear or the shame of awkwardness; it also means asking for clarification of things or

S. R. Amador-Corral (✉) • L. A. Escalera-Silva
Facultad de Trabajo Social y Desarrollo Humano, Universidad Autónoma de Nuevo León (UANL), Monterrey, Mexico
e-mail: sandra.amadorcrr@uanl.edu.mx; luz.escalerasl@uanl.edu.mx

E. F. Vázquez-Luna
Facultad de Derecho y Criminología, Universidad Autónoma de Nuevo León (UANL), Monterrey, Mexico
e-mail: evazquezln@uanl.edu.mx

S. Castaños-Cervantes, C. Atristain-Suárez (eds.), *Assertiveness in the Context of Human Rights, Ethics, and Classical Virtues*,
https://doi.org/10.1007/978-3-031-60962-6_7

situations and knowing how to say no in matters or affairs that require so (Egúsquiza, 2000).

From the humanistic approach of assertiveness, it is considered that it has to be conceived and developed as a technique for the self-realisation of people; in this sense, to be assertive one needs to accept and value oneself, respect other people, stay firm on one's own decisions, communicate on a clear and direct manner, in the right moment and place, all of which must be done using appropriate ways in how something should and needs to be said (Gaeta & Galvanovskis, 2009).

According to Naranjo (2008), assertive people, besides expressing their rights constructively without affecting other people, have some characteristics that support this practice: they are objective when they have a change in their opinion, give "no" for an answer when they think it is correct, try to reach goals, respect themselves and other people, express what they believe, communicate adequately, speak with objectiveness, are proactive and accept weaknesses as opportunities for improvement; assertive conduct improves communication, encourages mutual respect, helping to make satisfying personal relationships.

On the other hand, we can consider as characteristics of an assertive professional the ones referred to by Egúsquiza (2000) as those that assertive conduct implies:

- Liberty and confidence to show and express what someone is, thinks, feels, and needs without affecting other people.
- Communicates efficiently and freely with anyone, known or unknown, maintaining a direct, open, honest, and adequate interaction.
- In their actions and expressions, they respect themselves and their limitations, consider their self-worth, and work on their self-esteem, meaning they love and accept themselves.
- Has an active focus, knows what they want, works to get it, and is more proactive than functional.
- Freely shows emotions and expresses feelings, avoids both repression and aggressive or destructive expressions.

From the standpoint of Social Work, according to Valverde (2002), assertiveness implies adopting an attitude that fits with acting reasonably and responsibly and is guided by a scheme of ethical values that look after rights against exploitation, imposition, or manipulation in addition to freedom of thinking and acting; an assertive professional takes into account social and economic aspects of the people in the intervention and values them by putting themselves in the people's context. Specifically, the global definition of Social Work given by the International Federation of Social Workers [IFSW] (2018) mentions that this profession privileges and values change and social development, social cohesion, and the strengthening and liberation of people, ruled by principles of Social Justice, Human Rights, collective responsibility, and respect for diversity.

In this sense, we can see that Social Work, from its very own nature, is interested in people developing their assertiveness because this implies facing the challenges of life and bettering their well-being, the main objectives of Social Work (IFSW, 2018), therefore, it applies and develops values and ethical principles that rule the Social Work:

- ***Recognition of dignity inherent to the human being.*** Implies to value and respect every human being, in attitude, word, and action, defying the beliefs and actions of those who devalue or stigmatise themselves and others.
- ***Promotion of Human Rights.*** Social Workers work with people to find an adequate balance between every Human Right, which is fundamental and inalienable.
- ***Promotion of Social Justice.*** Means to reject discrimination and institutional oppression, respecting diversity, and promoting and giving access to recourses; for this, the social worker must be aware and alert of situations that risk their safety and protection to be able to make decisions in specific circumstances and are not bound to work on risky positions.
- ***Promotion to the Right of Self-determination.*** It implies respecting and promoting people's rights to make decisions if those choices do not threaten the rights or interests of other people.
- ***Promotion of the Right to Participate.*** It means developing self-esteem and people's innate abilities, promoting full participation in decision-making and actions that impact their lives.
- ***Respect for the rights to confidentiality and privacy of every person.*** Professionals respect and work under these rights unless there is a risk to them or other people or legal restrictions; they are also informed about the limits in privacy and confidentiality.

- ***Treating people as a whole***. Acknowledging their biological, social, and spiritual dimensions in their lives, treating people as a whole with the participation of other persons, organisations, and communities.
- ***Ethic use of technology and social media***. The ethical principle of Social Work applies in every context, including digital media, considering the needed abilities to protect against unethical practices regarding privacy, confidentiality, conflict of interest, and others.
- ***Professional integrity***. Organisations and Social Work associations must update their codes and ethical directions concurrent to each country. Validated by a professional degree, helping peace and non-violence, they care for themselves in the workplace, their private life, and society.

On the other hand, assertive rights can be defined as those that people possess to put themselves at the same level as anyone else; they can also be considered as an acquired capacity or competency (meaning, the exercising of those) beneficial for people to make their rights and the rights of others be respected, establishing adequate and healthy social relationships, acting on a responsible way, with conscience and a critical stance in the search for opportunities for themselves and others (Abanto, 2017).

An assertive professional will honour the fundamental rights of themselves and others; to achieve that, assertive training and instruction will favour a structure of thoughts, feelings, and emotions to prevent stressful or conflicting situations (Pérez, 2014). Next, Table 7.1 shows a list of assertive rights (Cusi, 2021) to show their relationship with the values and ethical principles of Social Work.

The relationship between assertive rights and principles and ethical values of Social Work can be reflected in the way in which needs, conflictive situations, and social problems are attended to; meaning, from professional practice, social intervention is a process of acting over reality to achieve growth change of betterment of situations, collectives, and groups with problems or needs. It facilitates their participation and integration into the social system, especially from the hermeneutic perspectives that put the person at the centre of intervention, starting from creating and applying intervention models with humanistic and existentialist approaches (Fernández, 2008).

Table 7.1 Assertive rights and values and ethical principles of Social Work

Assertive right	*Principle of Social Work*
Expressing feelings and emotions in their way	To treat people as a whole
Be heard and considered.	Right to self-determination Recognising the inherent dignity of human beings To treat people as a whole
Decision-making, prioritising one's own needs	Right to self-determination Promotion of Social Justice
Being able to say "no" without guilt	Recognising the inherent dignity of human beings
Being able to ask for something and being aware of rejection	Right to self-determination
Make mistakes	Recognising the inherent dignity of human beings To treat people as a whole
Making decisions about one's belongings and respecting everyone else	Right to self-determination Promotion of Social Justice
To rest and be alone	To treat people as a whole
To face challenges	Promotion of the right to participate
To praise and be praised	Promotion of the right to participate
To make decisions about one's own body and time without affecting anybody else	Right to self-determination
To achieve triumphs	Promotion of the right to participate

Source: Authors' elaboration based on García and Magaz (1992) and IFSW (2018)

Professional Intervention from Social Work

Social intervention is a dynamic, complex, and multifunctional process that involves the subjects' participation and collaboration in actions that allow them to change their way of being, thinking, and acting. It implies collective, group, and individual changes and transformations; the intervention aims to achieve modifications in the living conditions of the members to attain a quality of life according to their moment in time and social context (Chávez, 2014).

The complexity of the social situation requires basic plans in the practical orientation to achieve work with scientific methodological rigour, where professionals try to confront and explain many cases with valuable interpretative resources (Chávez, 2014). Social Workers use models to translate situations they encounter into languages that allow them to explain what is happening, generating and evaluating hypotheses to prove their adequate function in reality (Fernández, 2008).

In social sciences, models are human constructs developed by the continuous and critical reflection of a reality that uses the scientific method, submitting phenomena and aspects of society to experimentation and, that way, finding the best way to understand, modify, improve, or reduce a problematic situation. Models in Social Work integrate theoretical, methodological, functional, and philosophical aspects and work as a guide for a substantiated professional practice that guarantees better congruence to the social problem that will be intervened (Fernández, 2008).

The existence of models of Social Work is related to the need to merge concepts and theories from different professional practices within Social Work. A model involves action principles set focused on defining an experience or phenomenon; it explains why those principles are used, showing the methods or techniques that should be used, not only covers the "how" but also the "when," "where," "what for," and "why." According to Payne (1995), models in social work describe what happens in social practice; due to their structure, they can be applied to multiple situations because they extract principles and guidelines that provide coherence and uniformity to the practice.

The elements that form a model of social intervention are:

1. The type of phenomena for which the model is directed involves aspects of human experience considered or perceived as problematic, complex, or needing change.
2. The conceptual content that is used to describe, understand, analyse, or explain the problem systematically and scientifically that bases the objectives of intervention in Social Work.
3. The nature of the intervention in Social Work involves, on the one hand, the objectives assigned or reachable with intervention and, on the other hand, the active principles, proceedings, methods, and techniques that characterise the model.
4. The ways and normative and institutional frameworks in which the model is used.
5. The sociology of the practice within the model, meaning how the social worker and their preparation are considered not professionals by themselves or others.

6. The values and ethics that involve the model in practice.
7. How, within the model, the subject that lives the social problem is conceived or the one who needs help identifying conceptions that are attributed as the cause of the issues or difficulties, whether they are their traits as an individual or circumstances external to the person (i.e. the structural or social medium). This aspect includes personality and the strength of the capabilities of each person to face their problems.
8. The nature of the meaningful relationship between the social worker and the individual is subject to the intervention from asking for help.

Humanistic and Existentialist Models

The models of intervention in Social Work with humanistic and existentialist approaches consider essential the fact that human beings seek to give sense to the world where they live and that professionals (meaning Social Workers), from their interventions, can help them with this by giving them, with training, the tools to analyse themselves and the personal signification that they provide to the world what they perceive and by which they are affected; in addition to the fact that their interpretation that every person has of the world, and the self are valid and worthy of being taken into consideration.

These models establish questions concerning the human being: What is their existence? What is the reason for their existence? What is their purpose in life? These questions are made in a horizontal, equal, empathic, and evaluative way, favouring the active participation of people, considering it as a whole interacting with their environment, displaying every capacity and knowledge as a Social Worker, focusing on understanding and having respect for their experiences in life unconditionally, supported by the values of Social Work, which are essentially humanists (Payne, 2002).

From a conceptual standpoint, humanism brings an integrative and holistic vision of the human being that conceives people as a whole, with interrelationships between physical, emotional, ideological, and spiritual aspects; humanism sees individuals as complex beings, considering every part and its influence on the social whole. Conversely, existentialism argues that man exists, not things, and exists from freedom and conscience, starting from conquering their essence (Fernández, 2008).

The nature of intervention with a humanistic focus lies in the philosophy of considering people as a whole in interaction with their environment, respecting the understanding of their experiences: people who go through a problematic situation are the centre of everything; they are not regarded as sick people (*paternalism*) or a client (*welfarism*), they are conscient, capable, thinking, and reflexive beings capable of analysing situations and making choices. How people are conceived from humanistic and existentialist models is based on recognising people as civic agents, free, autonomous, and protagonists of their lives, capable of making choices and increasing possibilities and actions available to come out of conflictive or problematic situations (Fernández, 2008; Viscarret, 2014).

The humanistic social worker establishes a profound relationship with the subject of intervention, respecting their experiences, does not interpret or give diagnostics, accompanies and favours reflection of and with the other, and is an observer that serves as reflection (like a mirror) so that the subject achieves that realisation through dialogue and clarification of their emotions, easing their processes, making them manageable and non-pathologic (Quinche, 2021). Intervention must consider the objective dimension, which refers to the knowledge of factors that have driven a problematic situation, and the objective one focuses on knowing how this situation is experienced and lived, who are the implied subjects, and which the transcendence and importance that it has for them (Viscarret, 2014).

Moreover, existentialist Social Work is focused mainly on diminished collectives, namely vulnerable groups with capacities and problems that do not need an immediate cure; the professional makes deep analyses regarding the interests and capabilities of the users to find meaning in their lives; it must be understood from empathy, without judgement, concerning the lived experience; self-acceptance, expression free from affections, internal knowledge, confidence in oneself and healing all receive importance (Osvalde, 2017).

On an existentialist approach, life can be understood in two manners: in the first place, from the viewpoint of a senseless life, and in the second place, from the standpoint of finding sense to complicated situations like sickness, elderliness, pain, injustice, or death; a social intervention from an existentialist perspective tries to help the subject to find meaning to their existence, uncovering those elements that can achieve that life have a purpose and therefore, favouring the realisation of people.

The purpose of intervention from an existentialist approach is to lessen the suffering of the painful situations of life; problems are treated based on acceptance of the ways of life, the values of the user, avoiding oppression and paternalism starting from three basic principles: (1) emphasis on the change of experience, (2) centralisation on the user or subject of intervention, and (3) a personal commitment by the social worker, respecting values, feelings, and attitudes (Payne, 2002).

The frame of reference that humanism and existentialism offer to Social Work and interventions made from these approaches privilege freedom, dignity, and the potential of people; meaning, beyond techniques and specific structure (like the ones done in other models), these involve a particular philosophy under premises that understand that people create their personality employing choices and decisions, determined by freedom and conscience (Viscarret, 2014).

Social Work, with the humanistic and existentialist approach, respects diversity, ethical pertinence, culture, opinions, and lifestyle choices; plus, it respects the capacity of action and choice, fundamental aspects of assertive rights and those interventions that involve assertiveness. How the subject and nature of the intervention in humanistic and existentialist models are conceived evidence the relationship of these with assertive rights; also, we can notice that some of them are implicit in the process of intervention, like the right of expression of feelings and opinions, being listened to and considered, decision-making prioritising needs, facing challenges, and accomplishing triumphs (Payne, 2002).

Humanistic and existentialist models in Social Work are represented by four approaches that Viscarret develops in his work *Modelos y métodos de intervención en Trabajo Social* [Models and methods of intervention in Social Work] (2014):

- **The client-centric model** centres on the acknowledgement of singularity from the viewpoint of the person, created by Carl Rogers, assumes that people tend to development and constant growth that can be found hampered by aspects or complicated situations (opposing forces) that are presented in the context in which is developed (society); is the intervention that can mobilise actions of understanding and personal growth with the absolute respect for the capacity of development of the human being when they encounter practical situations. The essence of professional intervention of the model focused on clients can be found in the attitudes of the social worker or therapist towards the subject of intervention to generate possibilities and courses of action that will not refer to opinions or interpretations. For this model, the term "client" has a particular connotation because it moves away from the fact of regarding people as sick of being unfavored; besides, it refers to the voluntary participation, action, and responsibility of the person who seeks to help in an equality relationship and at the same lever with the Social Worker.

- **Gestalt therapy** is another humanistic focus developed by Frits Perls; it is framed in the movement of the human potential, with influences of psychoanalysis and existentialist philosophy. As the model focused on the client, this has significantly influenced Social Work. Gestalt is a word of German descent that means 'totality' or 'structure'; this focus does not centre on pathology. Instead, it focuses on the integral development of the human being and includes many aspects: physical, mental, emotional, social, and spiritual. It is an experiential therapy centred on the 'here and now'. Most importantly, people investigate 'how' a problem is experienced in the present, looking for its origins in the past. The philosophy of this focus centres on giving the 'client' the means to solve their current problems and experience more than understanding; the professional intervention is directed to a space of work that can share feelings and emotions.
- **The existentialist social work**: The existentialist philosophy prioritises four fundamental aspects: the importance of individual liberty, the recognition of human suffering, the participation in the current moment, and the sense of commitment. Existentialism is an approach of intervention centred on making efforts to establish in their clients' authentic lifestyles represented by freedom, responsibility, and learning from personal suffering; according to existentialists, actual (capitalist) societies empower anomie and alienation from the forces of oppression of the political and economic systems. In existentialist interventions, the singularity of the client makes every case unique and different from others; that is why processes and techniques in each case are different.
- **Transactional analysis**: This approach implies a theory of personality and human relations that gives a basic and straightforward formation in psychological and elemental aspects of personality; it consists of a philosophy centred on growth and personal or organisational change. Its concepts must be expressed in a simple vocabulary that seeks to understand problematic phenomena or situations of professionals, therapists, and clients—looking for straightforward and close explanations of people's life experiences. The theory of personality is a system that answers to specific aspects; the first is the external

> behaviour of people, and the second is the analysis of internal psychological processes. The transactional analysis (as a theory of personality) provides an image of the psychological structure of the person, using three parts of the 'I' or ego: the parent, adult, and child; it also develops a theory of communications can be applied to the transaction and interaction of the therapist with the client and can be used for the understanding of systems and organisations.

In Table 7.2, the general elements that make up every approach in relationship with Social Work are described and presented by Viscarret (2014) in his book.

Conclusions

An assertive professional will be capable of exercising their rights and enforcing the rights of their clients or users of their service; from an optic of Social Work, the defence of rights and social justice is made through the scientific application of specific methodologies and the knowledge of social theories, all of it is backed up by the principles and ethical values of Social Work that, depending on the context, function as a decalogue and a professional operation guide that can be supported and complemented by promoting attitudes of assertiveness and Assertive Rights.

The exercise of Assertive Rights must be an essential part of processes of change and social intervention, mainly in the active participation of people in resolving their problems and decision-making, as regarded in humanistic, existentialist, and phenomenological models of Social Work.

Humanistic and existentialist approaches of models presented in this chapter demonstrate that the client must actively participate in the intervention process, prioritising interpersonal and intrapersonal analysis. The analysis and the expression of feeling an emotion are present; in addition, the client must go through cycles of decision-making and facing challenges to diminish or resolve a problematic situation, which will be accomplished with the company of the therapist (social worker), who will be present in a horizontal relationship, facilitating the processes of realisation in an environment of trust and constant communication.

From Social Work, the processes of systematisation of the practice are scarce, and interventions between assertiveness and Social Work were not found. However, we can see that assertiveness is implicit in the practice of Social Work from its values and ethical principles.

Table 7.2 Approaches in humanistic and existentialist models in Social Work

Humanistic and existentialist model	*Client-focused*	*Gestalt therapy*	*Existentialist Social Work*	*Transactional analysis*
Basic elements	• Capacity of the individual to handle constructively every aspect of their life from conscience • Emphasises the active, voluntary, and responsible participation of people	• Centred in the here and now • Interested in what the client needs and seeks through: (a) Figure and background (b) Realisation (c) Homeostasis (d) Existentialist dialogue (e) Here and now (f) Polarities (g) Dreams (h) Prägnanz	• Privileges individual freedom • Recognises human suffering • Prioritises active participation in the current moment • Recognises the sense of commitment • Emphasises the change in experiences • Interest in values and philosophical and religious viewpoints	• Centred on the external behaviour of people • Based on the theory of persona lity, structured by the three parts of the "I" of ego: parent, adult, and child

Functions of the social worker and/or therapist	• Companion in the process • Their position towards the client is horizontal, away from the "superior" scientist role • Facilitator in the process of clarification of emotions • Sensibility to the experiences of the client • The main instrument of the intervention in the therapist through: (a) An empathic capability (b) Empathy, sympathy, and intuition in the diagnosis (c) Authenticity in the internal agreement (d) Positive conception of the liberty of man and human relationship (e) Emotional maturity (f) Understanding of oneself	• Generates the necessary conditions to achieve realisation • Accompaniment, non-directivity • Pedagogic function • Ability to communicate • Capacity to centre attention in the here and now • Capacity to display attractively without the need for charisma • Realise the creative and transcendent aspects of their labour	• Action focused on the client • Recognising the singularity of the client, far from prejudices • Promote in the client a realist action to face problems • Help clients give a new meaning to their life • Clarification of internal, mental, and emotional conflicts • Give affirmation to clients • Encourage an active and responsible attitude in the client that enables the observation of conducts and experience of new ones	• Facilitate the procurement of personal autonomy. • Increase awareness • Achieve the capacity to express needs and feelings • Develop in clients the ability to open up to other people • Accomplish the psycho-social well-being of the client • Induce change from the proposal of changes in behaviour

(*continued*)

Table 7.2 (continued)

Humanistic and existentialist model	*Client-focused*	*Gestalt therapy*	*Existentialist Social Work*	*Transactional analysis*
Relationship between the Social Worker and client	• Based on unconditional acceptance and respect for the client or intervention subject • The client is the one who drives the process of intervention • The therapist must be unlinked from emotional impact to have a clear perspective • The function of the professional is not passive; instead, they let the client "be and do" from a position of respect and non-directivity	• The therapist is the primary tool for change • The therapist is an observer who respects the experience of the client • Through dialogue, the client increases their capacity for realisation • The relationship between the therapist and the client is horizontal • The relationship between therapist and client is based on an equality principle in which both are active participants in the process	• Centred on the absolute value of the person and their freedom • Invigorating the client in the processes of treatment • Uses vitality, spontaneity, clarity, and humour in situations where the client might be defensive • Based on the development of five fundamental therapeutic concepts: (a) Disappointment (b) Freedom of choice (c) Meaning of suffering (d) Need for dialogue (e) Commitment	• The client can change in favour of their autonomy and has the resources to accomplish it • Based on clear, direct and opportune communication • Based on mutual respect and in establishing agreements and commitments

Intervention process and/or therapeutic process	• First stage: Obtaining harmony and empathy • Second stage: Establishing a therapeutic link • Third stage: Collaboration of tasks, easing the mutual implication in the objectives of therapy • Fourth stage: Experiential process, where the client is understood and accepted as they are • Fifth stage: Promote growth and self-determination of the client • Sixth stage: Finishing the task, there is a new way in which feelings are experienced • Seventh stage: End of the therapeutic process, can be developed in the therapeutic relationship outside of it	The goal is that the client obtains the support and acquires self-responsibility to obtain the best integration that facilitates their growth and development from the following concepts: (a) Figure and background (b) Realisation (c) Homeostasis (d) Existentialist dialogue (e) Here and now (f) Polarities (g) Dreams (h) Prägnanz (an organised whole)	• It is not a linear or structured process; phases comprise it: (a) change of specific conduct or symptom (b) change in the environment (c) change in relationships (d) directional change (personalisation of values) (e) Internal analyses	• Analysis of the person and their behaviour through interpersonal aspects and relationships, psychological games, and the growth of life. • Focuses on the interpersonal operation, relational, in communication, studying the analysis of the units of essential communication, named transactions • Focuses on how interpersonal relationships are structured by the need to receive, recognise, accept and belong

(*continued*)

Table 7.2 (continued)

Humanistic and existentialist model	*Client-focused*	*Gestalt therapy*	*Existentialist Social Work*	*Transactional analysis*
Intervention techniques	There is no specific technique Centred on the acceptance of the client's affirmations: (a) Verbal and behavioural definition (b) the use of a friendly attitude (c) Cathartic techniques (d) Techniques to obtain the client's insight (e) Verbal clarification (f) the response to feeling	Used to promote awareness, revolve around rules and games: (a) awareness (b) the empty chair (c) focusing (d) monogram (e) amplification (f) staging of signals (g) metaphoric expression (h) resolution of pending issues	Can vary depending on the interests of the client and the abilities of the therapist: (a) modification of conduct (b) Gestalt (c) Psychoanalysis (d) Insight techniques (e) Realist or rational techniques	Use the main instruments of intervention: (a) Open communication between the professional and the client (b) The contract: orients and guides the work in a mutual commitment. (c) Can use techniques of Gestalt therapy

Source: Authors' elaboration based on Viscarret (2014)

This work is the first approach to open the discussion and analysis about the relationship between Assertive Rights and the principles and ethical values of the social worker; in addition to being considered for the creation of proposals of intervention, applying models of Social Work, taking as a basis the hermeneutic perspectives focused in the individual and their value as a person, that has the ability and conscience to change their social reality, to come out of problematic situations and bettering their well-being.

References

Abanto, S. (2017). *Niveles de asertividad en docentes y tutores de la Institución Educativa Pamer (Levels of assertiveness in teachers and tutors in Pamer Educative Institution)* [Bachelor's Thesis]. Universidad Inca Garcilaso de la Vega, Lima, Perú. http://repositorio.uigv.edu.pe/bitstream/handle/20.500.11818/1682/TRAB.SUF.PROF.%20SELENE%20CONSUELO%20ABANTO%20CASTILLO.pdf

Chávez, J. C. (2014). Modelos de intervención en la acción del Trabajo Social (Intervention models in the action of Social Work). In M. C. Guzmán, J. C. Chávez, & S. Vázquez (Eds.), *Epistemología y Trabajo Social (Epistemology and Social Work)* (Vol. II, pp. 75–86). ACANITS.

Cusi, M. (2021). *Efectividad del Programa "Mejora tu Vida" en los Derechos Asertivos de Docentes de una Institución Educativa de Lima (Effectiveness of the program "Better your Life" in the Assertive Rights of Teachers in an educative institution of Lima)* [Doctorate Thesis]. Universidad Nacional de Educación. Lima, Perú. https://repositorio.une.edu.pe/bitstream/handle/20.500.14039/5140/Marisol%20CUSI%20LIMA.pdf?sequence=1&isAllowed=y

Egúsquiza, O. (2000). Asertividad: Modelo de comunicación en las organizaciones (Assertiveness: Model of communication in organizations). *Quipukamayoc, 7*(14), 119–121. https://doi.org/10.15381/quipu.v7i14.5704

Fernández, T. (2008). *Trabajo Social con casos (Social Work with cases)*. Alianza.

Gaeta, L., & Galvanovskis, K. A. (2009). Asertividad: un análisis teórico-empírico (Assertiveness: A theoretical-empirical analysis). *Enseñanza e Investigación en Psicología, 14*(2), 403–425. https://www.redalyc.org/articulo.oa?id=29211992013

García, M. y Magaz, A. (1992). *Ratones, dragones y seres humanos auténticos: manual de entrenamiento asertivo: libro de trabajo.* Editorial: CEPE Ciencias de la Educación Preescolar y Especial. ISBN 84-7869-084-0

International Federation of Social Workers [IFSW]. (2018). *Global Social Work statement of ethical principles.* https://www.ifsw.org/global-social-work-statement-of-ethical-principles/

Naranjo, M. L. (2008). Relaciones interpersonales adecuadas mediante una comunicación y conducta asertivas (Adequate human relationships through an assertive conducts and communication). *Actualidades Investigativas en Educación, 8*(1), 1–27. https://revistas.ucr.ac.cr/index.php/aie/article/view/9315

Osvalde, M. T. (2017). *Trabajo social y existencialismo: aportes críticos para la intervención profesional (Social work and existentialism: Critical contributions for professional intervention)* [Bachelor's Thesis]. Universidad de la República. https://www.colibri.udelar.edu.uy/jspui/bitstream/20.500.12008/23805/1/TTS_OsvaldeMarysTriana.pdf

Payne, M. (2002). *Teorías contemporáneas en Trabajo Social. Una introducción crítica. (Contemporary theories in Social Work. A critical introduction)*. Paidós.

Pérez, J. (2014) *Autoestima y asertividad: Frecuente relación (Self-esteem and assertiveness: Frequent association)*. https://www.psicomaster.es/autoestima-y-asertividad-su-frecuente-relacion/

Quinche, M. G. (2021). *El enfoque humanista y la influencia en la intervención del trabajador social con perspectiva de justicia social y derechos humanos (The humanistic approach and the influence in intervention of the social worker with a social justice and Human Rights perspective)* [Bachelor's Thesis]. Universidad Técnica de Machala. http://repositorio.utmachala.edu.ec/bitstream/48000/17002/1/ECFCS-2021-TRS-DE00018.pdf

Valverde, L. (2002). Asertividad y ética profesional (Assertiveness and professional ethics). *Revista Costarricense de Trabajo Social, 14*, 22–25. https://revista.trabajosocial.or.cr/index.php/revista/article/view/176

Viscarret, J. (2014). *Modelos y métodos de intervención en Trabajo Social (Models and methods of intervention in Social Work)*. Alianza.

PART III

Assertiveness for Building a Culture of Virtue, Peace, and Equity

Where there is Peace, there is Culture; Where there is Culture, there is Peace.
Nicholas Roerich

Following the analysis of assertiveness from a social perspective, the book's third part comprises three chapters through which assertiveness is depicted as a core skill for building a culture of virtue, peace, and equity. First, it analyses assertively through philosophical ethics and psychological lenses. It examines assertive communication as essential for making informed, responsible, and wise decisions. It emphasises the critical elements of assertive communication and the study of assertiveness, such as virtue, responsibility, and care.

Secondly, it addresses assertiveness as a pillar for building peaceful, harmonious societies free of conflict and violence. It emphasises the role of assertiveness in strengthening respect for human rights and fundamental freedoms and promoting actions aimed at preserving peace, specifically among victims of structural violence. Thus, assertiveness is crucial for diminishing and preventing structural violence.

Thirdly and lastly, it highlights how Universities are essential for fostering assertiveness, hence promoting human rights, gender equality, and inclusion. Therefore, Universities are vital for educating in human rights through assertiveness fostering intercultural competence.

As such, this part provides the knowledge for cultivating a culture of virtue, peace, and equity through assertiveness.

CHAPTER 8

Ethics, Decision-Making, and Assertive Communication

César Augusto García-Avitia

Introduction

In scientific psychology, the *assertiveness* concept began to be used in the late 1950s (Caballo, 1983). Since then, this topic has gained significant relevance and has even become popular outside the discipline's borders. Also, there have been changes in its meaning, and different perspectives about it have been developed through the years. Despite differences, there is agreement among authors and theories about considering communication as assertiveness' central feature, which is why it is often referred to as *assertive communication*.

Assertive communication is a behavioural type or style that can be qualified as good, in contrast to aggressive or passive styles, which are qualified as bad (Weliangan, 2022). Assertive communication is a person's ability to speak and interact in a way that considers and respects others' rights and opinions while defending their own personal rights, needs and limits

C. A. García-Avitia (✉)
Faculty of Psychology, University of Colima, Colima, Mexico
e-mail: garciaavitia@ucol.mx

S. Castaños-Cervantes, C. Atristain-Suárez (eds.), *Assertiveness in the Context of Human Rights, Ethics, and Classical Virtues*,
https://doi.org/10.1007/978-3-031-60962-6_8

(Pipas & Jaradat, 2010). Ethical aspects take part in this definition, such as consideration and respect for other people's rights and their own. Thus, assertive communication must be supported theoretically by ethics.

Recognising how ethics support assertive communication is relevant, but then a question arises: Which ethical theories could be applied to it? One philosophy's theoretical perspective related to assertiveness is Virtue Ethics, developed by Aristotle. This Greek philosopher discusses the concept of *phronesis*, typically translated as prudence or practical wisdom, which is one of the main topics in Nicomachean Ethics (Aristotle, 349 BCE/1926). Phronesis can support assertive communication, standing for the ability to discern how to act ethically in each situation, considering that communication always occurs in specific relationships and contexts.

In addition to Virtue Ethics, other ethical theories can also serve to support assertive communication in ethical theory, such as Responsibility Ethics, which considers behaviours' consequences before carrying them out (Jonas, 1984), or Ethics of Care, which is particularly interested in others' well-being based on specific relationships and circumstances (Gilligan, 1982). Both theories could also make highly relevant contributions to support assertive communication since it is about avoiding negative consequences through communication and showing care for others and oneself.

In addition to ethical theories, it becomes necessary to understand that assertive communication combines several psychological processes. Behavioural components include verbal and non-verbal communication (Calua et al., 2021) and cognitive-affective components, such as perception, evaluation, motivation, and decision-making processes. So, analysing assertive communication characteristics from a psychological perspective is relevant. In such a way, philosophical ethics and scientific psychology combine to support assertive communication's benefits and processes theoretically.

Communicating assertively requires that people execute processes as decision-making, through which it is possible to evaluate situations and deliberate on the consequences of communicative acts before performing them. Then, another question arises: What thought processes engage in assertive communication? In this sense, Kahneman's (2011) Two Systems Theory is pertinent. The theory distinguishes between two ways of thinking, called *System 1* and *System 2*. System 1 operates automatically and quickly, with little or no effort and without perceiving any voluntary control. System 2 focuses on mental activities that require effort, such as complex calculations, and is often associated with a subjective experience of concentrating, choosing, and acting. Therefore, finding which system of thought can support the process required for assertive communication is relevant.

Complementing the Two Systems Theory, Rest's Four Component Model of Morality can also be applied to assertive communication (1983; as cited in Bebeau et al., 1999). The components are sensitivity, judgement, motivation, and moral character. Moral sensitivity is a specific situation's interpretation to identify moral aspects, moral judgement evaluates if an action is ethically or morally correct or incorrect, moral motivation includes prioritisation of values or moral principles over other interests, and moral character is the ability to conduct moral actions. So, finding the decision-making process integrated into assertive communication is relevant.

To integrate all of the above, this chapter aims to analyse ethical theories of Virtue, Responsibility, and Care in addition to psychological theories, such as the Two Systems of Thought and the Four Component Model of Morality, to support that assertive communication is a type of ethical behaviour. On the one hand, ethical theories' characteristics will be analysed, and on the other hand, systems of thought and moral decision-making from psychology, in such a way that it will have an interdisciplinary perspective, allowing more theoretical support to assertive communication.

Assertive Communication

It is crucial to define assertive communication and explore how it has been theoretically described. The meaning of the verb *to assert* has changed over the years. Merriam-Webster dictionary shows its etymological root in Latin *assertus*, past participle of *asserere*, from *ad-* + *serere* to join. There, it will be found that it means "to state or declare positively and often forcefully or aggressively" (n.d.a, definition 1a), which even stands for aggressiveness, a characteristic opposite to what today is understood by being assertive. That first meaning is more related to the verb *to declare*. A second meaning is closer to what this chapter is based on since asserting is defined as "to compel or demand acceptance or recognition of (something, such as one's authority)" (n.d.a, definition 1b). The linguistic meaning most related to what will be discussed here is when the dictionary presents the phrase "assert oneself", defining it as "to speak or act in a manner that compels recognition, especially of one's rights" (n.d.a, phrase 1). If one seeks the meaning of *assertive* as an adjective, *assertiveness* as a noun, or *assertively* as an adverb, the given meaning is "disposed to or characterised by bold or confident statements and behaviour" (n.d.b, definition 1).

According to Caballo (1983), Joseph Wolpe used the word assertion as a psychological concept in 1958 in the book *Psychotherapy by Reciprocal Inhibition*. Before that, in 1949, Andrew Salter set up the theoretical bases for what would later be understood as assertiveness when he developed his model on excitement in the book *Conditioned Reflex Therapy*. Later, in 1966, Wolpe and Arnold Lazarus developed the assertive training technique in *Behaviour Therapy Technique: A Guide to the Treatment of Neuroses*. In 1970, the first book dedicated exclusively to assertiveness appeared, written by Robert Alberti, called *assertiveness: Innovations, Applications, Issues*.

Caballo (1983) also mentions that since the 1970s, the assertiveness construct has become popular and expanded significantly. In the United States, associations dedicated to assertiveness training were founded, which was considered the ideal treatment for any social relationship problem. It also began to disassociate itself from Behaviour Therapy, and the first magazine dedicated exclusively to the subject was created: *ASSERT: The Newsletter of Assertive Behaviour*. Various books and articles on the subject also began to be published. Over 50 years after the topic expansion, assertiveness is a concept that has become commonly used outside psychology, resulting in diverse and ambiguous meanings, sometimes very differently from what the theories describe. Table 8.1 compiles several of the most relevant psychological definitions of assertiveness.

To clearly understand assertiveness, it is necessary to recognise some of its primary qualities as listed by Alberti (1977, as cited in Caballo, 1983). Firstly, assertiveness is a behaviour characteristic that is not of the person, which means that someone can be assertive sometimes and sometimes not. Also, it is based on the individual's ability to choose their actions freely and is a characteristic of socially influenced and not harmful behaviour. Being assertive depends on a person's condition in a particular situation, so it is not universal. Another characteristic is that it must be considered in the individual's cultural context and based on the terms of other situational variables.

As the introduction explained, this chapter focuses on assertive communication. When discussing a communicative process that is qualified

Table 8.1 Definitions of assertiveness

Authors	*Year*	*Definition*
Rimm and Master	1974	Interpersonal behaviour that involves honest and relatively direct expression of feelings.
Rich and Schroeder	1976	The ability to seek, maintain, or enhance reinforcement in an interpersonal situation through expressing feelings or desires when such expression risks loss of reinforcement or even punishment.
Wolpe	1977	The appropriate expression directed toward another person of any emotion other than the anxiety response.
Alberti et al.	1977	Set of behaviours emitted by a person in an interpersonal context that express feelings, attitudes, desires, opinions, or rights of that person in a direct, firm, and honest way while respecting the other person's feelings, attitudes, desires, opinions, and rights.
Alberti and Emmons	1978	Behaviour that allows a person to act in their best interests, defend themselves without undue anxiety, comfortably express honest feelings, or exercise personal rights without denying the rights of others.
McDonald	1978	The open expression of preferences (through words or actions) in such a way as to make others take them into account.
Libet and Lewinshon	1979	The complex capacity to issue behaviours that are positively or negatively reinforced and not to issue behaviours that are punished or extinguished by others.
Brown	1980	Behaviour that occurs in an interpersonal context is primarily concerned with the acquisition of personal reinforcement and minimises reinforcement's loss by the receiver of the behaviour.
Rees and Graham	1991	Respect yourself and others by fundamentally believing that your own opinions, beliefs, thoughts, and feelings are just as important as anyone else's.
Flores	1994	Verbal ability to express desires, beliefs, needs and opinions, both positive and negative, as well as to set limits in a direct, honest, and timely manner, respecting oneself as an individual and during social interaction.
Robredo	1995	Self-confidence, tenacity, and persistence. It refers to knowing how to march through life with a firm step and your head held high, having the habit of expressing yourself based on your self-esteem and affirming, defending, expressing yourself and acting directly, with the responsibility and ability necessary to maintain social interactions.

(*continued*)

Table 8.1 (continued)

Authors	*Year*	*Definition*
Bishop	2000	Be able to express oneself confidently without having to resort to too passive, aggressive, or manipulative behaviours—which implies self-knowledge and control of one's own authentic self and requires knowing how to listen and respond to the needs of others without neglecting one's own interests or principles.
Elizondo	2000	The ability to express thoughts, feelings, and perceptions and to choose how to react and stand up for one's rights when appropriate.
Duckworth and Mercer	2006	Assertive behaviour usually centres on making requests of others and refusing requests that have been judged unreasonable. It also involves communicating solid opinions and feelings.
Chambers	2009	Assertiveness means speaking up for one's interpersonal freedoms or, as required by one's role responsibilities, engaging others in finding viable, stable solutions.
Malti and Perren	2011	The ability to reach one's goals for oneself through social interactions.
Litt	2013	Refers to expressing oneself directly and non-aggressively, particularly concerning one's needs or desires.
Omura et al.	2016, 2017	The ability to respectfully express concerns about issues that can impact patient safety and share opinions with other staff, including those in authority.
Ames et al.	2017	The degree to which someone stands up and speaks out for their own positions when faced with someone else who does not want the same outcomes.
Speed et al.	2018	Reflects individuals' disposition to stand up for themselves, expressing their wants or needs, thoughts, and feelings. Assertiveness is considered along a continuum, whereby problems with assertiveness can manifest as excessive agreeableness (i.e., submissive/unassertive) or excessive hostility (i.e., aggressive).
Mrvoljak-Theodoropoulou et al.	2020	Mode of personal behaviour and communication characterised by a willingness to openly and directly advocate for one's own needs and interests.

(*continued*)

Table 8.1 (continued)

Authors	*Year*	*Definition*
Pfafman	2020	Assertiveness involves appropriately expressing ideas, feelings, and boundaries while respecting other's rights, maintaining positive affect in the receiver, and considering potential consequences of the expression. It includes both positive and negative expressions and seeks to achieve personal and/or instrumental goals.
Cantero-Sánchez et al.	2021	Fundamental type of behavior for the creation and maintenance of positive relationships at work and the facilitation of team functioning.
Richard et al.	2023	Interpersonal communication skill that helps express opinions or knowledge while respecting similar competencies in others.

Note. This table presents a compilation of assertiveness definitions. Some of the information has been taken from V. E. Caballo (1983), L. Gaeta and A. Galvanovskis (2009), and T. Pfafman (2020)

with the adjective *assertive*, the authors usually refer to a type of communication between two extreme poles: passivity and aggressiveness. In passivity, an individual does not defend his rights, and his interlocutor expresses her feelings, attitudes, opinions, or desires without respecting him. In aggressiveness, the rights of others are underestimated, and feelings, attitudes, opinions, or desires are expressed without respect for them. In both kinds of communication, at least one person involved in the process will be upset. Sometimes, everyone involved in the communication gets upset, and the conflict can escalate, even reaching violence, and then highly negative consequences arise.

So, assertive communication balances self-affirmation and respect for the other, implying honesty, fairness, and responsible use of power. It is a fair middle ground, thanks to which no one is harmed. Respect for one's rights and those of others involved in communication must be considered. Feelings, attitudes, opinions, and desires must be expressed while being sensitive to those of others. This communication style allows people to argue their opinions without being aggressive and not feel humiliated (Pipas & Jaradat, 2010).

Assertive communication stands for a possibility where those involved will have a satisfactory ending. Whether in giving or receiving requests or evaluations, this style allows communication to be effective and prevents it from being distorted because someone feels attacked. It is essential in conflict situations, where all interests must be considered, and thus, reaching a consensual solution is possible. It should be noted that communicating assertively does not ensure that other interlocutors do so. However, it makes it easier for them to do so and helps avoid conflict escalation.

Ethical Foundation of Assertive Communication

Without a doubt, assertive communication stands for ethical and moral qualities considered positive, healthy, and constructive, while passive or aggressive communication is harmful and destructive. Assertive communication implies various ethical values, such as honesty, freedom, fairness, respect for one's rights and those of others, responsibility not to harm, and care for one's well-being and that of others. In addition, this kind of behaviour stands for a balance, a medium point of great relevance for interpersonal relationships. All these ideas have been reflected in philosophy, even for millennia. Therefore, in this section, philosophical theories of Virtue, Responsibility, and Care will be reviewed from which the ethical foundations of assertive communication can be better supported.

Virtue Ethics and Phronesis

In the West, virtue ethics was founded by Socrates, Plato, and Aristotle (Hursthouse & Pettigrove, 2018). According to these philosophers, Virtue is an excellent character trait, a disposition ingrained in its possessor to notice, expect, value, feel, desire, choose, act, and react in specific ways. Possessing a virtue means someone who is a particular kind of person, different from someone who does not have it. A virtue involves accepting various considerations, defending reasons and driving motivations to act in everyday life. Virtue makes whoever has it good, or in other words, a virtuous person is morally good, excellent, or admirable because he acts and feels as he should.

In Nicomachean Ethics' book II, Aristotle (349 B.C.E./1926) distinguishes between two types of virtues: intellectual and moral. The first comes from teaching, which requires experience and time, and the latter results from habit. Aristotle considers actions the primary source of habits, so how they are performed is essential. He also considers that no moral virtue arises naturally in individuals. The virtues are acquired by exercising them; they are learned in practice.

Another critical point of the Aristotelian Virtue theory is that excess and defect spoil human acts, and finding a middle ground, a golden mean, is desirable. Pleasure and pain, related to any action or passion, will manifest in a certain way in the virtuous, being moderate. Pursuing or avoiding pleasure and pain can make us wicked. In such a way, notions are presented as opposites: better or worse, right or wrong, opportune and inopportune. In that sense, three aspects are preferable: the good, the useful, and the pleasant over their opposites, the bad, the harmful, and the unpleasant, which are rejected. The middle ground is opportune and proper because Virtue is a selective habit that seeks an intermediate position determined by reason. However, Aristotle considers that there are actions that are ruinous in themselves (envy, imprudence, robbery, or homicide) which should never be conducted.

The notion of a middle ground as good or better is present in both theories, Aristotelian Virtue and modern assertive communication. Communicating assertively means not falling into the extremes of aggressiveness, where the other is disrespected and harmed, nor passivity, where one disrespects and harms oneself. In such a way, finding good, helpful, and pleasant results and avoiding evil, harmful, and unpleasant results require a balance where both one and the others involved are satisfied. Of course, someone could suggest that one who is aggressive and imposes himself on others could obtain pleasure and satisfaction; however, by causing the opposite to others, it becomes a vile action, which is neither virtuous nor ethical.

One more of Aristotle's ethical Virtue Theory's central components is phronesis, usually understood as practical wisdom or prudence. This Virtue allows knowing how to obtain tangible benefits effectively in each circumstance. It involves knowledge or understanding that allows one to do the right thing following the situation and its morally and ethically outstanding conditions. Phronesis has two characteristics: first, it is acquired through life experiences, and second, it allows recognising some situations' aspects as more critical than others. Thanks to phronesis, people can recognise what is worthwhile and vital in life and learn how to live well (Hursthouse & Pettigrove, 2018).

The notion of obtaining the best results in a specific situation is found in Aristotle's theory of Virtue and assertive communication. In interpersonal situations where communication happens, assertiveness is that all people involved can interact respectfully, allowing all practical and satisfactory ends to be reached for all. To make this possible, specific conditions of each situation must be considered, and universal formulas of behaviour cannot be followed. Likewise, the cultural context in which the interaction occurs must also be considered. All of this is related to phronesis since it is the adaptive ability and prudence to reach positive results for everyone. Phronesis requires understanding the conditions of each situation and adding knowledge arising from previous experience. Their combination can allow assertive communication since decisions can be made after considering previous successful experiences.

Ethics of Responsibility

At the beginning of the twentieth century, Max Weber proposed the Ethics of Responsibility, a theory later developed by Hans Jonas, a contemporary philosopher who raised a new imperative of responsibility. This imperative is to act in such a way that the effects of our actions are compatible with the permanence of an authentic human life (1984). Jonas emphasises that ethical action does not threaten the life and well-being of others or the subject himself. In a more basic way, the fundamental premises of this theory consider the consequences of actions and the prevention of adverse effects. In such a way, one must rationally deliberate about the consequences and choose actions that obtain the most ethically desirable results.

Another critical aspect of Ethics of Responsibility is the precautionary principle. For Jonas, it means a precautionary or care mandate, which means considering probable future damages, catastrophes or ills caused by any action (González, 2015). This principle is based on reasoning about the possible actions' effects, but it is not strictly probative since there is not always certainty of something that has not yet happened. Being cautious in the face of possible evil becomes an ethical responsibility. Therefore, a key point in the Ethics of Responsibility is the possibility of supporting decisions based on scientific knowledge because being responsible implies an understanding of cause–effect relationships. People must have the most accurate knowledge about the consequences of actions to be responsible. Ignorance implies a high probability of irresponsible actions, so seeking information, when possible, is necessary to recognise the consequences before taking action.

Ethics of Responsibility has a formal character because it refers to how a decision should be made and implies the intention of causing good and not evil with the action to be conducted. Psychological processes needed to make decisions are part of ethical behaviour, so an action cannot be judged only by its consequences but by how the decision was made. So, in assertive communication, responsibility implies predicting how a message can be expressed without being aggressive or passive. Communicating assertively implies acting responsibly. Avoiding damage is a crucial aspect of responsibility; thus, no one involved should be harmed in the social interaction process.

Not harming someone is a minimum condition of respect related to assertiveness, but there is also the ideal that all those involved are favoured in communication. The fact that one's rights and those of others can be considered goes beyond not harming. An example is assertive communication, which allows freedom of expression but is framed within the limits of responsibility. Alberti and Emmons's (1978, as cited in Caballo, 1983) definition of assertiveness says that people must act based on their most important interests, exercising their rights without denying those of others. Assertiveness is not only about defending oneself in situations of aggression but also about rights practice and freedom exercise.

Ethics of Care

This ethical theory was initially proposed by psychologist Carol Gilligan (1982), who collaborated with Lawrence Kohlberg in his studies on moral reasoning's development. Held (2006, p. 10) mentions that some advocates of the Ethics of Care see this theory "as a mosaic of insights and value the way it is sensitive to contextual nuance and particular narratives rather than making the abstract and universal claims", like other moral theories do. Held also shows five key features of this theory, compiled in Table 8.2.

Ethics of Care involves real situations where it is necessary to consider others' needs, avoid harm, and be responsible for each other. Care Ethics are related to Responsibility Ethics since the world is understood as a network of relationships, and from this arises the responsibility of recognition towards others (Alvarado, 2004). Commitment to others is understood as helping actions in this ethical theory since one must help others. It proposes that if someone realises that another has a need, they should help resolve that need. Hence, this theory also relates to Aristotle's ideas on Virtue and phronesis.

Ethics of Care opposes considering universal justice as the central value, which is what Kohlberg did. It has a feminist background since Gilligan

Table 8.2 Features of ethics of care

Feature	*Description*
Taking care of others	The central focus of the Ethics of Care is on the compelling moral salience of attending to and meeting the needs of the others for whom we take responsibility.
Value emotions	In the epistemological process of trying to understand what morality would recommend and what it would be morally best for us to do and to be, Ethics of Care values emotion rather than rejects it.
Focuses on specific relationships	Ethics of Care rejects dominant moral theories' view about abstract reasoning, avoiding bias and achieving impartiality. Instead, it focuses on the claims of others with whom we share actual relationships.
Reconceptualises public and private domains	Ethics of Care refuses to see "public" life as relevant to morality while missing the moral significance of the "private" domains of family and friendship.
Critique liberal individualism	The ethics of care usually works with a conception of persons as relational, rather than as the self-sufficient, independent individuals of the dominant moral theories.

Note. This table presents the features of Ethics of Care. Information from *The Ethics of Care: Personal, Political, and Global* (pp. 10–13) by V. Held, 2006, Oxford University Press

found existing gender biases in the moral development evaluation while working with Kohlberg and realised that women have another perspective about what is good based on care. This theory gives importance to specific circumstances in which interactions take place in daily life, as well as interpersonal relationships involved (García et al., 2018). It has a pluralistic perspective, considering principles such as justice, care, responsibility, reciprocity, and love.

Ethics of Care directly applies to assertive communication because both focus on relationships. However, assertive communication is not expected in all care relationships, as in the case of parents and children; in all assertive communication, there should be care and responsibility. Second, people actively seek to care for others and assume responsibility for ensuring their well-being based on emotions like affection and love. It should be noted that this care and responsibility must also be addressed to oneself to achieve a midpoint between one's well-being and that of others based on a relational conception of a person's well-being. So, Virtue, Responsibility, and Care ethical theories gather some features that make assertive communication possible.

Decision-Making and Assertive Communication

Behaviour can be driven by various processes, from biologically predetermined and automatic when faced with some stimulus, such as reflexes, to those that require a conscious, rational, and voluntary effort. In assertive communication, decisions' complexity involves various psychological processes, including decision-making. Decision-making theory analyses how choosing an action among possible alternatives leads to the best result according to specific preferences. A decision starts with having to choose between two or more behavioural alternatives. Decision-making is a daily process that can even be done automatically, as in the case of habits and customs. On certain occasions, decisions are part of a more complex process. This section will review the Two Systems Theory of Thought and the Four Component Model of Morality to relate them to assertive communication.

The Two Systems Theory

Daniel Kahneman, renowned psychologist and winner of the Nobel Prize in Economic Sciences in 2002, defends the theory that two different systems of mental processes can lead to decisions after perceiving a given situation. One is related to intuitions, and the other to reasoning. These were labelled System 1 and System 2 by Stanovich and West (2000; Kahneman, 2003). System 1, referring to intuition, is characterised by its typically fast, automatic, effortless, associative, implicit (which cannot be identified by introspection) and usually emotionally charged operations. These are also commonly governed by habits and are difficult to control and change. System 2, referring to reasoning, has slower, serial operations that involve effort, which can be more easily monitored by consciousness and deliberately controlled. They are also relatively flexible and potentially rule-governed (Kahneman, 2003).

System 1 can process perceptions but also concepts that language and representations about past, present, or future can evoke. As shown in Table 8.3, regarding its contents, intuition and reasoning are not restricted to the stimuli being captured at that moment. Perceptual and intuitive processes generate impressions about perceived stimuli and thought attributes. Such impressions are not voluntary or verbally explicit. In contrast, System 2 involves judgements, which are always intentional and explicit, though not overtly expressed. Such judgements can originate from

Table 8.3 Process and content in two cognitive systems

	Perception	*Intuition System 1*	*Reasoning System 2*
Process	Fast Parallel Automatic Effortless Associative Slow learning Emotional		Slow Serial Controlled Effortful Rule-governed Flexible Neutral
Content	Precepts Current stimulation Stimulus-bound	Conceptual representations Past, Present, and Future Can be evoked by language	

Note. This table represents the process and content of perception and cognitive Systems 1 and 2. It is taken from A Perspective on Judgement and Choice. Mapping Bounded Rationality (p. 698), by D. Kahneman (2003); *American Psychologist*, 58(9). Copyright 2003 by American Psychological Association

impressions or deliberative reasoning. Judgements based directly on impressions not changed by System 2 can be identified as "intuitive" (Kahneman, 2003). Table 8.3 details the processes and contents of these systems.

Therefore, what thought system takes part in assertive communication? The answer is System 2, since to behave as assertiveness requires rational processes must be involved, such as deliberation and regulation of emotions in decision-making. However, assertive communication can also occur automatically, being a System 1 process. It seems paradoxical, but it must be considered that practising specific communication skills can lead to these becoming good habits, just as Aristotle conceived virtues development. System 1 is also present in care relationships since emotional responses to others' needs represent relevant motivation. However, it is also necessary to conduct more neutral, slow, and controlled processes to be responsible. Systems 1 and 2 complement each other and are helpful for each situation because, as phronesis supports, each one must be faced according to specific requirements.

Four-Component Model of Morality

Not all decisions that people make are perceived to have ethical implications. Deciding what to wear or what to eat for breakfast before going to work does not usually require ethical deliberation. However, sometimes, we perceive situations with ethical or moral facets to consider. Many tend to perceive a moral duty when giving alms to someone on the street or helping someone who asks for help. Such situations have been studied in Moral Psychology, a field to which the Four Component Model of Morality belongs. In 1983, James Rest found the following phases of moral decision-making through empirical research: (a) moral sensitivity, (b) moral judgement, (c) moral motivation, and (d) moral character. Detailed descriptions of each component process can be seen in Table 8.4.

This theory allows us to understand that people will not always act morally, even though they consciously find ethical implications in some situations. Someone can realise that moral aspects engage in some cases but not go beyond them. Another could find the morally correct possibility to decide but not conduct in the face of some circumstances. Someone else could go one step further and feel a duty to act morally and still do nothing. Finally, another could go through all the above and conduct the action he recognised as morally correct. Nevertheless, there would also be those who do not even realise the moral implications of some events and continue their way without caring.

When relating assertive communication to Rest's Theory, it is found that to be assertive, people must go through the four processes described in it. When aggressive communication occurs, people may not realise the moral implications of their behaviour or may not care; there may be moral sensitivity, but they find dominance, power, or self-assertion more valuable. The same can happen in passive communication since the action is not taken to defend one's rights, even though these are valued. However, for there to be assertiveness, it is necessary to be sensitive to communication's moral implications in each situation, judge which behaviour alternatives could be morally right and wrong, choose the best one based on ethical and moral criteria, and have the motivation and strength to carry it out. This process, in addition, would have to imply the previously addressed elements of the Ethical Theories of Virtue, Responsibility, and Care.

Table 8.4 Four-component model of morality

Component	*Description*
Moral sensitivity	Interpreting the situation. Moral sensitivity is the awareness of how our actions affect other people. It involves being aware of the different possible lines of action and how each could affect the parties concerned (including oneself). Moral sensitivity involves imaginatively constructing possible scenarios (often from limited cues and partial information), knowing cause-consequent chains of events in the real world, and having empathy and role-taking skills. Moral sensitivity is necessary to know that a moral issue engages in a situation.
Moral judgement	Judging which action is morally right or wrong. Once a person knows that various lines of action are possible, he or she must ask which line of action is more morally justified. Even at an early stage, people have intuitions about what is fair and moral and make moral judgements about even the most complex human activities.
Moral motivation	Prioritising moral values over other personal values. People have many values (e.g., careers, affectional relationships, aesthetic preferences, institutional loyalties, hedonistic pleasures, and excitement). Why place a high priority on moral values over these other values? Some evil people in the world (e.g., the professional assassin) may be explained not in terms of deficiencies in Components 1 and 2 but in the low priority given to moral values. It is not necessary to infer that the assassin is deficient in terms of Component 1 (i.e., that he does not realise that shooting someone affects his/her welfare), does not have to infer that the assassin is deficient in terms of Component 2 (i.e., that he does not understand that cooperative arrangements have conditions of reciprocity). Instead, it is more likely to explain the assassin's values (i.e., he does not care to do the fair, decent thing—other values are more important to him).
Moral character	Having the strength of their convictions, having courage, persisting, overcoming distractions and obstacles, implementing skills, and having ego strength. A person may have the first three components (be sensitive to moral issues, have good judgement, prioritise moral values), but it is lacking in Component 4; the person will wilt under pressure or fatigue, will not follow through, will be distracted, or discouraged, and moral behaviour will fail. Component four presupposes that one has set goals, has self-discipline, controls impulses, and has the strength and skill to act according to one's goals.

Note. This table represents the four components of Rest's Morality Model. Information from Beyond the Promise: A Perspective on Research in Moral Education. (p. 22), by M. J. Bebeau, J. R. Rest and D. Narvaez (1999), *Educational researcher,* 28(4)

Conclusion

Assertiveness and assertive communication require behaviours whose consequences are appropriate for the person themselves, do not cause harm, and benefit them and others. Therefore, this construct has substantial moral and ethical implications. However, there is still no solid theoretical foundation for philosophical ethics beyond the liberal and individualist perspectives. Thanks to this chapter's Ethics of Virtue, Ethics of Responsibility, and Ethics of Care analysis can support the statement that assertiveness is ethically right.

From Virtue Ethics, the golden mean and phronesis can be taken as a core part of assertive communication, based on its definition as a midpoint between passivity and aggressiveness. Furthermore, any communicative processes' situational and relational nature is also relevant. From Ethics of Responsibility, the importance of predicting the consequences of people's behaviours and choosing the best possibility when interacting and communicating is taken to obtain the best results for those involved in communication and avoid harm. Care Ethics takes an interest in caring for others and ourselves in communication, which always occurs in specific relationships and contexts. Combined, these three theories allow a better understanding of the complexity of assertive communication and set the tone for further analysis.

On the other hand, research has empirically supported the Two Systems Theory and the Four Components of Morality Model. These theories complement the ethical foundations of assertive communication by adding a scientific perspective on decision-making. System 2 processes and contents are necessary for assertive communication based on responsibility and care. However, through practice, it is possible to develop assertive communication skills as a good habit, which could allow System 1 involvement. Furthermore, assertive communication requires the four components of moral behaviour: sensitivity, judgement, motivation, and moral character. Assertive communication is a type of behaviour; thinking and motivation are not sufficient but necessary.

Hopefully, this chapter has been interesting and opened some doors for assertive communication to be studied, analysed, and discussed from more perspectives. Even though some theories were chosen for this analysis, it does not mean that other theories could not apply. Classic ethics theories, such as Utilitarianism and the Ethics of Duty, can also be involved, and so can most contemporary ones, such as Dialogic Ethics. The same can be said about many theories in the fertile field of Moral Psychology, which will gradually allow us to understand how assertiveness can be expressed in our behaviour and how we can promote it to improve human coexistence.

References

Aguiar, F. (2004). Teoría de la decisión e incertidumbre: modelos normativos y descriptivo (Decision theory and uncertainty: Normative and descriptive models). *Empiria. Revista de Metodología de Ciencias Sociales, 8*, 139–160. https://doi.org/10.5944/empiria.8.2004.982

Alvarado, A. (2004). La ética del cuidado (Ethics care). *Aquichan, 4*(1), 30–39. http://www.scielo.org.co/scielo.php?script=sci_arttext&pid=S1657-59972004000100005&lng=en&tlng=es

Ames, D., Lee, A., & Wazlawek, A. (2017). Interpersonal assertiveness: Inside the balancing act. *Social and Personality Psychology Compass, 11*(6), Article e12317. https://doi.org/10.1111/spc3.12317.

Aristotle. (1926). *Nicomachean ethics* (H. Rackham, Trans.). 10.4159/DLCL.aristotle-nicomachean_ethics.1926. (Original work published ca. 350 B.C.E.)

Bebeau, M. J., Rest, J. R., & Narvaez, D. (1999). Beyond the promise: A perspective on research in moral education. *Educational Researcher, 28*(4), 18–26. https://citeseerx.ist.psu.edu/viewdoc/download?doi=10.1.1.637.7940&rep=rep1&type=pdf

Caballo, V. E. (1983). Asertividad: definiciones y dimensiones (Assertiveness: Concept and dimensions). *Estudios de psicología, 4*(13), 51–62. https://dialnet.unirioja.es/descarga/articulo/65876.pdf

Calua, M. R., Delgado, Y. L., & López, Ó. (2021). Comunicación asertiva en el contexto educativo: revisión sistemática (Assertiveness comunication in the scholar context: A systematic revision). *Boletín Redipe, 10*(4), 315–334. https://dialnet.unirioja.es/descarga/articulo/7917878.pdf

Cantero-Sánchez, F. J., León-Rubio, J. M., Vázquez-Morejón, R., & León-Pérez, J. M. (2021). Evaluation of an assertiveness training based on the social learning theory for occupational health, safety and environment practitioners. *Sustainability, 13*, 11504. https://doi.org/10.3390/su132011504

Chambers, D. W. (2009). Assertiveness. *The Journal of the American College of Dentists, 76*(2), 51–58.

Duckworth, M. P., & Mercer, V. (2006). Assertiveness Training. In J. E. Fisher & W. T. O'Donohue (Eds.), *Practitioner's guide to evidence-based psychotherapy* (pp. 80–92). Springer Science + Business Media. https://doi.org/10.1007/978-0-387-28370-8_7

Gaeta, L., & Galvanovskis, A. (2009). Asertividad: un análisis teórico-empírico (Assertiveness: A theoretical-empirical analysis). *Enseñanza e Investigación en Psicología, 14*(2), 403–425.
García, C. (2021). Fundamentos teóricos para una distinción clara entre el comportamiento ético y el normativo-moral en el desempeño profesional del psicólogo (Theoretical foundations for a clear distinction between ethical and normative-moral behavior in the professional performance of the psychologist). *Avances en Psicología Latinoamericana, 39*(3), 1–16. https://doi.org/10.12804/revistas.urosario.edu.co/apl/a.10321
García, C., Preciado, M., Ángel, M., & Luna, A. (2018). El desarrollo moral y la toma de decisiones éticas del psicólogo (Moral development and ethical decision making of the psychologist). *Investigación y Práctica en Psicología del Desarrollo, 4*. https://doi.org/10.33064/ippd41993
Gilligan, C. (1982). *In a different voice*. Harvard University Press.
González, G. (2015). Hans Jonas' 'principle of responsibility' in the light of ecological awareness. *Nomads. Critical Journal of Social and Legal Sciences, 46*(2), 125–146. https://doi.org/10.5209/rev_NOMA.2015.v46.n2.51421
Held, V. (2006). *The ethics of care: Personal, political, and global*. Oxford University Press.
Hursthouse, R., & Pettigrove, G. (2018). Virtue ethics. *The Stanford Encyclopedia of Philosophy (Winter 2018 Edition)*. https://plato.stanford.edu/archives/win2018/entries/ethics-virtue/.
Jonas, H. (1984). *The imperative of responsibility: In search of an ethics for the technological age*. The University of Chicago Press.
Kahneman, D. (2003). A perspective of judgement and choice. *American Psychologist, 58*(9), 697–720. https://doi.org/10.1037/0003-066X.58.9.697
Kahneman, D. (2011). *Thinking fast and slow*. Penguin Books.
Litt, M. D. (2013). Network support treatment for alcohol dependence. *Interventions for Addiction*, 67–76. https://doi.org/10.1016/B978-0-12-398338-1.00008-7.
Malti, T., & Perren, S. (2011). Social competence. *Encyclopedia of Adolescence*, 332–340. https://doi.org/10.1016/B978-0-12-373951-3.00090-9.
Merriam-Webster. (n.d.-a). *Assert*. In the Merriam-Webster.com dictionary. https://www.merriam-webster.com/dictionary/assert.
Merriam-Webster. (n.d.-b). *Assertive*. In the Merriam-Webster.com dictionary. https://www.merriam-webster.com/dictionary/assertive.
Mrvoljak-Theodoropoulou, I., Gari, A., & Mylonas, K. (2020). Young adults' assertiveness in relation to parental acceptance-rejection in Greece and in Bosnia and Herzegovina. *Psychological Reports*. https://doi.org/10.1177/0033294120980967.
Omura, M., Maguire, J., Levett-Jones, T., & Stone, T. E. (2016). Effectiveness of assertive communication training programs for health professionals and stu-

dents: A systematic review protocol. *JBI Database of Systematic Reviews and Implementation Reports, 14*(10), 64–71. https://doi.org/10.11124/jbisrir-2016-003158

Omura, M., Maguire, J., Levett-Jones, T., & Stone, T. E. (2017). The effectiveness of assertiveness communication training programs for healthcare professionals and students: A systematic review. *International Journal of Nursing Studies., 76C*, 120–128. https://doi.org/10.1016/j.ijnurstu.2017.09.001

Pfafman, T. (2020). Assertiveness. In V. Zeigler-Hill, T. K. Shackelford, & T.K. (Eds.), *Encyclopedia of personality and individual differences*. Springer. https://doi.org/10.1007/978-3-319-24612-3_1044

Pipas, M. D., & Jaradat, M. (2010). Assertive communication skills. *Annales Universitatis Apulensis: Series Oeconomica, 12*(2), 649. http://www.oeconomica.uab.ro/upload/lucrari/1220102/17.pdf

Richard, C., Lussier, T., Millette, B., & Tanoubi, I. (2023). Healthcare providers and patients: An essay on the importance of professional assertiveness in healthcare today. *Medical Education Online, 28*(1). https://doi.org/10.1080/10872981.2023.2200586.

Speed, B. C., Goldstein, B. L., & Goldfried, M. R. (2018). Assertiveness training: A forgotten evidence-based treatment. *Clinical Psychology: Science and Practice, 25*(1), e12216. https://doi.org/10.1111/cpsp.12216

Stanovich, K. E., & West, R. F. (2000). Advancing the rationality debate. *Behavioural and brain sciences, 23*(5), 701–717. http://www.keithstanovich.com/Site/Research_on_Reasoning_files/bbs2000_1.pdf

Weliangan, H. (2022). Mindfulness and Assertive communication effect towards husbands and wives marital satisfaction. *International Journal of Research Publications, 104*(1), 931–940.

CHAPTER 9

Assertiveness, Conflict, and Peacemaking

Alejandro Ernesto Vázquez-Martínez

Assertiveness: The Transformation of a Concept

Caballo (1983) indicates that assertiveness originates in behaviour therapy, especially in the work of Salter, Lazarus, and Wolpe, the latter being the first to use the word *assertion in* the book *Psychotherapy by Reciprocal Inhibition* in 1958 (p. 83). In the same sense, in the book *People Skills. Regarding asserting yourself, listening to others, and resolving conflicts*, Bolton (1979) points out that conflict cannot be avoided in human life and that in so-called realistic conflicts, there are opposing needs, goals, and values. Likewise, Alberti and Emmons (2017), in *Your Perfect Right. Assertiveness and Equality in your Life and Relationships*, address the importance of clarifying the "real needs" of those involved in a conflict situation.

The authors can establish a direct relationship between assertiveness and conflict by opposing values, goals and needs. In that order of ideas,

A. E. Vázquez-Martínez (✉)
Departamento de Ciencias Jurídicas, Instituto de Ciencias Sociales y Administración, Universidad Autónoma de Ciudad Juárez, Ciudad Juarez, Mexico
e-mail: alejandro.vazquez@uacj.mx

S. Castaños-Cervantes, C. Atristain-Suárez (eds.), *Assertiveness in the Context of Human Rights, Ethics, and Classical Virtues*,
https://doi.org/10.1007/978-3-031-60962-6_9

Ames et al. (2017, p. 2) consider assertiveness as "a dimension in behavioural judgments in situations where people have goals that are not aligned with the judgments of other people, even when these are interdependent". From an analogous perspective, the conflict has an *overt* element that "means that members of at least one of the contending groups engage in behaviours that attempt to change the behaviour of the other party in ways that move them closer to their goals" (Kriesberg & Dayton, 2012, p. 2). Townend (2007, p. 57) notes that assertiveness is related to the connection between people; moreover, "conflict can provide people with the opportunity to develop assertive relationships and connect more honestly". Furthermore, the experience of conflict implies that people "feel physically, intellectually, emotionally, and spiritually disconnected from themselves and others" (Townend, 2007, p. 58).

This last description of the experience of conflict complicates the dimensions that constitute people and, therefore, the conception of assertiveness itself. Güel Barceló (2006) observes that assertiveness does not resolve disputes by itself but raises them satisfactorily. Furthermore, he correlates assertiveness with culture and human rights: "To focus the meaning of assertiveness in our cultural context, we can relate it to commonly accepted ethical values: human rights, in their most universal sense" (p. 15). Thus, the understanding of assertiveness from the paradigm of human rights allows us not only to understand the cultural patterns or maps (Giménez, 2005) that societies re-produce but also define assertiveness relationally, that is, from the inter-relationships, practices, links, and socio-cultural and political representations created between the State-government and the various social groups that make up the citizenry.

In that sense, the following considerations must be made. The first is to emphasise that the conceptions that contextualise assertiveness within the paradigm of human rights do not necessarily imply the problematisation of conflicts within the framework of commonly accepted ethical values since conflicts also reconfigure the legal, political, cultural, identity-related, among others, concepts of rights and their philosophical, anthropological, and political foundations. In this transformation, issues related to justice, formally institutionalised and derived from social practice, undergo changes that, in turn, imply the emergence of practices and representations that may diverge from the notions of justice that prevailed before the conflict.

The other consideration, related to a conception of assertiveness that allows for more satisfactory approaches in conflict resolution, lies precisely in the prevailing conditions before the conflict and the recognition of its existence. It refers explicitly to disputes that oblige a rethinking of governance, that is, the legitimacy and legality of the *auctoritas* and the responsibilities that may arise from that exercise. This consideration can be explored based on what Pierre Clastres (2013) points out in his book (*Society Against the State. Essays in Political Anthropology*), about the appearance of the state machine and the transformation of social structure, as well as the question of the legitimate monopoly of force/violence, in this chapter, it is interesting to note how assertiveness can help in conflict resolution, mainly if it is considered as a power that is currently under construction based on various knowledge and understandings that indicate the absence of the state and, in its case, state responsibility in generating the violence experienced in conflicts.

In the context of human rights narratives and the foundations of the state, the last consideration is the logic of reasoning that, until the early 1940s, began to examine the relationship between victims and offenders. This reasoning founded a type of "scientific" knowledge based on the positivist idea of the "intervention" of "specialist technicians" in resolving the conflict between victims and perpetrators. It was precisely the work of Hans Von Hentig (1940), "Remarks on the Interaction of Perpetrator and Victim", which allowed the development of victimological analysis. Despite this perspective still being prevalent today, it is increasingly apparent that there is a need to find mechanisms for interpreting and transforming conflicts that focus on the *potestas* and the right of political communities to resolve conflicts through tools such as assertiveness.

Assertiveness and Pacification

Initially, it is necessary to identify the different formal definitions of pacification. The United Nations distinguishes between conflict prevention and mediation, peacemaking, peace enforcement, and peacebuilding (United Nations [UN], 2023). These operations must conform to general norms such as the United Nations Charter, Intergovernmental organisation treaties, and the Geneva Convention, as well as a set of specific standards, including the Security Council Resolution, the Agreement on the status of peacekeeping forces, the Rules of Engagement (Calduch Cervera, n.d.), and other international legal norms.

Pacification, on the other hand, has concrete expressions in historical, socio-cultural, and political developments. Neocleous (2016) shows the military origin of pacification and its relationship with counterinsurgency in the 1960s, particularly in the US–Vietnam War. In that context, pacification was to establish a new order. The same author notes that the term pacification has now been replaced by other concepts such as "low-intensity conflict", "operations other than war", and the "grey-scale phenomenon" (pp. 10–11). The author's critical theory states: "Pacification is a military act, adorned as the 'peace' of a civil society and achieved through the construction of new orders called 'secure'. Therefore, we could also say that the time and space of bourgeois modernity can be understood as the time and space of pacification" (p. 20).

From the same perspective, Francis (2010) observes how: "'Security', in turn, has been militarised [sic] to mean (more often than not) armed protection and control and the establishment of a newly fashioned state's monopoly of violence" (pp. 72–73). It is relevant to note that from Neocleous's perspective, pacification, militarisation and security are understood as a unified process, in contrast to Francis, who holds an interpretation where security has been perverted and used to reconfigure the monopoly of violence. However, one of the biggest challenges is establishing a starting point that defines the complexity of the processes experienced by societies or political communities, understood as a set of relationships between the state and citizenship. Mainly because these relationships are, in one way or another, determinant in the "sense that offenders and victims exist in recognition of a combination of legal definitions and social" (Lea, 1992, p. 27).

This determination of the state and citizens towards victims and perpetrators allows us to reflect on the socio-cultural and legal context in which assertiveness unfolds and, above all, to indicate two questions that will enable us to conceive it in its relational condition, as developed in the following section. On the one hand, it is necessary to stop at "the inability to theorise about the crime concept [as] a manifestation of a lack of understanding about the social categories role and processes associated with their development and interpretation. Understanding and classifying social categories are fundamental for any scientific investigation" (Matthews, 2014, p. 184). Furthermore, this inability to theorise about issues related to crime and the lack of understanding of social categories that are in some way associated with the knowledge of crime requires the establishment of analytical correspondences between assertiveness and pacification. Although it is evident that the limited literature that systematically categorises the types of theoretical and practical relationships between the two is minor, the approaches to pacification and transitional justice provide a plausible path for its practice.

Thus, Transitional Justice (TJ) is "the effort to build sustainable peace after a period of conflict, mass violence, or systematic violation of human rights. The objective of transitional justice involves bringing perpetrators to trial, revealing the truth about past crimes, providing reparations to victims, reforming abusive institutions, and promoting reconciliation" (Zyl, 2011, p. 47). Arias-Marín (2010) notes that TJ also seeks the identity and fate of victims and perpetrators, as well as establishing the facts related to massive human rights violations in situations of authoritarianism and armed conflict, as well as the design of the forms that society will address crimes and the needs for repair of damages (p. 20). In other mechanisms, TJ uses the so-called truth commissions, which function as spaces for:

> *(i) the (re)construction of more comprehensive public and participatory narratives about the contexts of widespread violence, its causes, consequences, and legacies, (ii) the expression of free versions, both from victims and perpetrators, (iii) the formulation, analysis, discussion, and reconsideration, from a social perspective, of the challenges involved in the reconciliation and reconstruction of the social fabric, as well as the reappropriation of public institutions, the promotion of substantive democracy, or the rule of law.* (López Ayllón, 2018, p. 43)

Undoubtedly, TJ processes involve complexity involving other variables; however, the importance of assertiveness from its relational property and political condition is emphasised here, as it allows for an approach to conflicts in their different spheres and dimensions, focused on the public and community understanding of violence, its causes and consequences, primarily from the narratives of victimised people, as well as from the participation of all subjects involved in understanding the conflict to systematise the set of experiences to conceive agreements from the oppositions and tensions that constitute the conflict. Without forgetting that the network of relationships that organises and configures the necessary conditions must count on the participation of the state government and the international community, this participation cannot be formulated without the certainty of a profound transformation in governance mechanisms, as well as in the reconfiguration of socio-cultural, legal representations and practices where the conflict emerged. Discussions and consensus-seeking on crime, pain, suffering, and legal co-responsibility mechanisms are unavoidable.

Assertiveness, Human Rights, and Politics

The relational property of assertiveness and conflict in the rights paradigm makes it possible to characterise social subjects as victimised persons; however, victimisation is not only caused by harm to the person as such but also by harm to the member of a community: "Human rights, therefore, refer to the person simply as a person, while fundamental rights concern the person as a member of a specific public entity" (Höffe, 2000, p. 168). Thus, "the relational property of assertiveness and its link with human and fundamental rights also makes it possible to define conflict as a constitutive part of politics (Balibar, 2013, p. 163) since, as Rancière (1996) indicates, politics is a matter of subjects, of modes of subjectification, that is, "the production through a series of acts of an instance and a capacity of enunciation that were not identifiable in a given field of experience" (1996, p. 52).

Assertiveness, then, in its political condition, is opposite to statements that, for example, indicate: "You can change the structure of your life by altering the structure of your mind. You can take away your pain" (McKay et al., 2011, p. 279), for it is a reversal to "hermeneutic visibility" (Mate, 2011, p. 11). This act interpellates its community and the state government. Assertiveness does not seek clarity for itself but to warn from the testimony of an absence of the "[l]oss has made a tenuous 'we' of us all" (Butler, 2004, p. 20). Therefore, Agamben (2014) reminds us that whoever testifies commonly does so in favour of truth and justice; however, "testimony is essentially worth what is missing in it; it contains, at its very core, something that is not testimonial" (p. 34). Implicit in this assertion is a conception of the human being, the social subject and conflict.

In this regard, it is necessary to conceive of conflict beyond opposing values or needs; it is also an "intentional clash between two beings or groups of the same species that manifest a hostile intention towards each other, [...]. Trying to break the resistance of the other eventually using violence, which can lead to the physical annihilation of the other if necessary" (Freund, 1983, p. 65). Likewise, the science that studies conflict, *conflictology*, points out that one should act "on the causes of conflicts rather than on their symptomatology and proposes methods of change as a system of conflict resolution [...] the objective is not focused on establishing an ideal system of peace, but on seeking, on trying to make it possible, to facilitate, that peace establishes itself" (Vinyamata, 2015, p. 17). Such conflict resolution, inevitably, is built from the people's testimony who have been victimised, that is, from the narratives of the victimisation processes.

Assertiveness, Language, and Collective Memory

Now, Veena Das (1996) evidenced that "even the idea that we should recover the narratives of violence becomes problematic when we realise that such narratives cannot be told unless we see the relation between pain and language that a culture has evolved" (p. 88). For this reason, it is essential to consider issues such as assertiveness relationally and, where appropriate, from the relationships that occur in the exercise of governance, "every regime of governance invokes its particular subject of governance" (Evans & Reid, 2014, p. 78). Moreover, there is *therapeutic governance* centred on self-esteem (Pupavac, 2001) that conceives the contemporary subject "under the discourse of human rights [that] takes the form of the fragile and vulnerable pre-political victim that must be protected and empowered through therapeutic intervention" (p. 360), without considering the political and historical specificity of conflicts and victimisations (Wolhuter et al., 2009, p. 27).

Relational assertiveness in its political condition must be understood as a fundamental element of the pacification process. It is "collective decision-making to resolve direct conflicts once they have become visible" (Bickmore et al., 2017, p. 283). The visibility of conflicts and their resolutions are closely related to the understanding made of the victimisations originated by them. The following questions contribute to this understanding and the pacification search: "How does the challenge of violence feel for the people who live within these communities? What are their responses to the events that unfold, their language and organisational metaphors for dealing with violence […] What are the reference points that help frame their experience and how they make sense of their challenges?" (Lederach & Lederach, 2010, p. 44).

In the following narrative, the author finds some answers to the questions proposed by Lederach. Daniela, interviewed on 12/06/2019, shares her experience after her father's murder in 2010 in the municipality of Ciudad Juarez, Chihuahua, in one of the highest homicides in the locality.

> *My mom took me [to the psychologist] and everything, but when I finished my sessions, the psychologist said to me, 'Do you feel ready? Do you think you can stop coming?' And I told her the truth: No, it has helped me because I started to do certain things, like write a letter, burn it, and so on, and I still do it. And I said no, she talked to my mom and everything, and my mom said no, I already brought you, and that is it! And that is why I still, well, because of what I've seen in psychology class, I feel like I did not close the stage, and again, I'm unconsciously looking for it. I mean, the government, yes, they did give me support: they gave me a psychologist, they paid for my school, and so on. Yes. It has helped me a lot, but I still feel that the violence has continued; I feel that nothing has been done. Everything remains the same. No, it is not worth anything.* (Daniela, 2019, cited in Vázquez et al., 2021)

In the narrative, the author finds the therapeutic intervention presence, as well as a correlation with the figure of the fragile and pre-political victim, since her process has developed outside the community, that is, without considering the relational aspects that define the human being and without approaching the conflict from the collective participation perspective. Moreover, the challenge of violence, as Lederach calls it, is, for Daniela, a spiral that does not stop since it remains the same. This experience, however, remains articulated with the current forms of violence.

It should be noted that this chapter refers to structural violence, understood as "the total of all the shocks embedded in social structures [...], such that the unjust, unequal results are almost immutable" (Galtung, 1998, p. 16). However, the conflict's visibility in a structural violence context is "only possible from the memory's social frameworks, that is, from the capacity of a community or society to reconstruct its past" (Halbwachs, 2004, p. 336). Not only that, but it is also about the "right to know" that all people have, the right to "know and make known their history" (Todorov, 2013, p. 19). This right makes it possible to rethink the understanding of conflicts and assertiveness from a different epistemological framework, "not only for the due evocation of the past but for the–complete—examination of the present" (Rivera Beiras, 2011, p. 52).

This correspondence between past and present allows us to understand the experience of Mireya, a young woman originally from Ciudad Juarez, Chihuahua, who lost one of her brothers in October 2010, first kidnapped and then murdered. In that circumstance, Mireya went to a psychologist and recalled:

> *For a long time, my mother did not want to eat; she did not stop crying, and we, therefore, did what we looked at. Then, I remembered that for a while, I did not want to go to school; I looked, well, at people as if they were all bad. -What did you think they were going to do to you?—Well, they were going to hurt me.* Again, without collective actions supported by the state government, Mireya points out: *Sometimes I feel... Well, there is much insecurity, but it's not like I will stay in my house forever locked up so that nothing else happens to me. We are exposed to much violence, but being locked up will not change things* (Mireya, 2019, quoted in Vázquez et al., 2021).

The author observes how, in both cases, structural violence persists. Although the intention to continue with life even though exposure to such violence is found, the accounts remain in individual memories, waiting to form collective memories that allow for the transformation of the lives of social subjects through an epistemology that generates recognition of victimisation processes to create political inputs directed towards the pacification of society. It not only eliminates the possibility of conceiving conflicts from state practices and concepts outside the logic of securitisation but also inhibits the participation of different social groups and prevents the incorporation of the experience of colonial subjects in understanding and responding to conflicts. In this sense, it is pertinent to transform dominant narratives about insecurity, particularly when state strategies integrate community pacification with military and police deployment.

Assertiveness, Structural Violence, and Pedagogy of Memory

Relational assertiveness, in its political context, also allows for perspectives encompassing the dimensions of structural violence, mainly through the practice of pedagogy of memory. With this purpose, it is pertinent to note that, to the defining qualities of structural violence, such as injustice and nearly immutable inequality, one must add the specificity that Galtung (1969) points out regarding structural violence, social injustice, and human rights.

> *One expression of what social justice means is in declarations of human rights, where several norms about equality are stated. However, they often suffer from the deficiency that they are personal more than structural. They refer to what*

> *individuals can do or can have, not to who or what decides what they can do or have; they refer to the distribution of resources, not to power over the allocation of resources. In other words, human rights as usually conceived of are pretty compatible with paternalism, where powerholders distribute anything but ultimate power over the distributions so that equalisation without any change in the power structure is obtained […], concessions are not enough, not even equality is enough, it is how decisions about distribution are arrived at and implemented that is basic. However, there is little reason to believe that this will not also, in due time, crystallise into some human right and be added to that list of philosophical and political battlefields.* (p. 188)

This development highlights issues related to the deficiency of human rights norms regarding equality, as they focus more on personal matters than structural ones, emphasising what an individual can do or have rather than the power to decide who can do or have. Therefore, these concessions to individuals do not entail changes in power structures. For this reason, the analytical division proposed by the author is significant:

> *We have baptised the distinction in two ways: personal-structural and direct-indirect, respectively. Violence with a clear subject-object relation manifests because it is visible as action. It corresponds to our drama ideas and is personal because persons are committing the violence […]. Violence without this relation is structural, built into the structure. Thus, when one husband beats his wife, there is a clear case of personal violence, but when one million husbands keep one million wives in ignorance, there is structural violence.* (Galtung, 1969, p. 171)

The narrative of the young woman Abril interviewed on 08/21/2023 allows us to observe how the conditions of structural violence experienced from an individual perspective are linked to collective practices and how direct and structural violence converge: "Structural violence is not, however, primarily about personal choice—it is built into the functioning of impersonal (bureaucratic, technocratic, and automatic) systems and applied to whole classes of people without regard to the characteristics of any individual case" (Farmer, 2004, p. 321).

> *Personally, I am someone who has not directly witnessed any violent events in my life (and I have known quite a few); only the fact that I saw an attempted murder during my childhood in elementary school stays with me. I had to be locked in the classroom for approximately two hours with other classmates, watching as teachers, janitors, and the vendors from the typical stands searched*

for [the assailant] and passed through the classrooms to calm the students. No one told us explicitly, but we knew we had to stay low, not leave the classroom, and avoid spending too much time near the windows; the knowledge was inherent for us children around 11 years old. Part of 'my 11-year-old self' routine was to wake up, get ready for school, hear the news report the death toll, see soldiers along the way, arrive at school, and go to the principal's office because the teacher had entrusted me with some messages. I could hear the principal in the distance reassuring a parent on the phone, emphasising that there were no threats to the elementary school, that they could bring their children in safely, and that this school was a secure place, unlike others where the drug cartels used to leave decapitated bodies with narco-banners. Whoever said the school was a safe place spoke from a reality entirely different from mine (Abril, 2023).

The reality that Abril experienced within a continuum of structural violence, distinguishable only by degrees and characterised by the violation and fragility of life, is significant due to the correspondence between childhood-death-soldiers-mutilated bodies-narco-banners. However, the everyday nature of these experiences brought about normalisation:

Another aspect that I realised I had normalised was when I began to have contact with people from other places who were shocked by my everyday anecdotes. They were horrified by things that were so routine for me, such as the fact that someone had been killed near my house, that I had been close to shootings, that I had met people who had been held at gunpoint, or that I had to attend virtual classes or work because the city was on alert due to shootings in various areas, fires at establishments, and related issues that affected everyone's route when they were outside their homes. One day, I wasn't sure if I could make it home because such a solid armed confrontation had been going on for a long time, and it was unclear when it would stop. It got to the point where I had to consider staying elsewhere because the route home was complicated. Fortunately, it wasn't necessary, but it was a challenging situation. It wasn't one of those shootings you hear a few blocks away that lasted for a few minutes; it was such a fierce confrontation that social media closely followed every event. (Abril, 2023)

The reflexivity expressed in Abril's words allows us to consider the pedagogy of memory as "a space for reflection and the production of experiences associated with the transmission of violent and conflict-ridden pasts in both Latin America and other parts of the world" (Legarralde & Brugaletta, 2017, p. 1), even when structural violence persists. As mentioned in the previous section, if it is possible to reconstruct a collective past through the social frameworks of memory, pedagogy of memory becomes a suitable methodology for reconfiguring the experience and, therefore, the past: "Locating memory temporally means referring to the 'space of experience' in the present. The recollection of the past is embodied but dynamically, as already incorporated experiences can change over time" (Jelin, 2003, p. 15). Finally, if pedagogy of memory entails reflecting on the following questions:

> *Through what formative and organisational practices do social groups, communities, non-governmental organisations, research centres, and mobilisation dynamics reconstruct their memories of political violence and armed social conflict? How do individuals confront the reconstruction of social relationships and their community life when they have experienced extreme violence? How do various social agents narrate, interpret, and remember individual and collective violent pasts?* (Herrera et al., 2014, p. 174)

The closing reflection by Abril leads to considerations of specific needs and possibilities that connect relational assertiveness in its political context with pedagogies of memory.

> *It is not normal what we have witnessed. It is not expected to have lived a childhood in which you would encounter soldiers on many streets. It is not likely to dream of going to your elementary school and finding decapitated bodies. It is unknown when and in which areas there were assaults outside the high school. It is not expected to see pink crosses on the lampposts around the city. It is not likely to experience events like a robbery or a shootout and then must continue with daily activities. Violence should never be normalised, yet in Ciudad Juárez, it still is.* (Abril, 2023)

This approach involves an analytical understanding of reality and the integration of epistemologies that first recognise the *absence* of *experience* (De Sousa Santos, 2017) that occurs in various victimisations. Second, mechanisms should be developed to recover those experiences, and third, the necessary inputs should be available to make viable proposals for state programmes and policies that prioritise citizen participation. However, this participation must be understood outside of traditional notions that assign a marginal role to communities in decision-making. Therefore, relational assertiveness in its political condition is closely related to the central role of communities and the victimisations that define part of their existence and the construction of collective decisions, as has already been pointed out.

Conclusions

Assertiveness allows for a comprehensive understanding of the human being from the human rights paradigm, considering its emotional, ethical, spiritual, and intellectual dimensions, among others, and its correlation with conflict. Initially, assertiveness originated from concepts that focus on the subject without considering its social nature, namely, the relationships and connections that define it. Nevertheless, from the earliest definitions, there have been notions about the relational quality that defines assertiveness. In the same way, assertiveness has not only been conceived as a mechanism for conflict resolution, but it has also provided a thorough descriptive and analytical precision about conflict, highlighting the need to delve into behaviours and conduct as well as to establish specific goals that allow for the conflict to be observed from other perspectives.

In developing practices guided by assertiveness, it has been necessary to reconfigure its qualities whenever understood and practised from the human rights paradigm. In this context, it is essential to conceive of assertiveness from its correlational property and political condition since rights can undoubtedly be seen from the individuality of subjects, but never without the political community where the paradigm's effectiveness is experienced differentially and the subsequent need to critically position oneself on the conditions of existence, particularly in a context of direct or indirect structural, cultural, or explicit violence.

The causes of violence production differ from one place to another, from one community to another. Nevertheless, any victimisation process invokes the collective victim figure who challenges formal and actual powers intending to find justice. One of the most relevant characteristics of these positions is the act of testifying in favour of reconstructing, through experience, the causes of victimisation and establishing the necessary measures to reverse and prevent its reproduction. Ineffable losses inevitably mark these processes; however, to understand the causes of such violence, it is essential to focus on the correlations between language and pain and the organisational metaphors proposed by Lederach to analyse.

For these reasons, assertiveness from its political condition is only possible if specific actions are recreated that are understood from the experiences of transitional justice, primarily to know what happened in the various victimisations, to articulate the needs for justice that arise from those victimisations, establish routes to understand which are the most appropriate practices to seek comprehensive reparations, and finally, prevent the causes that produced violence from finding reasons again. At this point, it is essential to assume that victimisation cycles have responded to different causes, even though the same social subjects and their communities have suffered the consequences.

Therefore, it is also relevant to outline proposals focused on social and collective memory since these categories used in methodologies such as the pedagogy of memory, aimed at "the articulation of [...] practices related to processes of signification and appropriation of our recent history" (Minatti, 2013, p. 2), contribute to a better understanding of victimisations. Therefore, this pedagogy also implies a pedagogy of conflict (Goldberg & Lasa, 2018) and, consequently, the possibility of using the qualities of assertiveness. As previously mentioned, in its relational form and political condition, this allows for the conception of relevant epistemologies to understand victimising experiences not from their absence but rather as the core that will enable the construction of actions, programs, or state policies directed towards pacification.

References

Agamben, G. (2014). *Lo que queda de Auschwitz. El archivo y el testigo. Homo Sacer III. (Remnants of Auschwitz: The Witness and the Archive. Homo Sacer III).* Pre-textos.

Alberti, R., & Emmons, M. (2017). *Your perfect, right. Assertiveness and equality in your life and relationships.* Impact Publishers.

Ames, D., Lee, A., & Wazlawek, A. (2017). Interpersonal assertiveness: Inside the balancing act. *Social and Personality Psychology Compass, 11.* https://doi.org/10.1111/spc3.12317

Arias-Marín, A. (2010). Justicia transicional y derechos humanos. La relevancia de las víctimas (Transitional justice and human rights. The relevance of the victims). *Revista del Centro Nacional de Derechos Humanos, 13,* 13–32.

Balibar, É. (2013). *Ciudadanía (Citizenship)* (Trad. R. Molina). Adriana Hidalgo.

Bickmore, K., Kaderi, S. A., & Guerra-Sua, Á. (2017). Creating capacities for peacebuilding citizenship: history and social studies curricula in Bangladesh, Canada, Colombia, and México. *Journal of Peace Education, 14*(3), 282–309. https://doi.org/10.1080/17400201.2017.1365698

Bolton, R. (1979). *People skills. How to assert yourself, listen to others, and resolve conflicts.* Simon and Schuster, Inc.

Butler, J. (2004). *Precarious life: the powers of mourning and violence.* Verso.

Caballo, V. (1983). Asertividad: Definiciones y dimensiones (Assertiveness: Definitions and dimensions). *Estudios de Psicología, 4*(13), 51–62. https://doi.org/10.1080/02109395.1983.10821343

Calduch Cervera, R. (n.d.). *Operaciones de pacificación (Peacekeeping operations).* https://www.ucm.es/data/cont/docs/835-2018-03-01Apuntes%20de%20Operaciones%20de%20Pacificacion.pdf.

Clastres, P. (2013). *La sociedad contra el Estado. Ensayos de antropología política (Society against the State. Political anthropology essays).* Hueders.

Das, V. (1996). Language and Body in the Construction of Pain. *Daedelus, 125*(1), 67–91.

De Sousa Santos, B. (2017). *Justicia entre saberes: Epistemologías del sur contra el epistemicidio (Justice between knowledge: Southern epistemologies against epistemicide).* Ediciones Morata.

Evans, B., & Reid, J. (2014). *Resilient life. The art of living dangerously.* Polity Press.

Farmer, P. (2004). An anthropology of structural violence. *Current Anthropology, 45*(3), 305–325.

Francis, D. (2010). *From Pacification to Peacebuilding: a call to global transformation.* Pluto Press.

Freund, J. (1983). *Sociologie du conflit.* Presses Universitaires de France.

Galtung, J. (1969). Violence, Peace, and Peace Research. *Journal of Peace Research, 6*(3), 167–191. http://www.jstor.org/stable/422690

Galtung, J. (1998). *Tras la violencia, 3R: reconstrucción, reconciliación, resolución. Afrontando los efectos visibles e invisibles de la guerra y la violencia (After violence, 3R: reconstruction, reconciliation, resolution. Facing the visible and invisible effects of war and violence).* Red Gernika.

Giménez Montiel, G. (2005). *Teoría y análisis de la cultura (Theory and analysis of culture)* (Vol. 1). CONACULTA.

Goldberg, C. & Lasa, L. (2018). *Pedagogía de la Memoria en construcción. La experiencia educativa en el Espacio para la Memoria y la Promoción de los Derechos Humanos (Pedagogy of Memory under construction. The educational experience in the Space for Memory and the Promotion of Human Rights).* Ex Centro Clandestino de Detención, Tortura y Exterminio (CCDTyE) "Olimpo" [Archivo PDF]. https://www.exccdolimpo.org.ar/publicaciones.

Güel Barceló, M. (2006). *¿Por qué he dicho blanco si quería decir negro? Técnicas asertivas para el profesorado y formadores (Why did I say white if I meant black? Assertive techniques for teachers and trainers).* Editorial Graó.

Halbwachs, M. (2004). *Los Marcos sociales de la memoria (The social frameworks of memory)* (Trans. M. Baeza & M. Mujica). Anthropos.

Herrera Cortés, M., Ortega Valencia, P., Cristancho, J., & Olaya Gualteros, V. (2014). *Memoria y formación: configuraciones de la subjetividad en ecologías violentas (Memory and formation: configurations of subjectivity in violent ecologies.)*. Universidad Pedagógica Nacional.

Höffe, O. (2000). *Derecho intercultural (Intercultural right)*. Gedisa.

Jelin, E. (2003). *Los derechos humanos y la memoria de la violencia política y la represión: la construcción de un campo nuevo en las ciencias sociales (Human rights and the memory of political violence and repression: the construction of a new field in the social sciences)*. Instituto de Desarrollo Económico y Social.

Kriesberg, L., & Dayton, B. (2012). *Constructive conflicts. From escalation to resolution*. Rowman & Littlefield Publishers.

Lea, J. (1992). El análisis del delito (The analysis of the crime). *Delito y Sociedad. Revista de Ciencias Sociales, 8*, 26–49.

Lederach, J. P., & Lederach, A. J. (2010). *When blood and bones cry out. Journeys through the sound-scape of healing and reconciliation*. Oxford University Press.

Legarralde, M., & Brugaletta, F. (2017). Dossier Pedagogía de la Memoria: políticas y prácticas de transmisión del pasado reciente en Argentina (Dossier Pedagogy of Memory: policies and practices of transmission of the recent past in Argentina). *Aletheia, 7*(14) http://www.memoria.fahce.unlp.edu.ar/art_revistas/pr.7891/pr.7891.pdf

López Ayllón, S. (2018). *Estudio para elaborar una propuesta de política pública en materia de Justicia Transicional en México (Study to prepare a public policy proposal on Transitional Justice in Mexico)*. Comisión Nacional de los Derechos Humanos/Centro de Investigación y Docencia Económicas.

Mate, R. (2011). *Tratado de la injusticia (Treaty of injustice)*. Anthropos.

Matthews, R. (2014). Realismo crítico: un análisis estructural (Critical realism: a structural analysis). *Politica Criminal, 9*(17), 182–212. http://www.politicacriminal.cl/Vol_09/n_17/Vol9N17A6.pdf

McKay, M., Davis, M., & Fanning, P. (2011). *Thoughts and feelings: taking control of your moods and your life*. New Harbinger Publications, Inc.

Minatti, A. (2013). *Pedagogía de la Memoria. Desafíos de la transmisión y debates en torno al abordaje del pasado reciente con jóvenes (Memory Pedagogy. Challenges of transmission and debates around addressing the recent past with young people)*. https://rdu.unc.edu.ar/bitstream/handle/11086/5879/7876-22157-1-PB.pdf?sequence=1&isAllowed=y.

Neocleous, M. (2016). La lógica de la pacificación: guerra-policía-acumulación (The logic of pacification: war-police-accumulation). *Athenea Digital, 16*(1), 9–22. https://doi.org/10.5565/rev/athenea.1738

Pupavac, V. (2001). Therapeutic Governance: Psycho-social intervention and trauma risk management. *Disasters, 25*(4), 358–372.

Rancière, J. (1996). *El Desacuerdo. Política y filosofía (The desagree. Politics and philosophy)*. Ediciones Nueva Visión.

Rivera Beiras, I. (2011). La memoria. Categoría epistemológica para el abordaje de la historia y las ciencias penales (The memory. Epistemological category for approaching history and criminal sciences). *Revista Crítica Penal y Poder, 1*, 40–55. https://revistes.ub.edu/index.php/CriticaPenalPoder/article/view/1984/2079

Todorov T. (2013). *Los abusos de la memoria (The abuses of memory)* (Trans. M. Salazar). Paidós.

Townend, A. (2007). *Assertiveness and diversity*. Palgrave Macmillan.

United Nations. (2023). *Terminology*. https://peacekeeping.un.org/en/terminology.

Vázquez, A., Camarillo, H., & Ramírez, A. (2021). Procesos victimológicos fronterizos (Border victimological processes). In E. Ortega (Ed.), *Derecho y Migración Forzada: aportes desde los estudios biopolíticos y necropolíticos (Law and Forced Migration: contributions from biopolitical and necropolitical studies)*. Instituto de Investigaciones Jurídicas, UNAM. https://archivos.juridicas.unam.mx/www/bjv/libros/14/6682/8.pdf

Vinyamata, C. E. (2015). Conflictología (Conflictology). *Revista de Paz y Conflictos, 8*(1), 9–24.

Von Hentig, H. (1940). Remarks on the Interaction of Perpetrator and Victim. *Journal of Criminal Law and Criminology, 31*(3), 303–309. https://scholarlycommons.law.northwestern.edu/cgi/viewcontent.cgi?article=2969&context=jclc

Wolhuter, L., Olley, N., & Denham, D. (2009). *Victimology: Victimisation and Victims' Rights*. Routledge-Cavendish.

Zyl van, P. (2011). Promoviendo la justicia transicional en sociedades post conflicto (Promoting transitional justice in post-conflict societies). In F. Reátegui (Ed.), *Justicia transicional: manual para América Latina (Transitional justice: manual for Latin America)* (pp. 47–72). Ministerio de Justicia/Comisión de Amnistía/Centro Internacional para la Justicia transicional.

CHAPTER 10

Assertive Leadership for the Protection of Human Rights: Inclusion and Gender Perspective in the Autonomous University of Nuevo León

Dave Alexander López-Mejía, Abraham Alfredo Hernández-Paz, and Gerardo Tamez-González

Introduction

In the University, promoting a gender perspective means recognising and addressing gender inequalities and working towards equity. At the Universidad Autónoma de Nuevo León, assertive leadership on these issues implies that academic and administrative leaders can foster an environment of respect and tolerance, where human rights values and

D. A. López-Mejía (✉) • A. A. Hernández-Paz • G. Tamez-González
Facultad de Ciencias Políticas y Relaciones Internacionales, Universidad Autónoma de Nuevo León, Monterrey, Mexico
e-mail: abraham.hernandezp@uanl.mx; gerardo.tamezg@uanl.mx

S. Castaños-Cervantes, C. Atristain-Suárez (eds.), *Assertiveness in the Context of Human Rights, Ethics, and Classical Virtues*,
https://doi.org/10.1007/978-3-031-60962-6_10

inclusion are promoted, establish policies and practices that ensure equal opportunities for all students and staff, regardless of gender or gender identity, as well as integrate the gender perspective in the planning and implementation of academic, research and student support policies and programmes, to collaborate with student groups and civil society organisations working on the promotion of human rights, inclusion and gender equality and education and awareness on these issues throughout the university community.

Globally, assertive leadership for the protection of human rights, inclusion and the gender perspective at the Autonomous University of Nuevo León implies an active and constant commitment of the institution's leaders to create an inclusive university environment that is fair and respectful of the fundamental rights of all people.

Brief Historical Review of the Recognition of Human Rights in Mexico

Since the Universal Declaration of Human Rights proclamation in December 1948, the evolution and international recognition of human rights have progressed in some countries, both practically and legally speaking. However, in Mexico, this has not happened in the same way, as a constitutional reform of human rights was published in the Official Journal of the Federation on June 10, 2011, which for the first time contained a mandate to create a new culture of human rights protection with a pro-human perspective.

This was a before and after in Mexican law since incorporating these changes corresponds to international human rights treaties. In this sense and under faithful compliance with the principle pacta sunt servanda, the nation has reached the slogan of protector of human rights since 2011, at least from the normativity, because in practical terms, its exercise has yet to be fulfilled.

Concerning the above, the legal imposition of human rights as inherent rights of individuals and not as constitutional guarantees with the 2011 constitutional reform paved the way for listing approximately 54 human rights that the State and all its institutions must protect, guarantee and ensure, including the right to life, to freedom and equality, to integrity and security, to freedom of expression and conscience, religion and worship, to justice, due process of law, legal certainty in detention, the principle of legality, to inviolability of the home, to access to information and protection of personal data, to property, to housing, to health and to education, to name a few.

Although it is true, the Autónoma de Nuevo León is an entity that leaves the direct hierarchy of any power of the State, and the breadth of its autonomy exempts not only from the direction of the executive but also the legislative one regarding the regulation of the provision of the service. This autonomy ensures that universities can define themselves, adopt their plans, programmes, budgets, internal organisation and governance, and define how their competencies are distributed within (Gónzalez, 2008, p. 11) by providing a public service that concerns the State to offer and protect it such as access to education, freedom of expression, thought, human development, among others. Precautions are taken so they are not obstructed or affected in exercising their functions.

In this sense, the Universidad Autónoma de Nuevo León's rectory and its departments have carried out actions that seek to promote a culture of respect for human rights through various means of action, strategies and dissemination, which has caused human rights to be desired, in some cases assertively and with deficits in others. Thus, the leaders, coordinators and directors of each unit must have—within their power to act—the knowledge and commitment to be assertive leaders to be effective in situations involving the protection of human rights. Therefore, leaders should first analyse the problem and then discover the critical factors in the organisation's tasks to improve or remedy shortcomings that involve any impairment in protecting human rights.

In the light of the preceding, this study shall be limited to the protection, recognition and observance of human rights established in the Political Constitution of the United Mexican States, international treaties and university institutions in Mexico, especially the Faculty of Political Sciences and International Relations of the Autonomous University of Nuevo León, as well as listing the challenges and implications that this entails.

Assertive Leadership Exercised at the University Level for Human Rights with a Gender Perspective and Inclusion

As mentioned in the general notions, assertive leadership is the activity that a leader does when respecting himself/herself and others, generating a synergy of collaboration that makes things happen and creates opportunities, using openness towards those around him/her, defending their rights without affecting those of others and communicating with all levels.

Although the literature on this topic is primarily inclined to business management and private initiative, this does not impede extending its analogy to the university field. In any organisation where activities are administered and managed with people and resources, there is an organisational chart, and service is provided, among other functions. Talking about leadership and assertiveness are matters of complete concern. Proper leadership is suited for working as a team and achieving a status quo within any organisation for continuous improvement.

In this sense, the international speaker, leader and senior management specialist Cornejo (2010) indicated that assertive leadership is the right one for growth since ideas and opinions are consulted on many decisions that concern all and are participatory, practical and listened to. Likewise, assertive leadership paves the way for seriously analysing the ideas of their subordinates and accepting their contributions whenever they are helpful and possible.

The assertiveness of the leader is characterised mainly by the communication that is given and received, but also that it is done with it because this gives direction to new ideas, allows generating agreements or receiving disagreements in some decisions and makes decisions by airing all the spectra of the subject. In this order of ideas, Lussier (2016) stated the following:

> Leaders use communication to influence others. As such, they need to have good skills in this area. Formal authority affects communication and, ultimately, performance. Information processing is relevant for structured organisations to meet the requirements of this processing, which is generated by interdependent activities. With changing technology, the way we communicate has changed over the years, as mobile technologies provide a constant communication pattern, influencing our work and personal lives. (p. 185)

Following this same ideological rhythm, Armas (2010) conceptualises assertive communication as the human capacity of leaders to interact with their peers to resolve differences and confront situations with a sense of rationality, where mutual respect, sincerity, spontaneity, honest expression of feelings and the strengthening of interpersonal relationships prevail

(p. 39). Through assertive communication, other people know their needs, concerns, desires and annoyances. It is a competition for all individuals at different levels, according to their personality, self-knowledge and personal and professional maturity.

Based on those mentioned earlier, in the university field, three major areas are taken with three great perspectives on human rights. On the one hand—without an order of superiority or inferiority—teachers, those in direct contact with students, then the administrative staff, who care for both teachers and students; and, finally, students, who perceive the treatment of both teachers and administrative staff and who, for reasons of age group, are those of lower ages.

Everyone has a point of view and needs to listen to make decisions in search of the defence and prosecution of human rights. For this, Ferrero (2013) propose assertiveness strategies. They explain that these originate when the leader, as a fundamental person in communication, helps others to position and affirm themselves. Likewise, leader and others exchange achievements in an environment of good language and expression (p. 26).

Consequently, it is required that the position adopted by the persons exercising managerial functions contains elements of leadership and not of directors—speaking in a material and non-formal sense because of the significant difference between one and the other. Leadership refers to influencing a person-leader concerning other people-groups in the search for a common goal (Blais & Sinclair-Desgagné, 2002). In contrast, the concept of the Director responds more to a core of administration, which focuses on routine actions and involves the leaders in coordinating and supervising the actions of the team members, seeking the fulfilment of their goals (Robbins, 2004). However, this does not constitute an incompatibility in both since the terms are intertwined when considering that leaders face high-order tasks such as improving the performance of people, leading, developing and maintaining daily operations, directing and managing resources and integrating both activities into a single function (Vázquez et al., 2014).

In addition to the above, Palomo (2013) is right when he says that good managers evolve and become good leaders, and usually most effective leaders are good managers (p. 18). Nonetheless, this equation is not an irrefutable elocution because there are good directors, but not with the characteristics of good leaders.

Once defined, talking about human rights with a gender perspective and inclusion is another fundamental element to consolidate assertive decisions. To begin with, it is essential to define it by operationalising its elements since human rights are the natural rights that all humans have on the face of the earth for the simple right to be human. For this, they place a list of rights, which serve as a guarantee of protecting their humanity concerning the tentacles of the State and the abuse of power that could be vented. To this, we add the gender perspective. We would understand it as that gaze that people with certain powers—legal or not—should have on those historically vulnerable groups to guarantee them special protection.

Since 2011, there has been a transformation of the Mexican legal system at the national level that has impacted a new transition towards promoting a culture of respect for human rights in the university community (Contreras & Cortina, 2021). At the constitutional level, article 3 of the Supra-Norm, in its part concerning education, indicates that education shall be based on unrestricted respect for the dignity of persons—when it expresses unrestricted, it refers to an absolute order of inescapable compliance—with a focus on human rights and substantive equality, which imperatively mandates broad transversality for the pursuit of human rights.

In this connection, the commitment was extended to the National Association of Universities and Higher Education Institutions (ANUIES) where it proceeded to develop appropriate strategies for the dissemination and promotion of constitutional reform in the field of human rights, signed with several universities in 2016 the University Charter, Commitment for Human Rights (2016), which consists of an explanatory preface and six commitments. The third commitment highlights:

> Promote or strengthen its functioning if there are already offices, mechanisms, instances, or institutions for protecting human rights in the university community. As bodies responsible for ensuring compliance with the university legal order governing the structure and functioning of universities, these governing instances are responsible for monitoring human rights fulfilment. In other words, they must be aware of individual conflicts between authorities and academic and administrative staff or students to protect and ensure respect for the rights granted to them by the university legislation. The functions carried out by these bodies are linked to the protection of the human rights of individuals against acts or omissions by university authorities, both academic and administrative. (p. 8)

Under the above, according to the constitutional ministry, higher education institutions in Mexico must educate for life. It is not only a matter of transmitting specific academic knowledge to a professional area for the development of professionals but also of forming citizens with a high ethical sense who promote the welfare of society through respect for and defence of human rights. Thus, it must be preached by example. The institutional channels, which are tools of the universities, must be used to open the field to the pursuit of human rights within and outside the institution.

Legislation on Higher Education and its Protectionist Approach to Human Rights with a Gender and Inclusion Perspective

On April 20, 2021, the new General Law on Higher Education was published in the Official Journal of the Federation, Article 3 of the Constitution of the United Mexican States on the recognition of the human right to education (Chamber of Deputies of the H. Congress of the Union, 2022); norm whose observance is *erga omnes* for the whole Republic, of public order and social interest, as provided for in article 1 of the same law. Although this rule is valid, it sets the tone for university form and management around specific guidelines that seek, among other things, free education. It is essential to mention that it contains explicit respect for the governance and autonomy of the University so that an express recognition of this autonomy is dedicated to it in several articles, which allows managers to continue making assertive decisions for better educational development that provides quality teaching with a strong culture of respect for human rights.

On the other hand, it is necessary to mention that this law is born with clear and specific objectives, which become thoracic points to analyse, which are detailed in Table 10.1.

Given the preceding, it should be emphasised that the law contributes in an interpretative manner and application to Article 3 of the Constitution. Nonetheless, for the development of this chapter, we will focus on the objective of contributing to Article 7, paragraphs V and VI, which quote:

> Higher education shall promote the integral human development of the student in the construction of knowledge based on the following: V. Social, economic, and cultural relations are constructed based on gender equality and respect for human rights; VI. Combating all types and forms of discrimination and violence, with particular emphasis on girls and women, persons with disabilities or persons in situations of social vulnerability, and the promotion of cultural change to build a society that promotes substantive equality between women and men. (General Law on Higher Education, 2021)

Table 10.1 Objectives of the general law of higher education

Objectives	Establish the basis for fulfilling the State's obligation to guarantee the exercise of the right to higher education. Contribute to the social, cultural, scientific, technological, humanistic, productive and economic development of the country, through the training of people with creative, innovative and entrepreneurial capacity with a high social commitment. To distribute the educational social function of higher education among the Federation, the federative entities and the municipalities. To distribute the educational social function of higher education among the Federation, the federative entities and the municipalities. To guide the criteria for the development of public policies on higher education with a State vision. Establish criteria for funding for the public service of higher education. Regulate the participation of the public, social and private sectors in higher education.

Source: General Law of Public Education (2021)

Article 8 states that:

> Higher education shall be guided by the criterion of substantive equality in order to contribute to the construction of a free, just and inclusive society… equal opportunities to guarantee people access to higher education without discrimination… the recognition of diversity… the culture of peace and the peaceful resolution of conflicts, as well as the promotion of the values of equality, justice, solidarity, the culture of legality and respect for human rights… mainstreaming the gender perspective into academic teaching, research, extension and cultural dissemination; as well as in administrative and managerial activities to contribute to equality and equity in the field of higher education and foster it within society… promotion of and respect for equality between women and men by generating alternatives to eradicate all types and forms of gender-based violence in higher education institutions.

In parallel, Title IV on Actions, Concurrence and Powers of the State, the law states in article 36, second paragraph, that:

> Their actions shall be based on the approach of human rights and substantive equality, respecting the principle of inclusion. They will have youth, gender, and intercultural perspectives with particular attention to indigenous peoples and communities, Afro-Mexicans, persons with disabilities and vulnerable groups. Consider measures to provide care for gifted students and adults at higher education levels.

Similarly, there are more precepts around promoting programmes—Article 37—that are based on the principle of equality between persons and shall be constructed following assertive actions that eliminate gender inequalities and promote timely and balanced discharge between women and men. The Act is also specific in stating that affirmative action should be taken to support women in gaining access to, staying in, continuing and graduating from higher education. In the same way, it states the eradication of any discriminatory circumstances, social, educational, economic, health, work, cultural or political; legal provisions, figures or legal institutions, actions, omissions, barriers or practices which have the object or effect of denying, excluding, distinguishing, impairing, preventing or restricting the right to higher education of individuals, groups or peoples, especially those who are socially disadvantaged or vulnerable (General Law on Higher Education, 2021).

It is essential to mention that the law contains arguments within its body to protect human rights and guarantee equality, diversity and inclusion in all its scope. Article 43 of the Act provides that the States must cooperate with the institutions to ensure that they are established as free spaces for all types and forms of violence, particularly gender violence and discrimination against women, to ensure full access to the right to higher education. By opening three areas, institutional, academic and in the provision of services, positive actions associated with assertive leadership can perpetuate and generate a culture of respect because, in the institutional sphere, the law establishes that programmes, diagnoses and protocols to prevent, address, punish and eradicate all types and forms of violence, particularly gender violence, must add that conciliation measures or their equivalents will be excluded as a means of dispute settlement. There is no doubt that this is legally consistent with criminal provisions on gender-based violence since conciliation in such crimes is not admissible in a court of law.

Moreover, the Act provides guidelines for establishing bodies with trained personnel to operate and monitor protocols to prevent, respond to, punish and eradicate violence, specifically violence against women, and strategies for taking action to consider violence against women as a severe cause of responsibility. The Act sets the norms for implementing positive measures, such as conducting programmes to identify problems related to violence against women in higher education institutions at an early stage. This Act also seeks a prompt and urgent response to avoid harmful situations against female students. All this must be strengthened through training actions, such as training all those involved in the provision of higher education services, that must be carried out with a cross-cutting approach with a gender perspective, whose function enables it to fulfil another legal prerogative such as the creation of a body for gender equality whose function is the incorporation of the gender perspective in all the actions carried out by the institution, the latter being empowered to monitor all situations involving a violation of human rights within the University.

Concerning learning units, the General Law on Higher Education mandates the inclusion of gender-sensitive content that promotes substantive equality and contributes to the elimination of all types and modalities of violence, as well as gender stereotypes in educational plans and multidisciplinary scientific research aimed at creating models for the detection and eradication of violence against women in universities. With the above, the legislative work on recognising gender equality, sexual diversity and inclusion is perceptible as a governmental response to social demands. Even though there are statistical numbers with severe violations of these human rights, the State seeks, through education, to generate a new culture of respect, tolerance and emotional responsibility towards historically vulnerable groups.

Review of Results on Assertive Actions for Pursuing Human Rights around Inclusion and Gender Perspective in Universidad Autónoma de Nuevo León

In recent years, Universidad Autónoma de Nuevo León has launched several projects to generate gender parity and equality at the material level. Recent reports of activities submitted by all faculties, 26 in total, have been perceived to address issues related to the realisation and guarantee of human rights. Likewise, affirmative actions are perceived to build inclusion and the gender perspective materially. Some of them are detailed below.

In 2014, the Unit for Gender Equality was created (Unit for Gender Equality, 2022) whose emergence was born within the framework of social responsibility and commitment between the Universidad Autónoma de Nuevo León and the Women's State Institute of the Government of the State of Nuevo León. This collaboration gave life to a body that promotes the management and development of projects and actions that seek to eliminate gender inequalities in the University. As a result, Gender Equality

Committees were created to support Uniigénero's activities and situations in each unit. They also carry out actions aimed at the training of administrative personnel from a gender perspective:

- Workshop on tools to detect gender inequality.
- Biannual planning meetings with the Gender Links of University Academic Units.
- Workshop on tools to detect gender inequality, the Gender Agenda.
- Analysis of the Protocol of Care for Sexual Harassment Cases, Attention to Complaints.
- Preparation of CEDAW shadow report in Nuevo León. UANL-UNAM.
- Gender awareness course for some Directorate of Social Prevention and University Protection members.
- Courses on Substantive Equality.
- Workshop on tools to detect gender inequality.
- Biannual planning meetings with the Gender Links of University Academic Units.
- Diploma on women's rights and access to a life free of violence. As part of the UNIIGÉNERO Liaison Training Program, Dra. Gloria Ramírez, head of the UNAM-based Chair of Human Rights Education at UNESCO, presented "The History of Women's Rights in the History of Human Rights and Universities".
- As part of the UNIIGÉNERO Liaison Training Program, Prof. Nayana Guerrero and Dr. Miguel Reyna of UNAM presented the theme "New masculinities and gender gaps in the Sustainable Development Goals".
- As part of the UNIIGÉNERO Link Training Program, Dra. Gloria Ramírez and Prof. Irma Ochoa presented the theme "Gender-based violence in the country and the Gender Violence Alert Mechanism against Women".
- As part of the UNIIGÉNERO Liaison Training Program, Dra. Gloria Ramírez, Chair of Human Rights Education at UNAM, presented the theme "Commemoration of the International Day of Human Rights and Women's Rights Mechanisms and its Implementation".
- As part of the UNIIGÉNERO Liaison Training Program, Dr. Gloria Ramírez, head of the Chair of Human Rights Education of UNESCO, based in the UNAM, presented the theme 'Gender-based violence in universities and tools for its eradication".

- On the International Day of Women and Girls in Science, organised by the UniiGénero and the Research Directorate of the UANL, the conference "The Importance of Women Training in Scientific Research" was held.
- Within this same framework, the Director of the Institute of Social Research of the Universidad Autónoma de Nuevo León, Advisory Counselor of the National Institute of Women in 2018, was presented in 2021. Member of the Civil Society Advisory Group of UN Women Mexico attended the event "Talk among Women", whose discussion served as the basis for seminars, dialogues and meetings to promote gender equality inside and outside the University. It should also be mentioned that on June 6, 2022, the University created the Commission for Research on Gender Equality of the University Council to establish a university structure to follow the vision and objectives of that body.
- One of the actions taken by the Director in collaboration with the members of the board of directors of the Faculty of Political Sciences and International Relations of the Universidad Autónoma de Nuevo León as a way of materialising the discourse of inclusion and equality was the construction and adaptation of inclusive bathrooms that contain the legend: "everyone can use this bathroom regardless of identity and gender expression", being the first faculty of the UANL to implement it and marking the pattern as good practice susceptible of adaptation in other faculties and even other universities of the Mexican Republic.

It is necessary to add that not only instances have been created that favour or promote gender equality and sexual diversity and inclusion in the academic and administrative area of our University, but also campaigns and events have been created focused on the student body of the university premises. These exercises can be considered as actions that do not have a high impact on the accumulation ofpeople who hold the Universidad Autónoma de Nuevo León—among students, teachers and administrative staff—about the total number of inhabitants of the State, but precisely because the universities are institutions with an edifying nature, these assertive actions contribute to a new culture of respect, and it also portrays the effort of modernity and the struggles that activist groups practice year after year, generating in the University a synergy of acting as a social commitment.

This is to list some assertive actions without prejudice to the existence of more. Considering the preceding, it should be noted that the decisions taken by the University's directors to incorporate all these actions are directly and proportionally responsible for the social commitment to respect for human rights, which acquires good practices that generate this culture of protection, inclusion and formal and material equality more effective.

The main objective of this research was to analyse the current State of assertive leadership in the Universidad Autónoma de Nuevo León (UANL) concerning the protection of human rights, inclusion and gender perspective. It also sought to identify best practices and challenges in this area.

Method

Given the nature of the research and its goal, the present chapter had a qualitative integration. This is due to the insertion and intervention of the intellectual author—and co-author of these lines—because it is actively involved in the decision-making process and selection of strategies adopted to develop human rights advocacy with a gender perspective and inclusion. Participatory action research is clearly and precisely explained by Greenwood (2016) when he mentions that:

> It is not just another "method" of the social sciences but a fundamentally different way of conducting joint research and action for social change. In action research, participation has a moral value. However, it is essential for the success of the process because the complexity of the problems addressed requires the knowledge and experience of a wide range of actors. Action research is neither a method nor a technique: it is a life strategy that includes creating spaces for collaborative learning and designing, implementing, and evaluating liberating actions. (p. 97)

This research strategy was the ideal one for the elaboration of this chapter because the intellectual authorship of the same one is built with the integration of the Director of a university institution—the same that belongs to the territory, space and object of the investigation—in collaboration with research teachers; which allows the association of variables such as assertive leadership and the actions studied around the protection of human rights protection, inclusion and equality in university management, to have material, practical and theoretical support.

Procedure

Identification of the Documentary Sample

The selection of documents was based on sophisticated criteria, including relevance, timeliness and authority of sources. It included academic documents, institutional reports, university policies, previous research and other related materials. Priority will be given to documents that provide quantitative and qualitative data on assertive leadership and its impact on human rights, inclusion and the gender perspective in the UANL.

An exhaustive search was performed in academic databases such as PubMed, Scopus, Web of Science and Google Scholar, using keywords related to assertive leadership, human rights, inclusion and gender in the university context. The UANL digital repository and other institutional sources were consulted for specific university-related documents.

In addition, this research includes a legal review, that is, a documentary review of primary and secondary sources of doctrinal and legal studies on the evolution and recognition of social rights as human rights; in the same way, hermeneutics was used as an analytical strategy and interpretation based on jurisprudential criteria of the Supreme Court of Justice of the Nation regarding the constitutional recognition of human rights, as well as the legislative study of the initiative of the General Law on Higher Education and its points of view on equality, inclusion and a gender perspective.

The selection criteria considered documents published in the last ten years to ensure the information's timeliness, prioritising documents written by experts in the field and empirical research that provided substantial evidence. Likewise, documents that address both theoretical and practical aspects of assertive leadership and its relationship with human rights, inclusion and the gender perspective, including those that offer diverse perspectives and interdisciplinary approaches, were considered.

Data Analysis

For the analysis process, a qualitative analysis of the selected documents was conducted using open and axial coding techniques to identify patterns, topics and significant relationships. In addition, qualitative analysis software tools such as NVivo facilitated the organisation and analysis of data, respecting the ethical principles of research, such as proper citation of sources and protection of confidentiality if necessary.

Table 10.2 Documents selected and analysed regarding assertiveness

Title	*Authors*	*Years*
Assertiveness: A theoretical-empirical analysis	Laura Gaeta González y Agris Galvanovskis Kasparane	2009
La conceptualización del liderazgo: una aproximación desde la práctica educativa.	Sandra Vázquez Toledo, José Luis Bernal Agudo y Marta Liesa Orús	2014
Liderazgo. Teoría, aplicación y desarrollo de habilidades.	Robert N. Lussier	2016
Investigación Acción Pragmática	Davydd Greenwood	2016
Estrategia de Equidad de Género en el Entorno Universitario.	Mireya Baute Rosales, Virginia Bárbara Pérez Payrol y Margarita Luque Espinoza de los Monteros	2017
La responsabilidad social universitaria en la actual sociedad del conocimiento. Un acercamiento necesario	Rolando Medina Peña, María del Carmen Franco Gómez, Leodanis Torres Barreiro, Kerslin Velázquez Rodríguez, Marina Alexandra Valencia VeraI y Ana Leonor Valencia Vera.	2017
Carta Universitaria, Compromiso por los Derechos Humanos. México.	Asociación Nacional de Universidades e Instituciones de Educación Superior en México.	2018
Comunicación asertiva y su relación en la convivencia escolar de docentes de una institución educativa.	Rossemery Meryam Arguello Davalos	2019
Responsabilidad Social Universitaria: el respeto de los Derechos Humanos en las Instituciones de Educación Superior	Helen Contreras Hernández, Marco Antonio Cortina y Saint André	2021

Source: Authors' elaboration

Of the number of documents that were finally selected and analysed, the following are found (see Table 10.2).

Results

The main results were broken down after the documentary review and the experience as binding participants of this chapter.

First, including a gender perspective and equality between men and women as guidelines for protecting human rights is no longer an option that should or should not be fulfilled since its mandate is constitutional and federal. Consequently, all Mexican universities must, by law, adapt their internal structures, regulations and structures so that they do not contradict the norms with greater hierarchy within the country's legal system.

Second, in a second finding, we observed the apparent need to promote teaching and research on the meaning and scope of equality, gender perspective and inclusion. Only in this way can we cultivate a culture of legality and respect for human rights. Hence, actions like those conducted by the Universidad Autónoma de Nuevo León and its dependencies are relevant as the discourse materialises with action around this problem.

Third, the introduction into the curricula, as a fundamental element of professional development, education in, by and for inclusion, equality and gender perspective in a transversal way is a crucial element.

Fourth, without a doubt, the leadership associated with assertive decisions, their own convictions or socio-structural movements and changes by the directors and directors of the Universidad Autónoma de Nuevo León represent an essential step forward for New Leonese society, as more spaces are created for the protection and guarantee of human rights around equality, inclusion and mainstreaming of the gender perspective.

More and more, a society firmly committed to this new and thriving culture of legality and respect for human rights is being built, and this alone meets the nature and raison d'être of universities.

Conclusions

Based on the qualitative findings obtained through the documentary review and our experience as binding participants in this study, we can conclude that promoting the gender perspective and equality between men and women is no longer an option but a constitutional and federal mandate in Mexico. Mexican universities have the legal obligation to adapt their structures and regulations to comply with these guidelines, aligning themselves with the highest standards within the country's legal system.

Furthermore, there is a need to promote teaching and research on equality, gender perspective and inclusion to cultivate a culture of legality and respect for human rights. The concrete actions carried out by institutions such as the Autonomous University of Nuevo León are notable since they demonstrate how the discourse materialises into concrete actions to address this problem.

The integration of education in inclusion, equality and gender perspectives transversally in academic curricula is presented as a crucial element for professional development and the construction of a society committed to these values.

Finally, assertive leadership by directors and rectors of institutions such as the Autonomous University of Nuevo León is essential to promote socio-structural changes that protect and guarantee human rights in areas such as equality, inclusion and gender perspective. These advances represent essential progress for society, building a culture of legality and respect for human rights that reflects the fundamental purpose of universities in the country.

It is pertinent to quote Baute et al. (2017, p. 50), who mention that gender as a tool for social analysis has been incorporated massively in recent years. Inclusion and gender equality are the result of a long social and political process, a product of the efforts of the women's movement, where the global political context and current conceptions and values have conditioned their assimilation in the public debate by other actors. In this sense, university campuses, with their particularities and characteristics, in the duty to be, have and remain entities of revolutionary disruption because the scientific and knowledge opening allows the construction of autonomous citizens with elements of self-sufficiency, which allows these, in turn, to be the promoters of initiatives around significant social and structural changes.

In this sense, as static infrastructure, universities must be transformed internally and externally for these changes they cause. Nonetheless, for this synergistic relationship to occur, they must make assertive decisions with a high sense of coherence between educational values as institutional pillars and the social demands driven by globalisation, which in turn leads to the expiry of obsolete customs and promotes the legal and material recognition of new forms of respect for human rights.

As a result, Universidad Autónoma de Nuevo León has confirmed its commitment to respect human rights in a cross-cutting manner, although it has gradually changed, not only in the discourse but also through actions, which is due in large part to the citizen and student participation and on the other hand to the assertive leadership of the University's directors and administrators, who, with a joint effort, have materialised their policies so that they are inclusive and with a gender perspective.

Although the constitutional and legal recognition of the protection and defence of human rights has progressed gradually and significantly, the challenge to ensure it palpably remains a Goliath. Mexican society has dragged for centuries customs that are naturally contradictory to the spirit of equality, inclusion and gender perspective; the struggle through education is a powerful ally to generate a new culture of legality and respect, and this is the most significant legacy.

References

Baute, M., Pérez, V., & Esponizo, M. (2017). Estrategia de Equidad de Género en el Entorno Universitario (Gender equality strategy in the university environment). *Revista Universidad y Sociedad, 9*, 50–57.

Blais, A., & Sinclair-Desgagné, B. (2002). *Le leadership en 3C: Capacités, conduite, circonstances.* Cirano.

Cámara de Diputados del H. Congreso de la Unión. (2022). *Constitución Política de los Estados Unidos Mexicanos (Mexican constitution).* https://www.diputados.gob.mx/LeyesBiblio/pdf/CPEUM.pdf.

Cámara de Diputados del Honorable Congreso de la Unión. (2021). *Ley General de Educación Superior (General law of superior education).* Diario Oficial de la Federación.

Contreras, H., & Cortina, M. (2021). Responsabilidad Social Universitaria: el respeto de los Derechos Humanos en las Instituciones de Educación Superior (University social responsibility: Respect for human rights in higher education institutions). *Dilemas contemporáneos: educación, política y valores, 8*, 00018

Cornejo, M. (14 de 11 de 2010). *Lides.* http://lidesbolivia.blogspot.com/2010/11/liderazgo-asertivo.html.

De Armas, L. (2010). *Test de autoconocimiento (Self-knowledge test).* Robinbook.

Ferrero, M. Y. (2013). *Comunicación asertiva (Assertive communication).* Biblos.

Gaeta González, L., & Galvanovskis Kasparane, A. (2009). Assertividad: Un análisis teórico-empírico (Assertiveness: A theoretical and empirical anaylsis). *Enseñanza e Investigación en Psicología, 14*(2), 403–425.

Gónzalez, Y. (2008). El reto de la autonomía universitaria (The challenge of university autonomy). *Universidades, 7*, 7–18.

Greenwood, D. (2016). Investigación Acción Pragmática (Pragmatic action research). In G. Damonte & M. García (Eds.), *La Investigación Acción Participativa: referente inspirador de investigación y docencia sobre el agua en América Latina (Participatory action research: Inspiring reference for research and teaching on water in Latin America).* Serie Agua y Sociedad.

Lussier, R. y. (2016). *Liderazgo. Teoría, aplicación y desarrollo de habilidades (Leadership. Theory, application, and skill development).* Thomson Learning.

Palomo, T. (2013). *Liderazgo y motivación de equipos de trabajo (Leadership and motivation of work teams).* Gráficas Dehon.

Robbins, S. (2004). *Comportamiento organizacional (Organizational behavior)*. Pearson Educación.

Secretaria de Gobernación, Subsecretaria de Derechos Humanos. (2016). *Carta Universitaria. Compromiso por los Derechos Humanos (University CHARTER. Commitment to human rights)*. Secretaría de Gobernación, Subsecretaría de Derechos Humanos.

Unidad Para la Igualdad de Género. (2022). *Unigénero (Unigender)*. http://unigenero.uanl.mx/unidad-para-la-igualdad-de-genero-informe-2017-2021/.

Vázquez, S., Bernal, J., & Liesa, M. (2014). La conceptualización del liderazgo: una aproximación desde la práctica educativa (The conceptualization of leadership: an approach from educational practice). *Revista Iberoamericana sobre la Calidad, Eficacia y Cambio en Educación, 7*, 70–97.

PART IV

Exercising the Right to be Assertive

To practice five things under all circumstances constitutes perfect virtue; these five are gravity, generosity of soul, sincerity, earnestness, and kindness.
Confucius

Having a clear understanding of cultivating a culture of virtue, peace, and equity through assertiveness, this edited collection's fourth and final part, consisting of three chapters, focuses on exercising the right to be assertive. It begins by exploring assertive rights as a basis for fostering human dignity, particularly among vulnerable people. Likewise, it emphasises the need to recognise assertiveness as a constitutional right, specifically by current Mexican legislation. Then, it proceeds by analysing the exercise of assertiveness as a human right in Mexican homeless girls. It examines sexual assertiveness among this vulnerable group and how it enables the exercise of their sexual rights. It delves into how sexual assertiveness is crucial for diminishing sexual violence and enhancing sexual health. Moreover, it highlights the need for sexual education to promote sexual assertiveness as one of the pillars of sexual health.

Finally, it brings closure with educating in assertiveness as a valuable tool for promoting social justice, equity, and human rights protection, all of which pave the way for social change and shared value. It pinpoints how Universities provide the ambience needed for educating in assertiveness so that students can harness this skill, become responsible and socially committed citizens, and help improve society and their communities.

Therefore, this part provides a comprehensive understanding of how to exercise the right to be assertive with examples among vulnerable groups.

CHAPTER 11

Assertiveness as a Human Right: Its Configuration from the Dignity of the Person in Situations of Vulnerability

Rogelio López-Sánchez
and Marlene del Toro-Granados

Introduction

This exploratory research proposes that human dignity is the starting point for any human being to be recognised as a person. This inherent quality of all people, by the mere fact of being a person, is not a metaphysical or abstract characteristic but has had a development from the constitutional culture and human rights to such a degree that it becomes a fundamental piece for the socio-legal scaffolding of any projection and materialisation of the rights of people in situations of vulnerability.

Shortly after the middle of the twentieth century, Western societies had a vital phenomenology as events arose that restructured the conception of human rights and how they are legitimised. The episodes have an

R. López-Sánchez (✉) • M. del Toro-Granados
Universidad Autónoma de Nuevo León, Monterrey, Mexico
e-mail: rlopezs@uanl.edu.mx

S. Castaños-Cervantes, C. Atristain-Suárez (eds.), *Assertiveness in the Context of Human Rights, Ethics, and Classical Virtues*, https://doi.org/10.1007/978-3-031-60962-6_11

immediate relation with vulnerable and disadvantaged groups in the United States of America, such as people taken as enslaved people to that nation of the African continent. Soon after, social movements such as the French May and struggle for women's rights and LGBTQ+ collective continued in Europe.

An analysis of assertiveness will be made following a hermeneutic and phenomenological methodology (Husserl, 2011), which Lebech (2009) applied to legal science to understand human dignity. Once human dignity has expired, a proposal will be developed around the possible configuration of an assertive bill of rights based on situations of vulnerability due to issues related to discrimination, segregation, hate, ideologies, and situations of structural, symbolic, and institutional violence suffered daily by millions of people.

The main objective of this research is to discover and justify conceptually that the foundations from which human rights emerge are based on the situations described above (of ignominy and opprobrium). It has led vulnerable groups and collectives to struggle for cultural changes based on attitudes and assertive behaviours of these people, such as manifestations, expressions of indignation, social struggles, and protests, which have been legally translated into the recognition of dignity as a starting point for the rest of human rights.

Approach to Assertiveness as Part of Dignity and Free Personality Development

From a psychosocial approach, assertiveness is a personality trait that aims to establish and maintain functional interpersonal relationships, invariably with positive results, achieve personal goals, and increase respect, situated in a specific sociocultural context (Castaños & Sánchez, 2016). However, the results obtained in the proposals for standardisation of the assertiveness inventory showed that the Mexican population is characterised by the inability to have confrontations face to face, to assert their rights in the face of situations of daily life or consumption, to say no, and to express their opinions, needs, and feelings to family, friends, and partner (Castaños-Cervantes et al., 2010), which reflects a style of passive confrontation in the face of challenges and problems of life (Díaz-Guerrero, 1994).

This last type of attitude and behaviour, contrary to assertive principles, reflects from an empirical-juridical perspective, a biased perspective of human dignity in Mexico, since the refusal of inherent recognition of the other as a human being is one of the essential elements, without which, people (Donnelly, 2013) are no longer and lose such character or quality.

To cite a few examples, the harassment and manifestations of contempt and humiliation against individuals highlight the femicide of women, the systematic killing of migrants, the alarming rates of domestic violence against women, the increase in the number of street children, the lack of inclusion of people with disabilities, hatred, and systematic discrimination of people from the LGBTQ+ collective, among other episodes. Moreover, as if that were not enough, empathy by the population in these traumatic situations is absent.

Given the above, the concept of dignity is coupled with that of ***non-humiliation*** in its manifestations: direct or subtle, individual or group, symbolic or representative (Neuhäuser, 2011), that is, the value of people for the mere fact of being them, this intrinsic dignity, which is not granted by a social status, talents, or powers but by the simple fact of belonging to the human species (Sulmasy, 2002). Therefore, it coincides with the broad definition that conceives it as: "the particular understanding of each culture of the moral value intrinsic to the human person and of its political relations with society" (Howard, 1992, p. 83.).

Likewise, human dignity is conditioned on the possibility of appearing before others and being recognised as unique and singular beings through speech and action (Arendt, 2009). Respect for dignity also implies recognising peers as builders of worlds or as encoders of an ordinary world (Arendt, 1998). In most liberal or illustrated constitutional texts, ***man*** is spoken of as a category, defining the image they project in society. Many social sectors would then be excluded, such as women, children, the disabled, people of colour, homosexuals, and the marginalised, will be the constitutionalism of a social nature that would come to claim from the halves of the twentieth century the rights of these minorities from an idea of human image (Benda, 1975) as well as a mandate for the State to make a conclusive and negative judgment on the individual (Dürig, 1993). Furthermore, human dignity will be part of the global Universal Declaration of Human Rights consensus.

Having formulated the above considerations, the kinds of response or behavioural dimensions that encompass assertiveness and that are directly related to the dignity of the person as they imply the recognition of the personality of a human being in all its integrity are, by way of a bill of rights, among others (Lazarus, 1973), the ability to say no, the ability to ask favours and make requests, the ability to express positive and negative feelings, and the ability to hold and end conversations, express opinions, and ignore other people's advice.

In this way, it immediately explains the situations in which various social movements, as well as the decisions taken in judicial instances, have transformed the State of affairs in Mexico, recognising, in the first place, through assertive conduct, the rights of people in situations of vulnerability, and thus, causing gradual transformations in the behaviour of these vulnerable groups by empowering them to exercise their rights.

The first appearance of human dignity as a principle in the Constitutions is found in the post-war texts, mainly in the German federal states like Bavaria, Bremen, Hesse, and Saarland, and at the national level, with the Basic Law of Bonn (Stark, 2005). These German laws were followed by States such as Sweden (1975), Greece (1975), Portugal (1976), Spain (1978), and Switzerland (1998), whose texts contemplate dignity as the basis of the political order or within their catalogues of fundamental rights (Stark, 2011).

At the international level, the incorporation of dignity begins with the Universal Declaration of Human Rights,[1] followed by the texts of the American Declaration of the Rights and Duties of Man (Preamble and Article XXIII), the American Convention on Human Rights (Preamble, para.3, articles: 5.2 (personal integrity), 6 (Prohibition of slavery), 11.2 (Honour), as well as the Inter-American Convention to Prevent, Punish and Eradicate Violence Against Women (Articles 4—respect for and protection of women's rights—and 8)).

However, as a relevant aspect, we introduce two critical texts for comparative analysis in this section: the Bonn Basic Law, in paragraphs 1.1 and 2.1 (human dignity and free development of the person), as well as the Spanish Constitution of 1978, in Article 10; in both texts, there is a mention of human dignity as the foundation of the political order and social peace; even in the German text a cosmopolitan and universal idea prevails.

The Basic Law of Bonn has undergone an enviable jurisprudential development through the introduction to the constitutionalism of figures, such as an image of man, non-instrumentalisation of the human person, and objective order of values (Benda, 1975). There is no doubt that its

[1]There are five explicit references to human dignity, two of which are in the Preamble (First and Fourth) and the remaining three in paragraphs 1, 22.2 and 23.3 (Social Security and the right to work).

jurisprudential development has much to do with the degree of progress as a civilisation, having overcome the ethical, political, and cultural traumas left by the Nazi period, and claiming as a society before the world that the violation and contempt for the dignity of the person would never happen again.

German constitutionalism has become one of the highest standards of that country (Barber, 2010), even opening this process of understanding rights to German society. Following this line of argument, that country's Constitutional Court has been one of the most active in Europe in terms of the development of human dignity. In this context, the image of man (*Menschenbild*) in the Bonn Basic Law is one of the contributions of German jurisprudence to constitutional law. In one of the most emblematic decisions, the Constitutional Court of that nation ("Conscientious objection" case against the obligation to defend the homeland in the Military Law) referred to the dual dimension of dignity in the individual and collective sense as follows.

The image of a man in the Fundamental Law is not that of an autocratic individual; it is what he has concerning his community, without his substantivity being undermined. The individual must assume those limits that, to cultivate and promote life together, the legislator imposes on his freedom of action within the required limits, provided the person's autonomy is guaranteed (BVerfGE, 1960). It follows from an overview of Articles 1, 2, 12, 14, 15, 19, and 20 of the Basic Law.

In addition to the above, Günther Dürig (1993), the author of the formula of non-instrumentalisation of the person (Objektformel), argues that the correct fundamental statement on human dignity has historically been the product of reaction against totalitarian collectivism in German constitutional life. However, the budget of man in the Fundamental Law (which must be the measure of all rights) does not correspond to the other extreme considered in the liberal, classic sense of the nineteenth century, with the autonomous and independent character of each action of the individual.

In this way, Benda (1996) asserts that not only are their individualistic conceptions of classical liberalism rejected but also collectivist temptations; by renouncing extreme requests, a middle line is sought. In this context, the German Court ruled on banning the Communist Party, recalling the experience during the Nazi period, referring to the condition of man as the object of a collective entity (BVerfGE, 1960). Returning to the formula of non-instrumentalisation (*Objektformel*), constructed by

Dürig from the reformulation of the classic Kantian imperative, the initial category has gone in the sense of not distinguishing individuals by their moral value. The idea of human dignity as a supreme value will now be approached from the idea of recognising the human being based on the idea of the human person's non-humiliation.

Human Dignity as the Supreme Value and the Idea of Recognition and Non-humiliation

There is no doubt that today the meaning given to the dignity of the human person is one of the most polysemic, complex, and heterogeneous in political philosophy, anthropology, ethics, and legal science. From a historiographical perspective, the recognition of people as autonomous beings, free and with full rights, is an idea that inspires most of the modern Constitutions (Donnelly, 2013). However, the full universal recognition of all human beings alike has been a slow and complex process, full of uncertainties and chiaroscuros in the history of the human family. As the philosopher Hans Jonas aptly puts it in his thesis called Heuristics of Fear, it can be said that in occasions of vexation and contempt (threats), those that help us to build an accurate idea of man (Jonas, 1995).

This constant fear of humiliation makes us more cautious and attentive towards vexation or contempt. It is not only the brutal and horrendous experience of the Holocaust that has marked us as a species to guarantee from international law (Capps, 2009) a minimum ethical standard of rights and guarantees such as the Universal Declaration of Human Rights; despite this, the subsequent terrible events in Cambodia (1975–1979), Guatemala (80s), Bosnia (1992–1995), Rwanda (1994), Peru (80s–2000) have also marked this painful experience of dehumanisation and extermination, ironically, in the name of racial, genetic, and even ethical improvement (Glover, 2001).

Professor Milton Lewis, in 2007, points out how world views have gradually modified certain norms, for example, slavery, which was considered permissible and even perceived as a sign of honour among enslavers, "until it was finally considered immoral, degrading, humiliating and prohibited by the authorities and international law" (Lickiss & Malpas, 2007, p. 65). Even in the twenty-first century, practices such as torture, rape as a military tactic, human trafficking, social exclusion, extreme poverty, labour exploitation, and forced labour, which are clear examples of degradation, persist. In this context, the concept of dignity is coupled with that of "no humiliation" in its different manifestations: direct or subtle, individual or group, symbolic or representative (Neuhäuser, 2011).

In this context, the person's dignity is aimed at the non-humiliation and the human being's recognition as such, that is, the value of people for the mere fact of being them; this intrinsic dignity, which is not granted by a social status, talents, or powers but by the simple fact of belonging to the human species (Sulmasy, 2002). For this reason, the broad definition provided by some authors (Howard, 1992) is as follows: a particular understanding of each culture of the moral value intrinsic to the human person and its political relations with society.

Human dignity originates in classical thought, mainly in the ideas of stoicism, which formulate the idea of humanity. Four indispensable elements move to modernity to understand this concept: "Caring for oneself," the "Sapere aude," the "Carpe diem," and the notion of "Citizen of the world" (Peces-Barba, 2010). Most of these categories will be recovered in modernity to rebuild the figure of dignity.

For philosophers of the Socratic period, human dignity is intimately related to the anthropocentric conception of the human being. For Plato, dignity must be achieved through actual knowledge; for this, it is necessary to master ourselves through virtues, as taught by his professor Socrates (Plato, 1996). Later, the author of *The Republic* states that the individual must produce knowledge and virtue as knowledge (wisdom, courage, temperance, and justice). In this context, the Greek educational model was based on the spiritual and technical formation of moral qualities or virtues, but from a kind of nobility or elite, excluding enslaved people and other social strata (Werner, 1996). Likewise, it rejects Athenian democracy, demonstrating their attachment to a hierarchy model of human nature (Pelé, 1996).

On the other hand, Aristotle defends an anthropocentric vision of man destined to fight to establish himself in the world, even without caring that human nature is flawed or not, thus striving to find a method to reach its essence better (Pelé, 2010). In this sense, the ethical virtues (courage, moderation, meekness, magnificence) are necessary to dominate the irrational part of man, which are acquired through habit (Aristotle, 1228b).

Cicero, Seneca, and Marcus Aurelius were strongly influenced by Greek stoicism; in the work of Cicero, there are several quotations from *Obligations of Man* by the philosopher Panetius of Rhodes (Middle Stoicism), who in turn had fused Socratic thought; for this reason, the virtues defended by this philosophical current referred to the four parts of honesty: justice, wisdom, fortitude, and temperance (Daraki & Romeyer-Dherbey, 1996). Likewise, in this period, we can find great wealth in stimulating the idea of individual autonomy and human will (Pelé, 2010).

One of the most comprehensive studies on the virtues of man concerning the State is found in the famous *De officiis* (*On Duties, or On offices*) by Cicero; this is one of the most representative works of profound philosophical content addressed to the field of public service (Cicerón, 1924). In this work, the qualities of man are embodied: prudence, justice, and strength. Greek philosophy, as well as its diffusion by Roman thinkers such as Cicero, served to develop virtues as a fundamental part of civitas in the Republic of Rome. Derived from the idea of Greek Polis, the human being went from being a political animal to a social animal (Sartori, 2003).

Cicero's idea of *humanitas* follows three directions: "The first, as anthropology, is relative to considering man as a rational, social being and member of the city. The second refers to a specific culture that is nourished by Greek influence. The third, finally, is dedicated to benevolence" (Pelé, 2010). Likewise, the Roman philosopher identifies piety and clemency as virtues to those responsible for administering justice (Cicerón, 1924). Finally, Seneca contributes an interiority defence of the human being as a defence to individual dignity. In ancient times, an idea of dignity prevailed over the fulfilment of moral and social guidelines, thus becoming a category of exclusive citizenship and opposed to the equal value of all human beings (Pelé, 2010).

As the Middle Ages began, the idea of human dignity became heteronomous through the medieval humanistic thought by authors like Saint Augustine, Gregory of Nicaea, and Thomas Aquinas, who merged the anthropological conception of a man with God, integrating it into the soul and human reason (Pelé, 2009). In addition, ecclesiastical thought will promote a pessimistic anthropocentric vision of the human being, of contempt for bodily identity and his reason since his dignity will be "derived from the image of God, projected on the creatures" (Peces-Barba, 2010, p. 421). This paradigm of human misery will be exhausted during the entry of Renaissance humanism.

At this time, thinkers of the stature of Giovanni Pico della Mirandola will appear, who, in his most important work, will build a concept of dignity based on man's self-healing freedom (Universidad Nacional Autónoma de México [UNAM], 2014). Also noteworthy is Giordano Bruno, who developed an idea of individual autonomy, free of religious dogmas

(Giordano, 1981). In addition, on the scene will appear two critical thinkers for constructing an idea of dignity in the peoples of America, Montaigne and Bartolomé de las Casas, who will defend the idea of equality between men (Pelé, 2008). The first of them, the conqueror of the new world, from a "secularised natural humanity" criticising the "good savage" (Montaigne, 1912, p. 959), while the second, the Dominican friar, criticising the idea of the cultural superiority of the conquerors of America (Beuchot, 1994).

In the same sense, Garzón Valdés defends this positive vision through a social dimension as a starting point for all rules of human coexistence that seek to have some moral justification, which promotes further development and consolidation (Garzón, 2006). Thus, after almost two hundred years of constitutional development, the German sociologist Jürgen Habermas affirms that it is precisely human dignity, the conceptual hinge, that joins the morality of equal respect for each subject with positive law and democratic legal production in such a way that its interaction in favourable historical circumstances could result in a political order based on fundamental rights (Habermas, 2010).

Throughout history, people have needed the recognition of others to form their identities. In this context, one of the foremost exponents of multiculturalism has developed a thesis on the politics of recognition. This idea consists in the formation of our own identity "starting from the recognition of others, or for lack of this, often also, by the false recognition of others" (Taylor, 2009, p. 68), suffering, when it happens. The difference, discrimination, and rejection of one's citizenship, as historical examples, is racial segregation in the United States of America or discrimination against homosexuals.

Thus, "respect for human dignity implies the recognition of my fellows or nations like mine, as subjects, as builders of worlds or as encoders of a common world" (Arendt, 1998, p. 203). The idea of recognition is a common element in understanding the subject's singularity and plurality. Fichte was one of the first to introduce the idea of mutual recognition around the construction of singularity (Gottileb, 1994). Hegel also later introduced the idea of intersubjective recognition as a condition for realising integrity, dignity, and freedom (Hegel, 2002). Therefore, recognition and identity are two indispensable elements for understanding the meaning and the meaning assigned to the person and the dignity of it.

One of the most recognised and employed conceptions in the Western legal tradition is Kant's illustrated idea of human dignity. The Könisberg philosopher sees law as a *universal obligation of all to act according to the freedom of all according to universal laws* (Kant, 1873).[2] In this sense, he elaborates the categorical imperative from practical reason about dignity as follows. *Only man, and with him the entire rational creature, is an end in itself. He is indeed the subject of the moral law, which is holy, thanks to the autonomy of his freedom.*

Following this guiding thread, with Kantian thought, the humanistic project of modernity is fulfilled; dignity will serve as a vehicle to legitimise the rights of the personality, which will have freedom and autonomy as its realisation (Pérez, 2001). The German philosopher's project will give the State a leading role "to develop and encourage the public use of reason" (Pelé, 2011, p. 21). This tradition has been recovered by authors such as Peces-Barba (2010).

Despite what has been said in advance, human dignity today faces sharp criticisms, such as uselessness, ambiguity, ethnocentrism, eurocentrism, and anthropocentrism that enclose the same concept. Some even prominent authors have tried to base human dignity on personalist philosophy, defending the thesis on the desacralisation of human life, which "is susceptible to suffering, but not to a greater degree than other living and sensitive beings" (Torralba, 2005, p. 202), as Peter Singer has repeatedly maintained (Singer, 1997).

Faced with the different senses that human dignity can acquire on the ontological, ethical, and theological plane, it is essential to ask some questions: Is human dignity an ethereal quality, difficult to apprehend in its essence and content due to polysemy in meanings? What should be the image of the human person before the complexity and plurality of senses granted to human dignity from the ethical, philosophical, and spiritual plane? Is there a minimum universal consensus, or should this issue be open to various interpretations in each case?

[2] According to Kant, the universal principle of law is that: "An action is by law (recht) when it allows, or whose maxim allows the freedom of each one's will to coexist with the freedom of all according to a universal law."d.

Conclusion: Configuration of Assertive Rights in Situations of Vulnerability

It is now essential to establish an assertive rights catalogue based on recognising the human person's dignity and free personality development from an approach to the various vulnerability situations in Mexico. The latter concept (free development) is a logical consequence of the development of the human being in its fullness. Therefore, it is impossible to manifest free behaviour without first fully recognising this principle, from which the will of the human being develops its full potential (López, 2018). A synthetic analysis will then be made of what has happened during the gradual constitutional recognition of these minorities through assertive behaviour and attitudes.

On the scene appears the Zapatista army of national liberation in Mexico, who, demanding recognition of their movement, caused during the 1990s, one of the most emblematic social movements that shocked the international community (United Nations [UN], 1997) after 400 years of invisibility. In 2001, this social struggle was finally enshrined in the Constitution by recognising its autonomy as a people to make decisions, deliberate, and be recognised in its dignity and worldview.

The most emblematic decisions that have hermeneutically guided the concept of human dignity relate to minority rights, especially the case of gender change (PC LXXII/2009d. December 2009; PC LXIV/2009a. December 2009; PC LXXIV/2009e. December 2009) and homosexual marriages (PC XXVIII/2011. August 2011). In the first decision, the Supreme Court orients its interpretation around the equality and autonomy of the person, considering it as a fundamental right and basis of all other rights, making an exhaustive list of the rights not recognised by, but derived from, the essential text, such as the right to life, physical and mental integrity, honour, privacy, name, self-image, free development of personality, civil status, and the right to personal dignity (PC LXV/2009b. January 2011).

In the same judgement, the Mexican court defines the free development of the person as a recognition by the State of the natural power of every person to be individual as he or she wishes to be, without undue coercion or controls; all this, in order to fulfil its goals or objectives that it has set in life, and without losing sight of its values, ideas, expectations, or tastes (PC LXVI/2009c. December 2009).

The same criterion is used in other relevant decisions on same-sex marriage in those states that are not recognised as such. The orientation and meaning given to these principles are based on the equality and autonomy of the person, invoking even precedents of some state courts of the United States of America, where it is reasoned based on the idea of equality and non-exclusion (Protection under Review, 581/2012).

On the other hand, the dignity principle is applied concerning the existential search for a dignified life. The meaning given to it is more precise in this decision since it relates it to the value of solidarity, "configured as the requirement that individuals have as their starting point conditions that allow them to develop an autonomous life plan, in order to facilitate the governed to participate actively in democratic life" (Isolated Thesis: 1a. X/2009).

There are also some attempts to define dignity in the ontological sense as "the origin, the essence and the end of all human rights" (Thesis: I.5o.C., 2011) or as "a quality unique and exceptional to every human being for the simple fact of being" (Thesis: I.5o.C., 2011). In principle, it has been determined that this quality is inherent and exclusive to natural persons (Thesis: VI.3o.A.1 K., 2013). Human dignity must act as a hermeneutic premise for understanding fundamental rights and give meaning to the various purposes of the Constitutional State, such as the realisation of freedom and the harmonious development of the person. The reconstruction of this principle occurs in modernity through its incorporation in the Constitutions of the mid-twentieth century, from the ancient, medieval, illustrated, and modern traditions. It is also important to note the multidisciplinary nature of this superior value of the system, which needs to be sufficiently understood through a reductionist view of legal norms.

The amendments to Article 1, the last paragraph, and Article 2 of the Constitution in 2001, which interpret and decipher human dignity based on the value of autonomy and equality, are essential for understanding the process of expansive evolution that human rights have undergone. For this reason, some courts, such as the German Courts, have reconstructed dignity based on three main aspects: formula of non-instrumentalisation, objective order of values, and human image. The latter may be an interesting proposal for Mexican jurisprudence.

It is also important to note that most ideas about human dignity in Mexico are visibly translated into equality and non-discrimination, proclaiming the value of individual autonomy. However, the origin and development of dignity since 2007 by the Mexican Constitutional Court are developed through an understanding of the rights of minorities, particularly the differentiated rights of transgender and homosexual persons. For this reason, the Mexican judge must change his paradigm to incorporate an inclusive and plural idea of a human person.

It is precisely through recognising the rights of minorities that it is possible to recognise socially disadvantaged groups not previously included in constitutionalism. This understanding has been realised not from the traditional concept of formal and even political equality but through different levels of analysis, such as sociological, political, philosophical, and anthropological. For example, when cases of sexually differentiated persons are resolved, the values of personal autonomy and dignity are invoked, recognising from a philosophical point of view the compatibility of their biological condition with their life project, an issue which no doubt heralds a neutral anthropological idea of a person, open and subject to scientific processes, related to the technologies of manipulation of the human body. However, above all, that from the philosophical plane seek the full realisation of the human being.

It is considered that the formula of non-instrumentalisation of the human person should be included in the catalogue of assertive rights to areas other than criminal law, such as civil law (conflicts over the right to honour, civil contracts), problems such as abortion, assisted suicide, women's rights, including the rights of the child (no instrumentalisation of the child in cohabitation trials), and labour rights (no exploitation of the worker as a mere factor of production).

In this context, there is still a long way to go; it is perhaps of great value to review the interpretation made by the Inter-American Court (in force for Mexican judges since 2011) on the dignity of the person in matters of personal integrity (IDH Court, July 29 1988; IDH Court, December 8 1995; IDH et al. 19 1995; IDH Court, November 19 1999), women's rights (IDH Court, August 30 2010, IDH Court, August 31 2010), private life (non-discrimination), (Corte IDH, February 24 2012), the dignity of the embryo (in vitro fertilisation) (COIDH, November 28 2012), rights of the child (Inter-American Court, September 2 2004; Inter-American Court, September 8 2005; Inter-American Court, April 27 2017), persons with disabilities (Inter-American Court, August 31 2010), migrant rights, (Inter-American Court, October 24 2012; November 23 2010), Indigenous rights (Inter-American Human Rights Court, Judgment of June 17, 2005; October 24, 2012), and protection of honour and dignity (Inter-American Human Rights Court, May 26, 2010).

Any process of construction of a category, such as a dignity and image of the human person since the Constitution, must be carried out under different horizons of understanding of the legal phenomenon, as explained in previous lines. The development of new technologies presents us with ethical dilemmas that must be resolved through a comprehensive and holistic understanding of the phenomenon in question; delimiting and circumscribing the subject of human dignity to the strictly juridical sphere would leave us out of the enormous conceptual wealth of other sciences and related areas, which ultimately also help to understand and harmoniously integrate law.

Today, human dignity and the free development of the personality are superior values of the legal order that serve to restructure and vindicate the rights of vulnerable persons. This deconstruction of the traditional positivist approach to human rights makes it possible to include interdisciplinarity, so providing a holistic understanding of these is necessary.

However, legal recognition is not necessarily on par with social or cultural movements; on the contrary, phenomena of discrimination and silent invisibility persist (Instituto Nacional de Estadística y Geografía [INEGI], 2017), which are directly related to non-assertive behaviours and attitudes of the population since they are reflected in acts of discrimination and denial of the individuality and autonomy of the other. It is, therefore, necessary to draw up interdisciplinary studies combining the psychosocial and intercultural vision of these phenomena to develop legal constructs compatible with the social and absolute effectiveness of legal institutions, which, as a science, is traditionally limited to regulating and subsequently monitoring human behaviour.

References

Arendt, H. (1998). *Los orígenes del totalitarismo (The origins of totalitarianism)*. Taurus.

Arendt, H. (2009). *La condición humana (Human condition)*. Paidós.

Aristoteles. (1228). *Ética Nicomaquea Libro V (Nicomachean Ethics Book V)*. Gredos.

Barber, C. (2010). *The making of a German constitution (a slow revolution)*. Berg.

Benda, E. (1975). Art. 1 Abs. 1 GG als Grundrecht (Europäische Hochschulschriften Recht). In V. Vortrag (Ed.), *Gefährdungen der Menschenwürde* (Vol. 198, pp. 7–45). Springer.

Benda, E. (1996). Dignidad humana y derechos de la personalidad (Human dignity and personality rights). In E. Benda, W. Maihofer, H. J. Vogel, K. Hesse, & W. Heyde (Eds.), *Manual de Derecho Constitucional (Constitutional right manual)* (pp. 119–125). Marcial Pons y Ediciones Jurídicas y Sociales.

Beuchot, M. (1994). *Los fundamentos de los derechos humanos en Bartolomé de las Casas (The foundations of human rights in Bartolomé de las Casas)*. Anthropos.

BVerfGE. (1960). Ley de Objeción de Conciencia I. *Primera Sala, 20 de diciembre de 1960, 12*, 45.

Capps, P. (2009). *Human dignity and the foundations of international law*. Hart Publishing.

Castaños, S., & Sánchez, J. J. (2016). Towards a psychosocial and cultural definition of Mexican homeless girls: A qualitative approach. *Anales de psicología, 2*(32), 516–527. https://doi.org/10.6018/analesps.32.2.204721

Castaños-Cervantes, S., Reyes-Lagunes, I., Rivera-Aragón, S., & Díaz-Loving, R. (2010). Estandarización del Inventario de Asertividad de Gambrill y Richey-II (Standardization of Gambrill and Richey's Assertion Inventory-II). *Revista Iberoamericana de Diagnóstico y Evaluación—e Avaliação Psicológica, 1*(29), 27–50. https://www.redalyc.org/articulo.oa?id=459645441003

Cicerón, M. (1924). *Los Oficios (The Trades)*. Librería y Casa Editorial Hernando.

Corte IDH. (2012). *Caso Nadege Dorzema y otros Vs. República Dominicana* (Serie C No. 251, § 233). Fondo, Reparaciones y Costas. Sentencia de 24 de octubre de 2012.

Daraki, M., & Romeyer-Dherbey, G. (1996). *El mundo helenístico: cínicos, estoicos y epicúreos (The Hellenistic world: Cynics, Stoics and Epicureans)*. Akal ediciones.

Díaz-Guerrero, R. (1994). *Psicología del mexicano. Descubrimiento de la etnopsicología (Mexican psychology. Discovery of ethnopsychology)*. Trillas.

Donnelly, J. (2013). *Human dignity and human rights. Universal human rights in the theory and practice*. Cornell University Press.

Dürig, G. (1993). Comentarios al artículo 1 de la Ley Fundamental de Bonn (Comments on article 1 of the Bonn Basic Law). In T. Maunz & G. Dürig (Eds.), *Grundgesetz (Kommentar)* (pp. 23–24). Beck'sche Editor.

Garzón, E. (2006). *Tolerancia, dignidad y democracia*. Universidad Inca Garcilaso de la Vega.

Giordano, B. (1981). *Sobre el infinito universo y los mundos (Iniciación filosófica) (About the infinite universe and the worlds [Philosophical initiation])* (p. 26). Aguilar.

Glover, J. (2001). *Humanity (A moral history of the twentieth century)*. Yale University Press.

Gottileb, J. (1994). *Fundamento del derecho natural según los principios de la doctrina de la ciencia*. Centro de Estudios Constitucionales.

Habermas, J. (2010). *La idea de dignidad humana y la utopía realista de los derechos humanos. Anales de la Cátedra Francisco Suárez, 11*(1), 111.

Hegel, G. (2002). *Lecciones sobre historia de la filosofía (Lessons on the history of philosophy)* (Vol. 2). FCE.
Howard, R. (1992). Dignity, community, and human rights. In A. An-Na'im (Ed.), *Human rights in cross-cultural perspective: A request for consensus* (pp. 81–102). Pennsylvania Studies in Human Rights.
Husserl, E. (2011). *La idea de la fenomenología (The idea of phenomenology)*. Herder.
Instituto Nacional de Estadística y Geografía (INEGI). (2017). *Encuesta Nacional sobre Discriminación. Principales Resultados (National survey on discrimination. Primary results)*. Instituto Nacional de Estadística y Geografía.
Jonás, H. (1995). *El principio de responsabilidad* (Ensayo de una ética para una civilización tecnológica) (p. 65). Herder.
Kant, I. (1873). *Principios metafísicos del derecho (Metaphysical principles of law)*, (de G. Lizárraga, Trans.). Librería de Victoriano Suárez.
Lazarus, A. (1973). On assertive behaviour: a brief note. *Behaviour Therapy, 4*(5), 697–699. https://doi.org/10.1016/S0005-7894(73)80161-3
Lebech, M. (2009). *On the problem of human dignity: a hermeneutical and phenomenological investigation*. Könighausen & Neumann.
Lickiss, N., & Malpas, J. (Eds.). (2007). *Perspectives on human dignity: A conversation*. Springer.
López, R. (2018). *La dignidad humana en México: su contenido esencial a partir de la jurisprudencia alemana y española (Human dignity in Mexico: its essential content based on German and Spanish jurisprudence). UNAM, 51*(151), 135–173. https://doi.org/10.22201/iij.24484873e.2018.151.12292.
Montaigne, M. (1912). *Ensayos (Libro I). (Essays. Book I)*. Miguel de Cervantes.
Neuhäuser, C. (2011). Humiliation: The collective dimension. In K. Paulus, H. Kuch, & C. Neuhäuser (Eds.), *Humiliation, degradation, dehumanisation (human dignity violated)* (Vol. 24, pp. 21–37). Springer.
Peces-Barba, G. (2010). Introducción (Introduction). In A. Pele (Ed.), *La dignidad humana. Sus orígenes en el pensamiento clásico (Human dignity. Its origins in classical thought)* (p. 421). Instituto de Derechos Humanos Bartolomé de las Casas-Universidad Carlos III.
Pelé, A. (1996). *Filosofía e Historia en el fundamento de la Dignidad Humana (Philosophy and history at the foundation of human dignity)*. Universidad Carlos III de Madrid.
Pelé, A. (2008). Montaigne y Las Casas dos defensores de la dignidad humana (Montaigne and Las Casas, two defenders of human dignity). In AA. VV (Ed.), *Estudios en homenaje al profesor Gregorio Peces-Barba (Studies in tribute to Professor Gregorio Peces-Barba)* (Vol. 3, pp. 959–974). Dykinson.
Pelé, A. (2009). Modelos de la dignidad del ser humano en la edad media (Models of the dignity of the human being in the Middle Ages). *Derechos y Libertades, 21*(2), 149–185.
Pelé, A. (2010). *La dignidad humana. Sus orígenes en el pensamiento clásico (Human dignity. Its origins in classical thought)*. Dykinson.

Pelé, A. (2011). *La dignidad humana. Sus orígenes en el pensamiento clásico. (Human dignity. Its origins in classical thought)*. Dykinson.

Pérez, A. (2001). El papel de Kant en la formación histórica de los derechos humanos (Kant's role in the historical formation of human rights). In G. Peces et al. (Eds.), *La filosofía de los derechos humanos. Historia de los derechos fundamentales (The philosophy of human rights. history of the fundamentals rights)* (Vol. II, p. 452). Dykinson.

Plato. (1996). *Writing by Jasper Neel*. Southern Illinois University Press.

Resolución P. (2009a). *Reasignación sexual. La sentencia que niega la expedición de una nueva acta de nacimiento en la que se rectifiquen los datos relativos al nombre y sexo de una persona transexual, es inconstitucional.* (*Sexual reassignment. The ruling that denies the issuance of a new birth certificate in which the data relating to the name and sex of a transsexual person are rectified is unconstitutional)* (LXIV, p. 4), December. https://desc.scjn.gob.mx/sites/default/files/2021-09/MÉX10-Criterios.pdf.

Resolución P. (2009b). *Dignidad humana. El orden jurídico mexicano la reconoce como condición y base de los demás derechos fundamentales.* (*Human dignity. The Mexican legal order recognizes it as a condition and basis of other fundamental rights)* (LXV, p. 1707), January 2011. https://www.google.com/url?sa=t&rct=j&q=&esrc=s&source=web&cd=&ved=2ahUKEwjy%2D%2Di1s_D9AhVuHUQIHda2B6sQFnoECDMQAQ&url=https%3A%2F%2Fwww2.scjn.gob.mx%2Fjuridica%2Fvotos%2F2012%2F2587.doc&usg=AOvVaw1OObALpkjaN-_rbN6zsvVH.

Resolución P. (2009c). *Derecho al libre desarrollo de la personalidad. aspectos que comprende.* (*Right to free development of personality. Aspects it includes)*, LXVI, December. https://www.corteidh.or.cr/tablas/r31089.pdf.

Resolución P. (2009d). *Reasignación sexual. La nota marginal en el acta de nacimiento de la sentencia que otorgó l demanda de rectificación del nombre y sexo, con la consiguiente publicidad de datos, viola los derechos fundamentales del interesado.* (Diciembre de 2009) (p. 4). (*Sexual reassignment. The marginal note in the birth certificate of the ruling that granted the request for rectification of the name and sex, with the consequent publicity of data, violates the fundamental rights of the interested party*) (LXXII, p. 4), December. https://desc.scjn.gob.mx/sites/default/files/2021-09/MÉX10-Criterios.pdf.

Resolución P. (2009e). *Reasignación sexual. no existe razonabilidad para limitar los derechos fundamentales de una persona transexual, impidiéndole la adecuación de sus documentos de identidad, bajo el pretexto de preservar derechos de terceros o el orden público.* (*Sexual reassignment. There is no reasonableness to limit the fundamental rights of a transsexual person, preventing them from adapting their identity documents, under the pretext of preserving the rights of third parties or public order*) (LXXIV, p. 1), December. https://desc.scjn.gob.mx/sites/default/files/2021-09/MÉX10-Criterios.pdf.

Resolución P. (2011). *Matrimonio entre personas del mismo sexo. La reforma al artículo 146 del código civil para el distrito federal, publicada en la gaceta oficial de la entidad el 29 de diciembre de 2009, no contraviene el contenido de la constitución política de los estados unidos mexicanos.* (*Marriage between people of the same sex. The reform to article 146 of the civil code for the federal district, published in the entity's official gazette on December 29, 2009, does not contravene the content of the political constitution of the United Mexican States*) (XXVIII, p. 877), August. https://sjf2.scjn.gob.mx/detalle/ejecutoria/22553.

Resolución Serie C No. 257. (2012). *Caso Artavia Murillo y otros (Fertilización in vitro) Vs. Costa Rica. Excepciones Preliminares, Fondo, Reparaciones y Costas. (Case of Artavia Murillo et al. (In vitro fertilization) v. Costa Rica. Preliminary Exceptions, Merits, Reparations and Costs)*, November 28. https://www.corteidh.or.cr/tablas/fichas/artaviamurillo.pdf.

Resolución Serie C No. 20, § 86. (1995, January 19). *Caso Neira Alegría y otros Vs. Perú. Fondo, Reparaciones y Costas. (Case of Neira Alegría y otros Vs. Perú. Preliminary Exceptions, Merits, Reparations and Costs).* https://www.corteidh.or.cr/docs/casos/articulos/seriec_29_esp.pdf

Resolución Serie C No. 22, § 53. (1995, December 8). *Caso Caballero Delgado y Santana Vs. Colombia. Excepción Preliminar, Fondo, Reparaciones y Costas. (Case of Caballero Delgado y Santana Vs. Colombia. Preliminary Exceptions, Merits, Reparations and Costs).*

Resolución. Serie C No. 215, § 118. (2010, August, 30). *Caso Fernández Ortega y otros Vs. México. Excepción Preliminar, Fondo, Reparaciones y Costas (Case of Fernández Ortega y otros Vs. México. Preliminary Exceptions, Merits, Reparations and Costs).* https://www.corteidh.or.cr/docs/casos/articulos/resumen_215_esp.pdf

Resolución Serie C No. 246, § 130. (2010, August, 31). *Caso Furlan y Familiares Vs. Argentina. Excepciones Preliminares, Fondo, Reparaciones y Costas. (Case of Furlan y Familiares Vs. Argentina. Preliminary Exceptions, Merits, Reparations and Costs).*

Resolución Serie C No. 4, § 154, 156, 158 y 165. (1988, July, 29). Caso Velásquez Rodríguez Vs. Honduras. Excepciones Preliminares, Fondo, Reparaciones y Costas. (Case of Velásquez Rodríguez Vs. Honduras. Preliminary Exceptions, Merits, Reparations And Costs). https://www.corteidh.or.cr/docs/casos/articulos/seriec_04_esp.pdf

Resolución Serie C No. 32, Serie C No. 63, Serie C No. 77. (1999, November 19). *Caso de los "Niños de la Calle" (Villagrán Morales y otros) Vs. Guatemala. Excepciones Preliminares, Fondo, Reparaciones y Costas. (Case of the "Street Children" (Villagrán Morales and others) v. Guatemala. Preliminary Exceptions, Merits, Reparations and Costs).* https://www.corteidh.or.cr/docs/casos/articulos/seriec_63_esp.pdf.

Resolución Serie C No. 112, § 159. (2004, September, 2). *Caso Instituto de Reeducación del Menor" Vs. Paraguay. Excepciones Preliminares, Fondo, Reparaciones y Costas. (Case of Instituto de Reeducación del Menor" Vs. Paraguay. Preliminary Exceptions, Merits, Reparations and Costs).*

Resolución Serie C No. 130, § 179. (2005, September, 8). *Caso de las Niñas Yean y Bosico Vs. República Dominicana. Excepciones Preliminares, Fondo, Reparaciones y Costas. (Case of de las Niñas Yean y Bosico Vs. República Dominicana. Preliminary Exceptions, Merits, Reparations and Costs).*

Resolución Serie C No. 213, § 205. (2010, May, 26). *Caso Manuel Cepeda Vargas Vs. Colombia. Excepciones Preliminares, Fondo, Reparaciones y Costas. (Case of Manuel Cepeda Vargas Vs. Colombia. Preliminary Exceptions, Merits, Reparations and Costs).* https://www.corteidh.or.cr/docs/casos/articulos/seriec_213_esp.pdf

Resolución Serie C No. 251, § 154. (2012, October, 24). *Caso Nadege Dorzema y otros Vs. República Dominicana. Excepciones Preliminares, Fondo, Reparaciones y Costas. (Case of Nadege Dorzema y otros Vs. República Dominicana. Preliminary Exceptions, Merits, Reparations and Costs).*

Resolución Serie C No. 251, § 233. (2012, October 24). *Caso Nadege Dorzema y otros Vs. República Dominicana Fondo, Reparaciones y Costas. (Case of Nadege Dorzema y otros Vs. República Dominicana. Preliminary Exceptions, Merits, Reparations and Costs).* https://www.te.gob.mx/juriselectoral/OEA/content/caso-nadege-dorzema-y-otros-vs-república-dominicana-0

Resolución Serie C No. 242, § 49. (2017, April, 27). *Forneron e hija Vs. Argentina. Fondo, Reparaciones y Costas. (Case of Forneron e hija Vs. Argentina. Preliminary Exceptions, Merits, Reparations and Costs).*

Resolución 1ª. X/2009. (2009, Enero). *Derecho al mínimo vital. su alcance en relación con el principio de generalidad tributaria.* (Right to minimum living. its scope in relation to the principle of tax generality), p. 547. https://www2.scjn.gob.mx/AsuntosRelevantes/pagina/SeguimientoAsuntosRelevantesPub.aspx?ID=114032&SeguimientoID=274

Resolución 581/2012. (2012, December). *Primera Sala de la Suprema Corte de Justicia de la Nación.* (*First Chamber of the Supreme Court of Justice of the Nation*), pp. 16–17. https://www.scjn.gob.mx/derechos-humanos/sites/default/files/sentencias-emblematicas/sentencia/2022-02/AR%20581-2012.pdf

Resolución I.5o.C. J/30. (2011, October). *Semanario Judicial de la Federación y su Gaceta, Quinto Tribunal Colegiado en materia civil del Primer Circuito, Libro I (Judicial Weekly of the Federation and its Gazette, Fifth Collegiate Court in civil matters of the First Circuit, Book I)*, p. 152. https://bj.scjn.gob.mx/doc/tesis/j_hxMHYBN_4klb4HpnRN/"Derechos%20humanos"

Resolución I.3o.A.1 K. (2013, Febrero). *Derecho a la dignidad humana. Es connatural a las personas físicas y no a las morales. 10a. Época; T.C.C.; S.J.F. y su Gaceta; Libro XVII (Right to human dignity. It is natural to natural persons and not to legal entities. 10a. Time; T.C.C.; S.J.F. and his Gazette; Book XVII)*, p. 1344. https://bj.scjn.gob.mx/doc/tesis/4DvNfYgBvbG1RDka3fU7/"Internet"

Sartori, G. (2003). *La política (Politics)*. Fondo de Cultura Económica.

Singer, P. (1997). *Repensar la vida y la muerte (El derrumbe de nuestra ética tradicional) (Rethinking life and death [The collapse of our traditional ethics])*. Paidós.

Stark, G. (2005). *Measurement and the eSourcing capability*. Carnegie Mellon University.

Stark, G. (2011). *A comparison of parametric estimation models*. Crosstalk.

Sulmasy, D. (2002). Human dignity and human worth. In N. Lickiss & J. Malpas (Eds.), *Perspectives on human dignity: A conversation* (Vol. XII, pp. 9–18). Springer.

Taylor, C. (2009). *La política del reconocimiento en El multiculturalismo y "la política del reconocimiento" (The politics of recognition in Multiculturalism and "the politics of recognition")*. Fondo de Cultura Económica.

Torralba, F. (2005). *¿Qué es la dignidad humana? (Ensayo sobre Peter Singer, Hugo Tristram Engelhardt y John Harris) (What is human dignity? (Essay on Peter Singer, Hugo Tristram Engelhardt and John Harris)*. Herder.

United Nations (UN). (1997). *Comité para la Eliminación de la Discriminación Racial de la Organización de las Naciones Unidas (United Nations Committee on the Elimination of Racial Discrimination)*. Asamblea General 52/2018.

Universidad Nacional Autónoma de México (UNAM). (2014). *Discurso sobre la dignidad del hombre (Discourse on the dignity of man)*. Universidad Autónoma de México.

Werner, J. (1996). *La Paideia: los ideales de la cultura griega (The Paideia: the ideals of Greek culture)*. Fondo de Cultura Económica.

CHAPTER 12

Sexual Assertiveness in Mexican Homeless Female Youth: A Qualitative Approach

Susana Castaños-Cervantes

Introduction

Human sexuality is rich and diverse since it is not biologically determined; as a result, it is possible to decide when, how, and with whom to be intimate, provided that the individuals involved give voluntary and free consent (López, 2009). Sexual encounters, however, are not always consensual: coercion and sexual violence can have significant repercussions on physical and psychological health. They can even impact the long-term ability to form healthy intimate relationships. Sexual violence has been defined as a sexual act committed or attempted by another person without the victim's consent or against someone who cannot consent or refuse (Basile et al., 2014). Among the female population and homeless men, homeless women are victims of sexual violence at a higher rate (Melander & Tyler, 2010).

S. Castaños-Cervantes (✉)
Escuela de Psicología, Facultad de Ciencias de la Salud, Universidad Panamericana, Mexico City, Mexico
e-mail: scastanos@up.edu.mx

S. Castaños-Cervantes, C. Atristain-Suárez (eds.), *Assertiveness in the Context of Human Rights, Ethics, and Classical Virtues*,
https://doi.org/10.1007/978-3-031-60962-6_12

Furthermore, homeless females are more inclined to sexual coercion and sexual compliance because they feel responsible for satisfying their partners' sexual needs, do not want to hurt their partners' feelings or make them feel rejected, want to avoid tensions and conflict, want to feel accepted by their partners, and believe that sexual activities will make their partners love them more and thus improve the quality of the relationship. They may find it difficult to risk being left by their partners. Therefore, they may tend to acquiesce to their partners' sexual requests despite being against their wishes (Kristanti et al., 2019). Many sexually active homeless women also perceive that they do not have the right to communicate about or control aspects of their sexual behaviour. Past research has demonstrated that women who have suffered abusive experiences, such as homeless females, have difficulty engaging in protective health behaviours even within consensual sexual unions and warding off further unwanted sexual interactions (Humphrey & White, 2000).

Among homeless women, homeless female youth are more vulnerable concerning sexual relations not only because they are facing multiple biological, psychological, behavioural, and social transformations but also because the pressures exerted by peer groups and adults are likely to give rise to an increase in risky sexual behaviours (Moyano et al., 2021). Moreover, such women, including homeless females, are more likely to carry out high-risk sexual behaviours, such as having unprotected sex or multiple partners (Hillis et al., 2001). Thus, homeless women are prone to experiencing further sexual re-victimisation.

One way to prevent and reduce further sexual victimisation, sexual violence and coercion, sexual compliance, and risky sexual behaviours and promote sexual health and healthy intimate relationships, encourage being sexually responsible, and foster the well-being of homeless female youth is through interventions targeting sexual-assertiveness skills.

Sexual assertiveness is the ability to communicate sexual desires effectively (Loshek & Terrell, 2015), including sexual consent and nonconsent (Greene & Faulkner, 2005), and to develop and establish healthy sexual interactions (Azmoude et al., 2016). To be "assertive" means to pursue one's goals or to state with assurance and self-confidence (East & Adams, 2002). As such, there are at least two forms of sexual assertiveness. One involves communicating one's sexual needs and desires. The other form of sexual assertiveness is reflected in the understanding that it is not okay for anyone to touch or kiss oneself when one does not want it, that one does not have to have sex if one does not want to, and that one needs not to be pressured into doing anything sexually with which one is not comfortable. These beliefs and the skills required to act on them are invariably rooted in how people feel about themselves and their bodies and allowing others to treat them accordingly.

Sexual assertiveness has numerous benefits. It fosters sexual health, being sexually responsible, sexual satisfaction, healthy intimate relationships, and exerting one's sexual rights (López-Alvarado et al., 2020). It diminishes sexual compliance (Darden et al., 2019) and reduces the risk of sexual victimisation among women with a history of assault (Fernández-Fuertes et al., 2020; Kelley et al., 2016) and unwanted sexual experiences (Zerubavel & Messman-Moore, 2013) and is related to fewer experiences of sexual coercion (Walker et al., 2011) and symptoms of depression. Hence, understanding young women's sexual assertiveness, particularly that of homeless female youth, is critical to developing effective interventions to promote sexual health and reduce sexual risk-taking and violence (Rickert et al., 2000). For purposes of this study, homeless female youth were defined as teen girls between 10 and 19 years old (World Health Organization [WHO], n.d.) that are sheltered, unsheltered, and emergency sheltered, as well as those at risk of homelessness because they lack stable housing and are victims of domestic violence and neglect.

Although sexual assertiveness is a critical factor for sexual health; being sexually responsible; healthy intimate relationships; and preventing and diminishing sexual violence, sexual coercion, sexual compliance, and risky sexual behaviours, research to date on sexual assertiveness in homeless populations, particularly underage groups, is limited and insufficient. To that end, this research aims to qualitatively explore the sexual assertiveness of a group of Mexican homeless female youth to identify factors shaping sexual assertiveness and plausible pathways that may explain its effects.

The theoretical framework adopted in this research will be the Psychosocial Theoretical Model for Sexual Health Promotion proposed by Wight et al. (1998).

This study will encourage designing and implementing effective research-based programs and policies to impact the sexual health of homeless female teenagers positively. When homeless female youth learn to behave sexually responsibly and to exert their sexual rights, they can learn to enjoy a healthy, developmentally appropriate sexuality free of violence, risk of pregnancy, disease, and exploitation, and that any partner who does not respect their wishes for adequate protection is not desirable.

Method

Participants: 200 participants were recruited from non-governmental organisations in Mexico City that serve homeless children and youth as their primary function using a purposive sampling method. Participants were required to (1) be between 10 and 19 years old, (2) reside within the selected shelter during the data collection period, and (3) consent to participate in the study. Participants with insufficient capacity to provide informed consent and a primary diagnosis of intellectual disability or head injury were excluded.

Assessment Measure: To examine some dimensions of sexual assertiveness, a semi-structured interview was developed based on multiple sexual assertiveness scales adapted to the Mexican population. Three psychologists, experts in the subject and qualitative methodology, reviewed the proposed semi-structured interview. The dimensions evaluated were sexual attitudes (e.g., Have you engaged in unprotected sex? Have you engaged in sex under the effects of drugs? Could you describe your sexual life?), sexual and reproductive health (e.g., Do you know how to use contraceptive methods? What barrier methods have you used? Do you know what menstruation is? How many sexual partners have you had? How satisfying were your relationships? Why?), and sexual violence (e.g., Have you been forced to have sex by your partner? Have you engaged in unwanted sex?).

Procedure: Because homeless female youth experience unstable living conditions (Coker et al., 2009), the researcher worked with non-governmental institutions that support homeless children and youth to acquire access to this population. These institutions were informed of the study's purpose and methods and assured that the researcher would follow ethical procedures and guidelines specified by the American Psychological Association (APA, 2017), the Mexican General Law of Health,[1] and the Mexican Law of Social Welfare.[2] The institutions provided permission to conduct the study instead of parental consent, as legal authority rested with the institutions to consent on teenagers' behalf. All participants in this study did so voluntarily and provided their fingerprints as written consent. Participants received information about the study's general objectives, use of data, and confidentiality agreement. The researcher took care

[1] https://www.diputados.gob.mx/LeyesBiblio/pdf/LGS.pdf
[2] https://www.diputados.gob.mx/LeyesBiblio/pdf/LASoc.pdf

to answer participants' questions without biasing participation choice. Participants were empowered to refuse to answer any question or to discontinue study participation at any time. The research took place in collaborating institutions' on-site classrooms. Participants were individually interviewed, and responses were recorded by the researcher with the prior consent of both the institutions and the study group. While interviews lasted approximately an average of two hours, no time limit was established. Participants did not receive compensation for their participation. This study was reviewed and approved by the Academic and Ethics Board of the collaborating institutions. This review serves as the Mexican equivalent of an American IRB Review.

Data Analysis: A content analysis was based on classic grounded theory principles (Denzin & Lincoln, 1998), reaching saturation at 50 interviews. The Atlas TI Version Six computer program was used to identify relevant categories, codes, and units of analysis and quantify the categories in percentages. To establish consensus among the final categories, two experts in qualitative research reviewed the categories and the coding system used.

Results

The consensus on the categories had an inter-rate reliability of 0.82 according to Cohen's Kappa index (Cohen, 1968), which indicates a high degree of agreement. Therefore, the results are reliable and valid for interpretation and analysis.

Outcomes revealed that more than 70% of the homeless female youth interviewed initiated their sexual activity due to sexual abuse by a family member, a friend, a neighbour, or an unknown person. Participants stated they were not believed when they reported the sexual abuse to other family members, mainly their biological mother or grandmother. They were blamed if it happened; it was because they provoked it. If they decided to report the case of abuse to an authority, they were further abused, and the authorities did not provide help or assistance in any way. They did not receive support and care and were left unprotected and vulnerable to greater victimisation.

After being sexually abused, more than 75% of the sample engaged in health risk behaviours such as substance use and abuse, risky sexual activities, and criminal activities (e.g., theft, drug selling, and, to a lesser degree, prostitution). This sexual abuse was their main reason for abandoning their homes for a life on the streets. The risky sexual activities present in 80% of the cases were:

- Engaging in sexual relationships with multiple partners
- Engaging in sexual relationships with other people that are having sex with other people
- Engaging in casual sex encounters
- Engaging in sex under the effects of alcohol or drugs (e.g., inhalants, marijuana, ecstasy, LSD, cocaine)
- Engaging in sex with people not using barrier methods
- Not using barrier methods

Involvement in risky sexual activities led them to become pregnant, abort frequently, and suffer from sexually transmitted infections. Approximately 20% have been pregnant, and 10% have aborted or lost the baby. More than 50% claimed they had suffered a sexually transmitted infection, the most common being the Human Papillomavirus (HPV), followed by chlamydia, gonorrhoea, and genital herpes. It was found that 7% of the participants presented with HIV-AIDS.

Once homeless, participants reported being re-victimised, abandoning school, using and abusing alcohol and drugs, engaging with risky groups (e.g., juvenile offenders, gangs, organised crime), engaging in illicit activities that caused them legal problems, and being convicted in the juvenile justice system.

Concerning sexual and reproductive health, less than 20% of the homeless female youth interviewed knew their right to receive sexual education, 12% knew essential aspects of a woman's anatomy and physiology, 15% have visited a health care centre to receive information or services, and 25% knew their right to have sexual relationships only when they wanted to. Likewise, only approximately 10% of the population knew about menstruation and their menstrual cycle.

The main topics of the three categories of risk behaviours identified in the qualitative analysis are broken down below: sexual attitudes, sexual and reproductive health, and sexual violence.

Sexual Attitudes

Permissiveness was present in the sexual attitudes reported by 65% of the participants, such as: "*I have sex because it is fun,*" "*When you are homeless, it is okay to get paid for sex*," "*I have three sexual partners, but my friends have at least four*," "*What is the point of commitment when you are going to be abandoned or betrayed?*," "*Love is unnecessary before consenting to sex*," "*If you are from the gang, you have to have sex with everyone*," and "*I prefer to keep sex casual and uncommitted.*" These behaviours were contrary to other observed sexual attitudes measured by communion.

Communion (i.e., meaningful connection between two persons) was present in the sexual attitudes reported by all participants. Because in their life history participants mentioned having lacked significant emotional relationships or being dysfunctional, they sought love and emotional attachment to satisfy their emotional needs. They long for commitment and dedication to one partner. They want to experience what it means to be loved and cared for. They must be accepted, recognised, and loved by someone who provides them affection, security, attention, a sense of belonging and identity: "*I want to be loved and cared for*," "*Although he hits me, he is there for me*," "*He cares for me because he makes me feel that I am loved*," "*If he abandons me, I do not want to live, he means the world to me*," "*Even though he sometimes forces me to have sex with him and his friends, he is all I have, I do not want to be alone again, I want to be cared for and protected*," "*I work to pay for everything he wants, I am willing to sacrifice myself so he can be happy*," "*I feel that I am worthy when I am with him*," "*We have a special connection*," and "*I am faithful to him, and we have a child together; finally I have a true family.*" Hence, their self-concept is embedded with the views of others, especially their significant persons. Therefore, they engage in sexual relationships to belong to a group, avoid abandonment, and obtain protection and affection. Their sexual attitudes are influenced by the relative importance they give to people who are significant to them. Thus, in this way, if they have broken their family ties, they will be more willing to follow their group or their partner since adolescents require generically and naturally daily coexistence, affective ties, and interdependence to subsist and meet their needs of affection, attachment, care, love, company, and love.

15% of the sample exhibited birth control attitudes since they asserted they did not want to get pregnant and repeat their family's vicious cycle. Remarks such as "*I do not want to be like my mother*," "*If I have suffered, I would not want for my baby to suffer*," "*I am a bad person, a demon, so I cannot give birth to a child*," *and* "*I will not become a good mother*," are some examples of sexual attitudes measured by birth control (sex should involve pregnancy prevention).

Instrumentality was present in the sexual attitudes reported by 87% of the participants with behaviours such as rewarded sex or the exchange of their body for money, food, or material resources (e.g., clothing, hygiene products, spending the night at a hotel): "*You want me to have a normal job with a schedule to fulfil so that I earn much less than what I earn now*," "*I can do what I want when I want, and there are no rules to follow*," "*I earn more than you* [addressing the researcher] *and you work eight hours a day*." The participants indicated that they engaged in rewarded sex to survive, satisfy physical needs, and obtain resources in a quick and accessible way, even if this exposed them to suffering greater victimisation. When they come from low-income households characterised by the lack of access to essential services (e.g., drinking water, sanitation facilities, electricity, waste removal, health care, and education, among others) and families with poorly paid jobs or those unemployed, with addictions, and with a low academic level, they often fall into rewarded sex. Participants usually engage in sex-rewarding behaviours, characterised by the trade of sexual activities for food, clothing, or housing. If they become part of a prostitution network, they usually become victims of human trafficking. Although they know that prostitution makes them prone to suffer greater physical violence, including sexual and psychological abuse, to contract diseases and to be easy prey to all kinds of aggressions, once they dabble, they are afraid to leave and express, which is practically impossible since they would place themselves and the lives of their relatives at a higher risk (*e.g.*, "*I do not have any other option, I am already here,*" "*I do not want anything to happen to my children,*" "*They threaten me with taking away my children or that I will no longer see my brothers*"). In addition, they accept their current situation by rationalising the supposed associated rewards (*e.g.*, "*I already know that I put myself in danger, that I can die or that something bad can happen to me, but at least they pay me well, I can do whatever I want with the money they give me, and I earn more than what you earn in a week* [addressing the researcher]"). Moreover, they expressed that it is crucial to satisfy the client's desires (*e.g.*, "*It does not matter if they want you to do weird things, touch whatever and wherever, in the end, they pay and afterwards you bathe and you already try to forget*").

Finally, the permanence in a shelter or facility helps them to be gradually rescued from the networks of prostitution and organised crime, although it is necessary to change their identity and locality to get out of this criminal world. Furthermore, when sheltered, homeless female youth engage in same-sex relationships characterised by communion and permissiveness. This ambivalent behaviour was present all along in their statements.

Sexual and Reproductive Health

More than 80% of the participants have little information and knowledge about their sexuality. They did not receive sexual education. They did not know essential areas of their anatomy and physiology and how to care for themselves. About contraceptive methods, they know of the existence of condoms and the contraceptive pill. However, they rarely use them, especially when they engage in sex under the effects of some drug or alcoholor preferring to satisfy the desires of their partner who does not want to use condoms. It is to avoid being abandoned and because the partner expressed his desire to feel more pleasure without a condom (*e.g.*, "*My partner does not like us to use a condom,*" "*My partner says that it does not feel the same,*" "*I do what my partner says to make him happy,*" "*Sometimes I do want to use a condom but then he gets angry and tells me he is going to leave me,*" "*If I do not do what he says, he hits me or insults me*"). Likewise, they have many myths, prejudices, and distortions. For example, "*menstruation is to get rid of what the body does not need,*" that "*you cannot get pregnant the first time and if you do not get pregnant at the first time, it means that you cannot have children at all,*" that "*you stop being a virgin if you are kissed on the lips,*" that "*the condom can be used several times if you wash it well,*" that "*the female condom can be used more than once*", and that "*sexually transmitted infections are not so serious as they seem.*" More than 50% of the participants did not know what AIDS or HIV was and were unaware of the effects of most sexually transmitted infections, including whether they are curable and treatable. Finally, it is essential to highlight that this group of homeless female youth did not have access to institutional health systems. At least 10% of the participants reported being discriminated against in health centres. Besides, they were not attended to, and when they received the care, they were victims of sexual harassment (*e.g.*, "*The doctor who treated me told me that he would cure me if I did him oral sex,*" "*When they treated me, the doctor put his hand inside my vagina without gloves,*" "*The doctor touched my intimate parts without my consent,*" "*The doctor threatened me that if I exposed his little secret that I would be sent to jail or I would become homeless once again*").

Sexual Violence

The main findings showed that in at least 50% of the participants sexual activity began before age ten due to intra-familial sexual abuse. It was the primary reason for running away from home. Once homeless, females suffered even greater sexual abuse by police officers, adults, and other homeless adults and youth. In approximately 50% of the cases, they were forced into prostitution or became victims of human trafficking. Moreover, if they decide to form part of a homeless group to receive support, protection, and satisfaction of basic needs, they are sexually abused by all of the group's male members, thus increasing their sexual victimisation.

As victims of sexual violence, they acquire sexually transmitted infections or become pregnant. While seeking access to institutional health systems, at least 10% of the participants reported being discriminated against in health centres. Besides, they were not attended to, and when they received the care, they were victims of sexual harassment, as previously stated. Therefore, they were also sexually victimised in health centres. It may be explained since their homeless status makes them invisible to law enforcement. Lastly, as a survival strategy, while homeless, they sell their bodies for food, shelter, or protection.

Discussion and Conclusions

This study is one of the few studies carried out in Mexico with homeless female youth. It adds to the growing body of literature on the field. Findings revealed that Mexican homeless female youth exhibit low sexual assertiveness and high levels of sexual violence.

The high levels of sexual violence observed may be explained by the fact that homeless women of all ages suffer sexual violence at a high rate (Feitel et al., 1992), even more so than the non-homeless population (Timmons et al., 2018). Furthermore, in many settings worldwide and particularly in Mexico, the health services that respond to survivors of sexual violence are non-existent or, at best, limited, especially for vulnerable groups such as homeless people. Likewise, many survivors may not seek care and, thus, suffer even more health consequences. Females often also face subsequent stigma and rejection from their families and communities, making them vulnerable to further sexual violence (WHO, 2019). Particular characteristics of sexual violence and its psycho-social effects on homeless girls and young women are partially and superficially known (Williams, 2018). In addition, actions aimed at studying and reducing the problem of sexual violence have been insufficient, ineffective, and limited (García-Moreno & Watts, 2011). Moreover, sexual permissiveness has been associated with unwanted sexual experiences and sexually risky behaviour (Martyniuk & Štulhofer, 2018). Lastly, child sexual abuse has been associated with sexually risky behaviours, sexual permissiveness, and sexual violence (Rong et al., 2022).

The following factors may explain the low level of sexual assertiveness:

- *Sense of belonging.*

Given that in their life history participants mentioned having lacked significant emotional relationships or being dysfunctional, they must be accepted, recognised, and loved by someone who gives them affection, security, attention, a sense of belonging, and identity. Women feel responsible for satisfying their partners' sexual needs, do not want to hurt their partners' feelings or make them feel rejected, want to avoid tensions and conflict, want to feel accepted by their partners, and believe that sexual activities will make their partners love them more and will improve the quality of the relationship. Therefore, they may tend to consent to their partners' sexual requests despite being against their wishes. Sexually assertive women can behave sexually according to their desires, despite their partner's needs, without feeling guilty or worried. She also knows and is sure of what she wants sexually and the boundaries of the sexual behaviours she is willing or unwilling to cross. She can communicate these to her partner (Kristanti et al., 2019).

- *Apparent satisfaction of essential needs.*

Lacking the necessary resources for subsistence and having broken with their family, school, and community ties, they alleged that they do not usually meet their basic needs for food, clothing, and housing. Rewarded sex allows them to adjust and face the harsh reality to survive on the streets.

- *Pleasure*

It is to feel an apparent satisfaction and temporary gratification without any commitment.

These results are typical in homeless groups, particularly the female population. After severing ties with their family and communities and becoming homeless without the proper academic formation and the necessary resources to support themselves, they engage in detrimental survival strategies that negatively affect their well-being. Also, they become an invisible group without law protection since they are homeless.

Lastly, engaging in sexual activities to feel a temporal gratification may be explained as a way for them to escape their reality and adjust to their extremely adverse circumstances (Castaños-Cervantes & Sánchez-Sosa, 2016; Castaños-Cervantes & Vélez-Agosto, 2018).

- *Lack of knowledge about sexual rights, sexual and reproductive health, and lack of sexual education.*

The outcomes obtained are similar to those reported in previous studies carried out in Mexico with Mexican youth and teenagers. Concerning sexual and reproductive health, only 54.5% of Mexican adolescents in high school know their right to receive sexual education, 46.8% have visited a health care centre to receive information or services, and 33.7% know their right to have sexual relationships only when they want to (Instituto Nacional de Salud Pública [INSP] y Centro Nacional para la Prevención y Control del VIH y el SIDA [CENSIDA], 2014). Globally, Mexico has the highest teenage pregnancy rate of the countries of the OECD. More than 1,000 Mexican teen girls between 12 and 19 become mothers daily without wishing it or planning it (Guillén, 2022). In 2018, 46% of female adolescents reported being pregnant at least once. 52% of adolescent pregnancies are unwanted, and 91% of female pregnant teenagers come from low-income and lower-middle-income households (Campero et al., 2021). In fact, during the COVID-19 pandemic, unwanted and unintentional adolescent pregnancies increased by 30% between 2020 and 2021. The majority of these early pregnancies derive from violations of sexual and reproductive rights.

Furthermore, in Mexico, not all women can fully exercise their reproductive rights: not all can decide autonomously and without discrimination whether or not to have children, with whom, how many, and how often. This situation in Mexico has been the same for over 20 years, so little progress has been made on this crucial matter. Likewise, adolescents between the age of 15 and 17, indigenous women, low-income females, and women who live in rural areas or are unschooled have little to minimum access to healthcare centres and rarely use contraceptive methods. In fact, generally speaking, Mexico is characterised by limited access to sexual information and sexual education, which increases sexual vulnerability, unequal access to contraceptive methods, and conducting inefficient sexual and reproductive health programs that mainly target indigenous people, migrants, and persons with disabilities without considering many other vulnerable groups such as homeless females (Arvizu et al., 2022).

The Psycho-social Theoretical Framework for Sexual Health Promotion (Wight et al., 1998) seeks to provide a theoretical foundation for effective and sustainable sexual health programs. It provides an understanding of the most critical determinants of young people's sexual behaviour that can be used to explain the results achieved:

- *Gender*: In Mexican culture, women are taught to be submissive, dependent, and obedient. Feminism is associated with submission, affiliative obedience, and weakness. It is how Mexican children grow up with an ideology regarding how they should behave and react to certain situations (Díaz-Guerrero, 2007). As such, they are more prone to sexual unassertiveness and victimisation. Women should be taught ways to develop a progressive sexual attitude that makes them stand up for themselves, be responsible for their needs and desires, and express their feelings and thoughts assertively. Perhaps sexual education is necessary to discuss strategies and inform how women can continue to prioritise sexual intercourse while incorporating safe sex practices and sexual well-being related to the intersections of gender, race, and sexuality (Armstrong et al., 2020).
- *Power*: Homeless female youth lack personal power because they engage in sexual activities in which their integrity is at risk and their well-being is severely impaired. Hence, sexual empowerment should be fostered in this particular group as it is related to positive sexual outcomes such as feeling good about one's sexuality, being able to ask for what one wants and refuse what one does not want sexually, and enjoying sexual encounters (Erchull & Liss, 2014).
- *Risk*: Homeless female youth engage in sexually risky activities due to their sexual attitudes, their lack of self-esteem, self-acceptance, self-efficacy, and emotional needs, and as a survival strategy. Even though they acknowledge the risks associated with their behaviour, they engage in such actions, which is common in young people, particularly when they do not have parental support and supervision and associate with risk groups. Other research has shown that survival is one of the main reasons for engaging in risky behaviours, especially when it comes to risky sexual activity (Heerde & Hemphill, 2017).

- *Individual cognitions*: Homeless female youth have sexual attitudes that make them more prone to subsequent victimisation and abuse. They are consistent with a cultural perspective, with being a woman and facing homelessness as a female. Hence, their sexual decision-making increases the probability of experiencing higher rates of sexual victimisation and of being less assertive sexually (Darden et al., 2019).
- *Social approval*: Homeless female youth lack quality relationships. Thus, being accepted by a group is crucial for them to have a sense of belonging, develop an identity, and feel protected, secure, and cared for. It is consistent with Mexican behaviour in which social belonging is more relevant than individual well-being and personal needs (Díaz-Guerrero, 2007). Likewise, the self-concept of homeless female youth is built upon the basis of their social relationships because they are a vital part of their self-concept. Therefore, their self-construal is mainly developed by how they relate to others (Treger & Schmitt, 2018).

When homeless female youth learn to behave sexually responsibly and to exert their sexual rights, they can learn to enjoy a healthy, developmentally appropriate sexuality free of violence, risk of pregnancy, disease, and exploitation. Consequently, this knowledge, which provides an understanding of the origins and control of sexual behaviour in Mexican homeless youth, should be applied to design evidence-based programs that promote safer sexual behaviour among homeless female youth, improve the quality of their sexual relationships, particularly in terms of reducing anxiety and regretted sexual behaviour, reduce the incidence of unsafe sex, and diminish the rate of unwanted pregnancies. One way to prevent and decrease further sexual re-victimisation, sexual violence and coercion, sexual compliance, and risky sexual behaviours, is to promote sexual health and healthy intimate relationships, encourage being sexually responsible, and foster the well-being of homeless female youth through interventions targeting sexual-assertiveness skills. Cognitive behavioural interventions and assertiveness training have proven efficient and sustainable for enabling assertive behaviour (Speed et al., 2018; Swee et al., 2018).

One of the limitations of this study was that, although qualitative interviews are the most appropriate method to address research objectives, the study had to rely exclusively on this method. Limited resources did not make it possible to add other forms of data collection through which the information could be triangulated and contextualised. In addition, the interview focused on some aspects of sexual and reproductive health due to practicality, lack of time availability, and being a high-floating and transitory population. Finally, since it was a non-probabilistic sample, the findings cannot be generalised to similar people in other contexts and to different risk behaviours.

References

American Psychological Association (APA). (2017). *Ethical principles of psychologists and code of conduct.* http://www.apa.org/ethics/code/.

Armstrong, J., Thorpe, S., & Williams, D. (2020). Sexual attitudes, religious commitment, and sexual risk behaviours among college-aged women: A feminist theory approach. *Journal of Gender Studies,* 1–12. https://doi.org/10.1080/09589236.2020.1838888.

Arvizu, V., Flamand, L., González, M., & Olmeda, J. (2022). *Embarazo temprano en México: panorama de estrategias públicas para su atención (Early pregancy in Mexico: Overview of policy strategies for its attention).* El Colegio de México, Red de Estudios sobre Desigualdades. https://desigualdades.colmex.mx/embarazo/embarazo-temprano-mexico-panorama-estrategias-publicas.pdf.

Azmoude, E., Firoozi, M., Sadeghi Sahebzad, E., & Asgharipour, N. (2016). Relationship between gender roles and sexual assertiveness in married women. *International Journal of Community-based Nursing and Midwifery, 4*(4), 363–373.

Basile, K. C., Smith, S. G., Breiding, M., Black, M., & Mahendra, R. (2014). *Sexual violence surveillance: Uniform definitions and recommended data elements, version 2.0.* Centres for Disease Control and Prevention.

Campero, L., Estrada, F., Hubert, C., De la Vara, E., & Villalobos, A. (2021). *Educación integral de la sexualidad en adolescentes: una tarea pendiente en México. Síntesis sobre políticas de salud (Whole sexual education in teenagers: A pending task in México. Synthesis about health policies).* Instituto Nacional de Salud Pública.

Castaños-Cervantes, S., & Sánchez-Sosa, J. (2016). Towards a psycho-social and cultural definition of Mexican homeless girls: A qualitative approach. *Anales de Psicología, 32*(2), 516–527. https://doi.org/10.6018/analesps.32.2.204721

Castaños-Cervantes, S., & Vélez-Agosto, M. (2018). Psycho-social risk behaviours in Mexican young women experiencing homelessness. *Children and Youth Services Review, 95,* 235–242. https://doi.org/10.1016/j.childyouth.2018.10.041

Cohen, J. (1968). Weighted kappa: Nominal scale agreement with provision for scaled disagreement of partial credit. *Psychological Bulletin, 70*(4), 213–220.

Coker, T., Elliott, M., Kanouse, D., Grunbaum, J., Gilliland, J., Tortolero, S., Cuccaro, P., & Schuster, M. (2009). Prevalence, characteristics, associated health and health care of family homelessness among fifth-grade students. *American Journal of Public Health, 99*(8), 1446–1452.

Darden, M. C., Ehman, A. C., Lair, E. C., & Gross, A. (2019). Sexual compliance: Examining the relationships among sexual want, sexual consent, and sexual assertiveness. *Sexuality & Culture, 23*, 220–235. https://doi.org/10.1007/s12119-018-9551-1

Denzin, N., & Lincoln, Y. (1998). *The landscape of qualitative research.* Sage Publications.

Díaz-Guerrero, R. (2007). *Psicología del mexicano. Descubrimiento de la etnopsicología (Mexican psychology. Discovery of ethnopscyhology).* Trillas.

East, P., & Adams, J. (2002). Sexual assertiveness and adolescent's sexual rights. *Perspectives on Sexual and Reproductive Health, 34*(4), 212–213.

Erchull, M., & Liss, M. (2014). The object of one's desire: How perceived sexual empowerment through objectification is related to sexual outcomes. *Sexuality & Culture, 18*(4), 773–788. https://doi.up.elogim.com/10.1007/s12119-013-9216-z

Feitel, B., Margetson, N., Chamas, J., & Lipman, C. (1992). Psycho-social background and behavioural and emotional disorders of homeless and runaway youth. *Hospital & Community Psychiatry, 43*(2), 155–159.

Fernández-Fuertes, A. A., Fernández-Rouco, N., Lázaro-Visa, S., & Gómez-Pérez, E. (2020). Myths about sexual aggression, sexual assertiveness and sexual violence in adolescent romantic relationships. *International Journal of Environmental Research and Public Health, 17*(23), 8744. https://doi.org/10.3390/ijerph17238744

García-Moreno, C., & Watts, C. (2011). Violence against women: An urgent public health priority. *Bulletin of the World Health Organization, 89*(1), 2. https://doi.org/10.2471/BLT.10.085217

Greene, K., & Faulkner, S. L. (2005). Gender, belief in the sexual double standard, and sexual talk in heterosexual dating relationships. *Sex Roles, 53*, 239–251.

Guillén, B. (2022). 1.000 *embarazos de adolescentes al día: México se estanca en uno de sus grandes retos demográficos (1000 teenage pregnancies per day: Mexico . stagnates in one of its great demographic challenges*). https://elpais.com/mexico/2022-08-31/1000-embarazos-de-adolescentes-al-dia-mexico-se-estanca-en-uno-de-sus-grandes-retos-demograficos.html.

Heerde, J. A., & Hemphill, S. A. (2017). The role of risk and protective factors in modifying risk for sexual victimisation, sexual risk behaviours, and survival sex among homeless youth: A meta-analysis. *Journal of Investigative Psychology and Offender Profiling, 14*(2), 150–174. https://doi.org/10.1002/jip.1473

Hillis, S. D., Anda, R. F., Felitti, V. J., & Marchbanks, P. A. (2001). Adverse childhood experiences and sexual risk behaviours in women: A retrospective cohort study. *Family Planning Perspectives, 33*(5), 206–211.

Humphrey, J. A., & White, J. W. (2000). Women's vulnerability to sexual assault from adolescence to young adulthood. *Journal of Adolescent Health, 27*(6), 419–424.

INSP & CENSIDA. (2014). *Análisis sobre educación sexual integral, conocimientos y actitudes en sexualidad en adolescentes escolarizados. Informe Final (Analysis of holistic sexual education, sexual knowledge and attitudes in shool adolescents).* INSP and CENSIDA.

Kelley, E. L., Orchowski, L. M., & Gidycz, C. A. (2016). Sexual victimisation among college women: Role of sexual assertiveness and resistance variables. *Psychology of Violence, 6*(2), 243–252. https://doi.org/10.1037/a0039407

Kristanti, I., Poerwandari, E. K., Pohan, L. D., & Primasari, I. (2019). Cognitive-behavioural intervention to enhance sexual assertiveness in women who exhibit premarital sexual compliance in the Greater Jakarta area, Indonesia. *Pertanika Journal of Social Sciences and Humanities, 27*(3), 1927–1943.

López, F. (2009). *La educación sexual (Sexual education)*. Biblioteca Nueva.

López-Alvarado, S. L., Van Parys, H., Jerves, E., & Enzlin, P. (2020). Development of sexual assertiveness and its function for human sexuality: A literature review. *Revista Interamericana De Psicología/Interamerican Journal of Psychology, 54*(2), e948. https://doi.org/10.30849/ripijp.v54i2.948

Loshek, E., & Terrell, H. K. (2015). The development of the sexual assertiveness questionnaire (SAQ): A comprehensive measure of sexual assertiveness for women. *The Journal of Sex Research, 52*, 1017–1027. https://doi.org/10.1080/00224499.2014.944970

Martyniuk, U., & Štulhofer, A. (2018). A longitudinal exploration of the relationship between pornography use and sexual permissiveness in female and male adolescents. *Journal of Adolescence, 69*, 80–87. https://doi.org/10.1016/j.adolescence.2018.09.006

Melander, L., & Tyler, K. (2010). The effect of early maltreatment, victimization, and partner violence on HIV risk behavior among homeless young adults. *Journal of Adolescent Health, 47*(6), 575–581.

Moyano, N., Granados, R., Durán, C. A., & Galarza, C. (2021). Self-esteem, attitudes toward love, and sexual assertiveness among pregnant adolescents. *International Journal of Environmental Research and Public Health, 18*(3), 1270. https://doi.org/10.3390/ijerph18031270

Rickert, V., Neal, W., Wiemann, C., & Berenson, A. (2000). Prevalence and predictors of low sexual assertiveness. *Journal of Pediatric & Adolescent Gynecology, 13*(2). https://doi.org/10.1016/S1083-3188(00)00016-4

Rong, Z., Wen, Z., Maoxu, L., Ya, L., Song, F., Hui, W., Xiaozhen, T., & Yunli, Y. (2022). Relationship between childhood sexual abuse and attitudes toward premarital sexual permissiveness among middle school students in Luzhou, China. *BMC Public Health, 22*(71). https://doi.org/10.1186/s12889-021-12490-1

Speed, B. C., Goldstein, B. L., & Goldfried, M. R. (2018). Assertiveness training: A forgotten evidence-based treatment. *Clinical Psychology: Science and Practice, 25*(1), e12216. https://doi.org/10.1111/cpsp.12216

Swee, M. B., Kaplan, S. C., & Heimberg, R. G. (2018). Assertive behaviour and assertion training as important foci in a clinical context: The case of social anxiety disorder. *Clinical Psychology: Science and Practice, 25*(1), e12222. https://doi.org/10.1111/cpsp.12222

Timmons, V., Coomber-Bendtsen, M., & Zederayko, A. (2018). *Gender-based violence and homelessness: Two sides of the same coin*. https://www.schoolofpublicpolicy.sk.ca/documents/research/policy-briefs/JSGS-policybriefs-Gender-Based%20Violence%20and%20Homelessness.pdf.

Treger, S., & Schmitt, D. P. (2018). Independent, autonomous, and permissive: Examining the links between self-construal and sexual permissiveness. *The Journal of Sex Research, 1–13*. https://doi.org/10.1080/00224499.2018.146588410.1080/00224499.2018.1465884

Walker, D. P., Messman-Moore, T. L., & Ward, R. M. (2011). Number of sexual partners and sexual assertiveness predict sexual victimisation: Do more partners equal more risk? *Violence and Victims, 26*, 774–787. https://doi.org/10.1891/0886-6708.26.6.774

Wight, D., Abraham, C., & Scott, S. (1998). Towards a psycho-social theoretical framework for sexual health promotion. *Health Education Research, Theory and Practice, 13*(3), 317–330.

Williams, M. (2018). *Women's hidden homelessness*. https://www.homeless.org.uk/connect/blogs/2018/feb/27/women%E2%80%99s-hidden-homelessness.

World Health Organization. (2019). *Displaced or refugee women are at increased risk of violence. What can WHO do?* https://www.who.int/reproductivehealth/displaced-refugee-women-violence-risk/en/.

World Health Organization. (WHO). (n.d.). *Adolescent health*. https://www.who.int/health-topics/adolescent-health#tab=tab_1.

Zerubavel, N., & Messman-Moore, T. L. (2013). Sexual victimisation, fear of sexual powerlessness, and cognitive emotion dysregulation as barriers to sexual assertiveness in college women. *Violence Against Women, 19*(12), 1518–1537. https://doi.org/10.1177/1077801213517566

CHAPTER 13

Assertiveness: A Tool for Social Change and Shared Value

Mary Paz Agudín-Colmenares

Introduction

We make soul with our behaviour.
—Hillman (1996)

Assertiveness is a difficult concept to define due to the multiplicity of its components. Townend (2007) offers an explanation enriching it with elements such as positive emotions, connection with others, purpose, imagination, ability to listen, and alignment and connection between body, mind, and brain.

This broad term's meaning needs to be clarified for the simple onlooker. It requires the effort of self-observation to go beyond oneself and decipher this code of essence, feeling, and thought. With a systemic-qualitative approach, the author points out that such a mixture, organised in synergies, would be a powerful tool for social change and shared value due to

M. P. Agudín-Colmenares (✉)
Facultad de Derecho, Universidad Panamericana, Mexico City, Mexico
e-mail: magudin@up.edu.mx

S. Castaños-Cervantes, C. Atristain-Suárez (eds.), *Assertiveness in the Context of Human Rights, Ethics, and Classical Virtues*,
https://doi.org/10.1007/978-3-031-60962-6_13

its heterogeneous alignment of possible formulas, such as respect for both oneself and other; meaning and purpose; empathy; dialogue and negotiation; awareness and physical, intellectual, emotional, and spiritual integration; acceptance and attention; curiosity and openness to change; honesty and respect in support of diversity; confidence and self-esteem; positive emotions and treating conflict management as an opportunity; integration of different types of intelligence; a sense of belonging and collegiality and many other synergies that serve to support the projection of an honest influence on others.

Assertiveness at the Micro and Macrosocial Levels

Sociological theory has generated a multi-paradigm debate central to this research's terms: The discussion on the existence or nonexistence of links between micro and macro social levels. As Alexander et al. (1987) point out, the controversy focused on establishing whether the actions of individuals are rational or interpretative and whether the social order is negotiated between people or imposed by some collective power. Beginning in the 1980s, the need emerged for a new approach based on the general conviction that both levels of analysis did not contradict each other but instead were complementary and synthetical to avoid the reductionism of polarities regarding the constitution of social reality and to link and thereby discover empirical relationships between their differing spheres.

It substantiates the significance of social and communicative skills regarding the contexts in which they reverberate. Unlike those who maintain that the micro-macro have little influence on each other and those who believe that one level is more fundamental than the other or that both are entirely independent of each other, this research corresponds to the view that there are mutual interrelations between both paradigms, and thus that in order to understand and explain social life and its expressions, it is necessary to take into account the results of the actions by both individuals and groups, since if there is reciprocity, correspondence, and connection, linking the whole with its parts and those parts with the whole becomes fundamental.

It is thus pertinent to ask ourselves whether the negative aspects of institutions, culture, and collectivity might result from poor formation in individual assertiveness and personal interaction. Faced with societies lacking in formative education, which is instead based on principles of extreme rationalisation, authors such as Olusanya (2014) warn us of the consequences: The perils of depersonalisation—which dilutes responsibility for denatured decisions such as going to war and normalises situations that in reality should not be so—and the dehumanisation and impoverishment of healthy emotions which, following diverse disciplines such as psychology, biology, or labour and organisational sociology, are essential to human progress.

Humanity has the propensity to act on beliefs about what the majority think must be done, and commonly, social pressure determines the behaviour in the face of fear of the consequences of failing to follow the rules, be they just or otherwise. It can be seen in innumerable cases, but to cite one example, the sale of girls by their own families in the State of Guerrero, Mexico, is something so ordinary and rooted in local customs that this cycle cannot be broken as it is a natural practice that the families in the community violate human rights and their daughters' wellbeing.

Bicchieri (2017) points out that, in addition to the possibility of rectifying behaviours, another possible means of remedying social norms and improving everyone's lives by altering empirical expectations is to ensure that others are changing in order to distance from a given established social norm and thereby weaken normative expectations to the point of collapse. She puts forward means such as constant long-term exposure to examples of alternative behaviours to achieve this. She emphasises that this change requires the modification of cognitive scripts, that is, values and beliefs of those who uphold such norms; nevertheless, this approach does not reach the crux of the issue since it focuses instead on symptoms, while it is a behavioural change that gets to the root of the problem.

An absence of assertiveness leads to social norms that need to be changed, as they are accepted passively due to a lack of emotional education. Therefore, unacceptable and unjust situations are normalised. To achieve this, beginning in a preventative sense to teach assertiveness in a generalised way would be far more advantageous than eliminating deeply rooted, ancestrally buttressed cognitive scripts. It would avoid the reactivity of waiting for anyone to believe that the rest of the community would transform and would, therefore, adopt a more proactive stance to break down harmful patterns.

Manipulating social norms and expectations is not a practical solution because it implies an exterior–interior change, but if the renovation comes from the inside–out, the chances lessen that social norms of this type develop, and, although this is not a panacea either, it is a preventive approach oriented towards avoiding the creation and proliferation of harmful social norms instead of labouring to correct them.

It is worth working towards proactivity that involves the certainty that it is necessary to start somewhere and to understand that transformations imply a type of movement identical to that of a Möbius strip, as shown in Fig. 13.1; that is, a non-orientable mathematical object that has a single surface is not possible to distinguish between the inner and outer surfaces, as its point of view is that of unity.

Communities based on mistaken belief systems can be reformed like many cases of abuse and illicit behaviours that societies may indulge in to exercise power. Assertiveness is the key that unlocks the door to change and can be taught and learned, more so if education aligns our minds and beliefs with our acts; however, the educational system, in general, has lent greater importance to cognitive learning, a reduced approach that plunges humanity into disastrous consequences. For Weller and Wilson (2018), the cognitive domain that involves learning with the head is not the only guise in which learning can change the world, as evidenced by its inclusion of an awareness of the cognitive mental plane by compassion for the affective map of the heart—a territory of feelings and attitudes where beliefs gain power—and the psychometrics of our hands, closely intertwined and supplementary. Thus, when doing something with conscious attention, thoughts turn to the "why?" behind this and to the compassion relating to the critical reflection of examining actions and the importance that these have either to the benefit or to the detriment of everyone else.

It is why—given the interwoven nature of social scales—thinking about systems contributes to aligning actions and values with mind, heart, and body and conquers internal and external changes since this form of introspection expands the brain towards the macro so that it visualises realities from perspectives other than just its own, an idea enlarged upon by

Fig. 13.1 Dynamics of change. (Source: Author's own elaboration)

Walther (2021) for whom the soul is another additional factor that adds to the equation by which to align actions to the benefit of the collectivity.

Ison and Straw (2020) point to the concealed power of systemic thought to effect profound and complex changes in this era in which the need for new ways of thinking and acting is pressing in terms of a sustainable and fairer world in the face of obsolete corporate and political interests, given that the *raison d'être* of such obstacles is the collective inability to tackle the emergencies of our time. Governance at every level should be replaced by systemic governance exercised by agents of change or public administration, activists, and decision-makers who embody the value of realising challenging transformations.

Reasoning about systems involves making oneself see the broader reality and, through the numerous tools that assertiveness contributes, makes the permeation of new stories and beliefs throughout society possible. Professionals should likewise be trained in intuitive and rational decision-making models as they are called upon to lay the foundations of new normative concepts.

Once people learn this way of concentrating and reflecting through implementing transformations from within, the assertive brain will be equipped with tools for accessing the outer world that will allow it, through the reconfiguration of histories and beliefs aligned with our values, to project norms that will not need to be changed due to their intrinsic fairness. It is helpful to point out some preliminaries regarding the functioning of the brain and all the possibilities that this organ is not exploiting at present but which assertiveness enables since the adoption of critical, creative, and systemic thinking throws into question social beliefs and offers solutions.

Innovative studies by Buzsáki (2019) demonstrate that our brain is not just a coding device that limits itself to absorbing information as is often claimed, but that it instead possesses truly expeditionary qualities such that it can control the body in order to prove hypotheses that it is not limited to processing information but also can create it by operating from the inside–out. It represents an inflexion point to which one pays the strictest attention. Following on from this, the education system should be reformed because up to now, it has been conceived in terms of the brain working from without to within, absorbing whatever information it is taught, favouring thereby reactive attitudes, and hindering proactive ones when the discoveries referred to here show that, in reality, it is underestimated by ignoring that it is perfectly capable of operating in the opposite direction.

Assertiveness is the mental planning that human beings need to trust their brains more and unblock all their capacities rather than passively waiting for change to come from outside. Assertiveness teaches the importance of quotidian actions when pitched towards the exterior. Hypotheses aligned with values that go beyond the merely economic or an exacerbated and poorly understood egoism, instead of being limited to taking on already existing histories and beliefs, and prove that the more creative and assertive the thinking, the more integral ways of doing things will be found. Emotional education can produce the mental schema necessary for interacting in a way nurtured by reality. The assertive hypotheses that the brain emanates would be projected outward and could bring about meaningful changes through their influence on creating equitable social norms instead of undertaking the titanic task of trying to change the unfair ones.

To achieve this, it is necessary first to forge the brain and the mind. Macrolevel social norms influence individuals at the micro level, but this can also work in reverse. An example is the agents of change and trend leaders who, with the ability to think critically and creatively, influence and alter entire macrolevels.

Assertive Education: A Formative Proposal for High-End Professionals

Since the brain is an organ that can be programmed, or even better reprogrammed, there exists an association that goes beyond mere metaphor between technology and the mind that means that this can manifest itself in people who are, to a greater or lesser degree, emotionally repressed but also, *contrario sensu*, among what might be termed "high-end professionals" who, via the elevated status of their jobs, contribute to social change and shared value. For this reason, it is essential to go beyond a simple assertive facade and properly rewire transformation in both the behaviour and the foundations on an individual level to achieve significant conversions in the macro strata.

Although change can be initiated on any scale, the proposition here is to refocus professional life on this mental strategy through universities since these form the bridge that unites paradigms of a diversity of thought and proposals aimed at achieving social change as well as being—or at least should be—natural laboratories of transmutation. In terms of social norms, the law is fertile ground as these are its tools and goals, and it is suggested through law schools that there be created an educational model that duly adapted to the needs of each profession can be extended via the work of interdisciplinary groups, to all areas of knowledge. The proposal that follows below is to pursue in a general way three steps to create generations of high-end professionals, as described in the next section.

Identifying the Consequences of a Lack of Assertiveness

An example of the connections between the micro and macro levels, whose consequences justify the strengthening of individuals' assertive skills, is put forward by Walker et al. (2020). It deals with the importance of democratic resilience by exposing the perils of sharp power, that aggressive domain whose most successful form of operation is probably via technological exploitation to repress and erode objective truth, hinder pluralism, and neutralise responsibility, as the values that supposedly govern new technologies lie on the margins of the most fundamental norms of human rights. However, the use of technoscience depends on the populations that interact with it, the rights that individuals and societies manage to establish, and the degree of success that societies achieve in defending their values when confronted with these behaviours that share data according to terms of service that are legal but which really should not be so as they undermine human rights in the face of a judicial system that permits algorithms to disseminate misleading content and enshrines economic, emotional, and behavioural biases.

Assertiveness needs to be fortified at the core of civil and governmental institutions and equally all other kinds of organisations to prevent opacity; lack of accountability; abuses; archaic, unjust, and unyielding customs; social narcissism; attacks on human rights, and any other elements that may frustrate effective responses when faced with the ambitions of macro power and its desire to reformat the world according to the isolated perspective of its exclusive whim, thereby favouring corrupt, bureaucratic, and highly and unjustifiably litigious societies.

Empathy is relevant in transformative learning, whose underlying purpose is to live life open to the capacity to ask questions, listen, observe, and benefit all living beings as they progress through the world (Weller &

Wilson, 2018). The brain has been taught to react in the face of reality, but given that it can project hypotheses outward and confirm these, it needs to be taught assertive premises and understood as an effective weapon of social change.

Centuries of legal tradition have taught us that law operates as an abstraction exterior to the human being. There is a substantial need for openness in law schools to the adoption of this point of view. However, it is of value to attempt to put forward something based on prevention and proactivity rather than reaction, even though the law and teaching have been based on litigiousness and reactivity, hence the need to teach to dialogue, empathise, and reach a compromise on the types of hypotheses that can be taught and which the brain can progressively confirm in the legal practice of every future lawyer.

Identifying the Causes of a Lack of Assertiveness

It also implies recognising the obstacles to overcome. In law, causes are multiple, and some are dealt with below.

Lack of Idealism

Some authors, as Levit and Linder (2010), now have a hazard to denounce what is failing to work in law schools and the profession, which is increasingly viewed as more a business than a mission, when the most desirable case would be an equilibrium between these goals; they question why curricula do not contain courses on professional satisfaction or lawyers' happiness and underline the idealism among students who usually enter academic life with a sense of happiness and balance and are transformed into significantly different people than those who first arrived: more depressed, less service-oriented, and tending more towards superficial goals and values; their personalities tend to spontaneously imitate the expressions and behaviours of other members of the field and absorb and reflect the emotions of others via largely unconscious feedback mechanisms evidencing thereby that teaching methods and the implied messages that they assimilate from professors can contribute to shaping them negatively, and that unhappiness gives them a greater propensity to be discourteous, take shortcuts, and to see others as enemies or adversaries as well as to engage in unethical practices.

False Stereotypes and Beliefs

Law schools ought to employ professors who do not feed stereotypes that undermine the autonomy and self-esteem of their students. Rigid mental models reflect a theatrical logic, such as that lawyers should be imperious, extroverted, combative, intimidating, sarcastic, competitive, and opinionated. Anyone who does not walk in the shoes of insensibility will never be a good lawyer.

However, it is common to encounter bias that favours extrovert loquacious students fitted to a world dominated by the Socratic method and dizzying discourse, such that silent or introverted thinkers often question their place in the legal sphere regardless of possessing gifts such as active listening, empathy, contemplative analysis, and impactful writing when faced with a legal community that appears to have no room for more subtle voices; the stereotypical extroversion of lawyers, judges, and professors and students of law affects calmer personalities and feeds more significant anxiety in a vocation that is already plagued with mental problems (Brown, 2017). Law school requires understanding professors who do not crush the value of individual growth of all personalities.

Stereotypes, because they operate from the outside–in, are demolished by assertiveness, a value with an all-encompassing meaning, perhaps because reality reveals an almost infinite number of possibilities of how things can be done.

Excess Narcissism and Lack of Diversity, Empathy, and Humility

Durvasula (2019) calls attention to taking better care of mind, body, and soul, as narcissism and a lack of civic consciousness and antagonism have become a new world order that normalises these without any regard for the fact that they are manifestations of pathological insecurity at both an individual and social level and incentivises them via consumerism and social networks to the degree that they are endemic in political, corporate, and academic leaders who infect everything they touch, filling others with doubt, desperation, confusion, angst, depression, and a feeling of inadequacy.

Changing directionality from within to without, rather than the reverse, is the significant difference between the assertive individual and the narcissist who would never dare attempt the art of self-observation. Likewise, specificity is the inverse of diversity, whose openness should be understood broadly to take the best that different thinkers offer. Failure to do so is a mental model that impoverishes thinking with prejudices and leads to biases when, in reality, it fertilises greater comprehension of the human species.

Annihilation of Creative Thinking and an Abundance of Analytic Thought

There is a need for professionals educated equally in scientific and intuitive thinking, in an interchange like that produced between the micro and macro levels, as the world is neither flat nor dual but rather a rich three-dimensional reality. As Wilson (2014) points out, to understand reality entirely means interpreting all the feelings and structures of the human mind, having intimate contact with people, and having knowledge of endless personal histories that illustrate how thought is translated into a symbol and how a large part of human creativity is the fruit of that conflict between the individual and the group dimensions, which is so necessary to an understanding of the reality that enables people to decide wisely with a vision that is complete and opposed to that almost bacterial rhythm with which science fragments reality into specialities.

The more mental models are employed, the greater the opportunities for creative thinking, and better still, if it is intertwined with other species. That occurs when, according to Siaud-Facchin (2008), developing numerous mental axes in a tree-like pattern, along which images, sensations, and emotions feed that ever-more complex arborescent thinking whose branches can spread themselves towards infinity to foster the birth of new creative ideas bolstered by multiple representations and emotions.

The transformation of conscious knowledge into unconscious knowledge and letting the latter guide decision-making in an integral and aligned manner without the wear and tear and effort that conscious knowledge requires (Linder & Levit, 2014) can be achieved through rhizomatic thinking and nurtured through assertive openness given that the more things you learn, the easier it is to learn a whole lot more. This fluidity of thought makes professionals true experts by endowing them with mental patterns obtained via a parallel emotional learning process that should become as normal as any other everyday activity.

Technology, Dispersion, and Lack of Concentration

Poorly understood and used technology is building entire generations of addicts in a veritable act of plunder that pillages presence, mental peace, and concentration to the detriment of the alignment of actions and values, making it easy to lose sight of our goals. The diminishment of presence dilutes objectives and makes it impossible to identify the "why" behind the actions, as without concentration, there is no wholeness.

Popular culture offers numerous metaphors for concentration aligned with spirituality, from the knight bravely donning his armour before a battle to someone firming up their tie before a meeting or the mere fact of taking three deep breaths before heading out in front of an audience. These are potent symbols of self-control intended to valorise oneself through a language of gestures that symbolise a profound reflection that calls for courage and brings about health. Think of a vertical vertebral column that, by not curving, provides firm support and eliminates back problems. Traditional Chinese medicine has for centuries taught that when organs and emotions are aligned, health comes from this equilibrium and that any contrary imbalance breaks the cycle of health and then illness results (Forbes, 2017). Here, the shared value lies for anyone who decides to behave assertively. Individuals who improve internally improve their posture because they change their body language for integration based on an ordered mind that favours their health by achieving an elevated mood that has repercussions on the outside.

These types of questions should be considered with all seriousness. Alignment is satisfaction with oneself and its absence, a form of cognitive dissonance that leads us to think in one way but to act in another, which then leads to survival mechanisms such as alcoholism or other means of escape that strip away the freedom of all those who lack the self-esteem that assertiveness provides.

Just as technological stress impedes alignment and makes us lose equilibrium, professions are also thrown off kilter by moving away from their origins. In the case of law, although it is legitimate to make money off work, it is preferable to stay within the noble cradle of the profession situated in the equity of ancient Roman law. This harmony lies in the vocation of service and negotiation over and above the litigation culture.

Identifying Possible Solutions

The following are among the potential solutions to some of the above-mentioned points.

Faced with a Loss of Idealism and False Stereotypes and Beliefs: Different Professors

One suggestion to combat the excess of analytical thinking and the impoverishment of other forms of reasoning would be to vary law schools' criteria for hiring professors and give education all the importance it ought to enjoy. According to Wilson (2014), the relationship between the sciences and the humanities should occupy a place at the centre of the liberal education of any academic subject, and the principal criterion for the hiring of new professors should not be preeminence in some speciality, since creative thinking—that which is truly important—does not arise from the puzzles of specialist areas but rather from understanding that the most competent scientists are those who think like poets and work like accountants.

Additionally, the hiring criterion should be based on something more than the economic success of those giving classes. It is essential to teach the student body to preserve a healthy relationship with money and to relocate their motivations, not an easy task in the face of the stereotype that law professors represent; that is, that of a lawyer who has—and ought to have—many relationships on the political and economic planes and more significant than average financial rewards.

Without criticising the legitimacy of honourably earned money when there is a synergy with the idea that the essence of the legal profession is service, it should lose its power and cease to teach students to look up to the lawyer with the most prominent car, who works in the partnership with the longest most bombastic name, and who has the most significant amount of connections and fame in order to begin praising truly admirable traits such as professionals who take the trouble to go beyond immediacy and who endeavour to interpret the symbols that enable them to read and understand their client's needs, who do not make them languish for hours in their law firms' waiting rooms, who maintain regular communication with them and inform them about everything to help them stay calm because they have empathy for them, or who do not charge them exorbitant fees to solve their problems because they know how to value their work fairly.

Education for assertiveness aligns and relocates motivations and, through this resignification, dilutes the stress and dissatisfaction that causes students to struggle to fulfil unbalanced expectations. It is a true paradox that a profession whose purpose is to achieve change through the law fails to provide emotional education as a mandatory subject and that assertiveness is understood solely as the ability to express disagreement while ignoring the universe it embraces, which has been demonstrated.

Professors ought to teach analytically and intuitively. The excess of rational thinking at law schools causes harm at the micro and macro levels. It is not an *a priori* statement as there are brave lawyers who dare to break the closed circle of the profession in order to demand a practice with meaning and who raise their voices to expose the standardised rationalisation involved in performing work that is not aligned with its values, and the disequilibrium caused by overvaluing reasoning while undervaluing emotions (Haskell, 1998; Linder & Levit, 2014; Levit & Linder, 2010; Melcher, 2014; Monopoli & McCarty, 2013; Rhode, 2015; Sommerlad et al., 2015).

Faced with Narcissism and a Lack of Diversity, Empathy, and Humility: More Negotiation

Strengthening the negotiating skills of future lawyers would not create less efficient professionals but rather the complete opposite. It is important not to confuse assertiveness with aggressiveness, as is the tendency in the judicial sphere where there is a noticeable and widespread lack of humility. One must ask how much this is due to the lack of emotional education that results in low self-esteem, contrary to what ought to be understood as good leadership open to otherness and reconciliation.

There are many ways of educating agents of change. Bicchieri (2017) suggests that it can be done by attenuating sensitivity to risk, reducing loyalty to permanent norms, and increasing autonomy and perceived high self-efficacy, traits characteristic of trendsetters and assertive people. Humility is not opposed to healthy self-esteem; it is quite the contrary, being a good conciliator who knows when and how much to give in requires much self-confidence.

Faced with Analytical, Linear Thinking: Creative Thinking and Interpretation of Signs

A high-end lawyer who places negotiation before litigation based on knowing how to read a client's needs and interpret beyond the immediate situation needs a way of thinking far more entirely than merely analytically. Law students should be instructed on acquiring knowledge of and recognising the existence of codes other than those of the legal sphere. A code is not solely a set of laws. It can also be understood as a series of guidelines and rules that encrypt and read secret messages. There is also a need to train students to read those codes and not only the letter—often a dead one—of the law.

The symbolic interactionism posited by Blumer (1986) shows how language is not only words but also symbols such as gestures or vocal intonation. It is based on the premise that individual actions always involve an understanding of the scope of physical, social, and cultural objects, finding in them a connotation by seeing them in the context of a specific idea or symbolic construction, all of which evidences the fact that to impose macrostructures on microstructures, individuals must first interact with them and endow them with meaning after interpreting them.

It is the reason for the importance of a global perception that relies equally on mind, body, and heart since this integrality in learning increases our capacity to communicate with others in a way that goes beyond mere exchange and broadens our field of interpretation. While using words alone can lead to confusion, assertive synergies forestall inaccurate readings by aligning values with the meanings given to things and with the efforts to understand others.

Faced with Dispersion and Lack of Concentration: Art to Deal with Technology

It helps to admire artworks as they represent a case of expressions that have taken a long time to create, and even though silencing the outside world is not an easy task, art shows how to do it so that our purposes are not diluted. As Yanklowitz (2019) justly asserts, working on the concentration necessary for spiritual activists—as he terms agents of change—to achieve constant innovations instead of mere outbreaks of fantasy, in times in which it appears that it is an obligation to achieve the most significant possible number of things in the shortest time possible, concentration is a natural and healthy way of flooding the prefrontal cortex with dopamine with the result that many cases of attention deficit, addiction, and hyperactivity disorders could be eradicated.

Nevertheless, the combination of technology and a lack of emotional education is like a bleak personal landscape symbolised by a clump of straw tossed by the wind through a deserted street. Teaching people to live healthily with technology combats dispersion, and the lack of concentration it eventually brings is indispensable. Including artistic media in teaching law and human warmth is helpful as students are not being taught to face up to their era.

Faced with the madness of technological solutionism denounced by Morozov (2013), who warns us of the dangers that algorithmic mediation and the dichotomy between intelligent devices and stupid humans imply for critical thinking, assertiveness can return to students what technology has stripped from them: the satisfaction and personal growth derived from overcoming complex tasks and from valuing not only the end—at least if this is solely financial—but the entire path because technology, by making life easier and turning them into addicts, has taken away the assertive right of feeling proud of themselves when they surmount difficulties. There lies the actual shared value:

> Learning to focus spiritually can save our lives physically and allow us to achieve our dreams for a better world. This delicate art must be mastered to achieve more effective social action within local communities and (inter) national progress... To be spiritually attuned, we need times of wholeness free of fracturing interruptions... To engage in the world with spiritual vigour, we must prepare ourselves for intense focus, concentration, disappointment, and triumph. (Yanklowitz, 2019, Holiness of Process section, paras. 19–20)

A New Academic Subject: Assertive Rights

Suppose assertiveness has the power to change behaviour. In that case, it is evident that it creates aligned social norms, so it is indefensible that it is not taught in all the degree courses at all the universities. Every department of every discipline should teach forms of conscious autonomy that instil in students the mental clarity to distinguish between the fundamental and the accessory and to face up the world with all the potentialities of what could be. In the case of law, this new mandatory subject could—and should—be taught; a mix of human rights and psychology which would deal with, among other issues, how to understand assertiveness in all its capacities and to learn how to be agents of change, trendsetters, and peacemakers; how to have a healthy relationship with technology, consumerism, and money; how to handle frustration; how to control thoughts and actions and give the latter their full importance as these are the sources of the change that arises from their repetition based on the creation of new cerebral patterns and connections, alongside techniques of mindfulness, meditation, and organisation in order to reduce stress.

Although it is the case that the origin of the term assertiveness lies in psychology, it fits in with any area of knowledge. For that reason, it is an entire concept as its content is highly varied and can continue to be augmented as it interacts with the various professions and emerging social needs. In the legal area and psychology, the field of interconnectivity should be highlighted. In the sphere of psychology, and with a behaviourist approach, Smith (1975) introduced the Declaration of Assertive Rights—similar to the Declaration of Human Rights—initially putting forward ten basic principles, such as the right to change one's mind; to make mistakes; to say "I do not know," "I do not understand," or "I do not care"; to make decisions that go beyond logic; to not provide reasons or excuses to justify our actions; to judge our reasoning, emotions, and behaviour, and—of course—to accept our responsibility for all of the preceding.

Over time, this has expanded to constitute an assertive education to affirm the rights themselves without any need to affect others negatively. This opens up an entire field of disciplinary interaction that is reflected in aspects such as the fact that what, for psychology, is an expression of one's desire to conform with self-esteem and a sense of personal security, for the sphere of human rights is freedom of expression; or that what for psychology is the capacity to commit oneself to other people instead of seeing everything from an individual and self-centred perspective, in law is the capacity for negotiation. Research remains open to the ongoing discovery of new areas of convergence.

The results obtained would be diverse, but in the case of law, assertive education would generalise and normalise the audacity of daring to refocus, that is, a possibility as necessary as it is rare in the legal domain which continues to teach, in an almost medieval fashion, that arguments from authority must not be questioned. For example, for decades, the idea has been taught that animals do not possess rights by the simple argument that they are incapable of demanding them.

Fearing to confront contradictions, few people dare to take the trouble to involve themselves in the effortful thinking necessary to see whether a different way of framing a problem might generate a different answer, and so many abuses are committed due to the dearth of bravery to moving off script and to adopt different ways of conceiving problems (Linder & Levit, 2014); however, bravery is assertiveness and fortunately, in many corners of the globe, the discourse now is of animal rights, and there are even university courses that employ that term, such as the master's degree in Animal Law and Society offered by the University of Barcelona (UAB), a powerful example of reframing.

There are now universities that are starting to treat feelings with the seriousness they deserve, such as the Kama Muta Lab of the Norway University, which is at the forefront of emotion studies and with which Fiske (2020) participates in the research on Kama Muta, a so-called new emotion that has arisen as the most profound that human beings can experience when they are allowed themselves to be moved to tears when faced with triggering factors that originate above all in the exterior, but also on an inner plane. Assertive people who are capable of changing their behaviour, of being alive to a perception that goes beyond immediacy, and which, instead of being frightened of what they do not understand, try to do so, have greater chances of experiencing Kama Muta. Those who look back and understand that they are the sum of all their parts and experiences and who manage to be emotionally moved by their selves and their work can initiate the continuous, reintegrated, and infinite movement implicit in the path of shared value.

It is not a romantic proposal. To think of it that way is a false belief that must not be converted into a social norm written in stone and will subsequently have to be changed. On the contrary, it is necessary to attempt it because it is a need for our times. All professionals deserve to be educated differently, one that will enable them to decipher the secret codes of assertiveness, something which Goethe (2013, p. 131–134), in his poem "Elegy," had already confided to us two centuries ago: "But courage! Open lies the world to you, / The glorious heavens above, the earth beneath; / Observe, investigate, with searching eyes, / And Nature will disclose her mysteries." It is time to pay attention.

References

Alexander, J. C., Giesen, B., Münch, R., & Smelser, N. J. (Eds.). (1987). *The Micro-Macro link*. University of California Press.

Bicchieri, C. (2017). *Norms in the wild: How to diagnose, measure, and change social norms*. Oxford University Press.

Blumer, H. (1986). *Symbolic interactionism: Perspective and method*. University of California Press (Original work published 1969).

Brown, H. K. (2017). *The introverted lawyer: A seven-step journey toward authentically empowered advocacy*. American Bar Association.

Buzsáki, G. (2019). *The brain from inside out*. Oxford University Press.

Durvasula, R. S. (2019). *Don't you know who I am? How to stay sane in an era of narcissism, entitlement, and incivility*. Post Hill Press.

Fiske, A. P. (2020). *Kama Muta: Discovering the connecting emotion*. Routledge.

Forbes, R. (Ed.). (2017). *Chinese medicine: A comprehensive guide*. Library Press.

Goethe, J. W. (2013). *Elegy. Delphi collected works of Johann Wolfgang von Goethe* (Illustrated; E. A. Bowring, Trans.). (131–134). Delphi Classics (Original work published 1827).

Haskell, P. G. (1998). *Why lawyers behave as they do*. Westview Press.

Hillman, J. (1996). *The soul's code: In search of character and calling*. Random House.

Ison, R., & Straw, E. (2020). *The hidden power of systems thinking: Governance in a climate emergency*. Routledge.

Levit, N., & Linder, D. O. (2010). *The happy lawyer: Making a good life in the law*. Oxford University Press.

Linder, D. O., & Levit, N. (2014). *The good lawyer: Seeking quality in the practice of law*. Oxford University Press.

Melcher, M. F. (2014). *The creative lawyer: A practical guide to authentic professional satisfaction* (2nd ed.). American Bar Association.

Monopoli, P., & McCarty, S. (Eds.). (2013). *Law and leadership: Integrating leadership studies into the law school curriculum*. Ashgate.

Morozov, E. (2013). *To save everything, click here: The folly of technological solutionism*. PublicAffairs.

Olusanya, O. (2014). *Emotions, decision-making and mass atrocities: Through the lens of the Macro-Micro Integrated Theoretical Model*. Ashgate.

Rhode, D. L. (2015). *The trouble with lawyers*. Oxford University Press.

Siaud-Facchin, J. (2008). *Trop Intelligent pour être heureux? L'adulte surdoué [Too smart to be happy? The gifted adult]*. Odile Jacob.

Smith, M. J. (1975). *When I say no, I feel guilty: How to cope using the skills of Systematic Assertive Therapy*. Bantam Books.

Sommerlad, H., Harris-Short, S., Vaughan, S., & Young, R. (Eds.). (2015). *The futures of legal education and the legal profession*. Hart Publishing.

Townend, A. (2007). *Assertiveness and diversity*. Palgrave Macmillan.

Walker, C., Kalathil, S., & Ludwig, J. (2020). The cutting edge of sharp power. *Journal of Democracy.*, *31*(1), 124–137. https://doi.org/10.1353/jod.2020.001

Walther, C. C. (2021). *Technology, social change and human behaviour: Influence for impact.* Palgrave Macmillan. https://doi.org/10.1007/978-3-030-70002-7

Weller, F., & Wilson, M. (2018). *Changemakers: Embracing hope, taking action, and transforming the world.* New Society Publishers.

Wilson, E. O. (2014). *The meaning of human existence.* Liveright Publishing Corporation.

Yanklowitz, S. (2019). *The soul of activism: A spirituality for social change.* Changemakers Books.

CHAPTER 14

Assertiveness in the Context of Human Rights, Ethics, and Classical Virtues: Final Reflections

Susana Castaños-Cervantes

Emerging and developing countries face numerous challenges, particularly regarding human rights protection, promotion, and exercise. These circumstances aggravate existing development challenges and lead to societies immersed in corruption, violence, conflict, injustice, discrimination, inequity, social exclusion, and marginalisation, among other aspects, and to communities where assertiveness is not encouraged but rather aggressiveness and passiveness. Aggressive behaviour permeates those in power who exercise their rights coercively, placing their needs and interests above everyone else and everything, not seeking social well-being. In contrast, passive behaviour arises from those in need and lack the means to express their voice firmly, fairly, and confidently and who have been ripped from their rights, succumbing to those in power. After the COVID-19

S. Castaños-Cervantes (✉)
Escuela de Psicología, Facultad de Ciencias de la Salud,
Universidad Panamericana, Mexico City, Mexico
e-mail: scastanos@up.edu.mx

S. Castaños-Cervantes, C. Atristain-Suárez (eds.), *Assertiveness in the Context of Human Rights, Ethics, and Classical Virtues*,
https://doi.org/10.1007/978-3-031-60962-6_14

pandemic, such conditions escalated, and the capacity of governments to respond has been tightly constrained. These societal challenges require new development models conducive to resilience, sustainability, and social well-being and essential to sustain our existence as humans.

One way to achieve such social well-being is by addressing the complex and intertwined interactions among culturally diverse people whose backgrounds and origins are complex and multi-faceted. To effectively manage these interactions, we should begin by educating people in assertiveness as a human right and as the ethical behaviour and communication style that paves the way for promoting a culture of respect, equity, justice, and peace, where inclusion and diversity are stimulated. As a result, we will be able to build societies in which the voice and needs of its people are listened to, considered, and encouraged, and where everyone has the whole exercise of their rights and respect is forged. In this way, assertiveness in the context of human rights, ethics, and classical virtues shapes societies based on principles and moral values.

Throughout its 12 chapters and using a mixed-methods approach, this interdisciplinary edited collection has provided a comprehensive understanding of assertiveness rights and how assertiveness can be cultivated as a human right in the context of emerging and developing countries so that these studies can help researchers, scholars, governments, and the people build societies based on ethics, justice, peace, inclusion, diversity, and equity, and cultures grounded in human rights.

The book has delved into the origins and concepts of assertiveness from a philosophical and social perspective, particularly the Aristotelian view and Reflexivity, thus affirming that assertiveness is the ethical way to righteous behaviour and communication as it is originated in virtues and principles where each person has the same value and where personal needs, wants, and desires are balanced with those of others. As an ethical behavioural and communication style, this collection has demonstrated that assertiveness lays the foundation for self-assurance and drawing power from this to get our points firmly, fairly, and empathetically. Hence, after a thorough analysis of assertive rights, the authors of this book have stated that being assertive helps manage conflict effectively based on win-win solutions, which lead to peacemaking. Consequently, assertiveness helps build societies characterised by justice, equity, inclusion, and diversity in which human rights are fostered and protected and where people's rights are exercised fully, particularly among vulnerable groups like homeless girls. Nonetheless, assertiveness as a human right has yet to be included in current laws and regulations, resulting in assertive rights infringement, especially among the vulnerable sectors of society.

Considering those mentioned above, we can conclude that the main ideas of the book are as follows:

Assertiveness as a Human Right and Virtue

Being assertive involves expressing thoughts, feelings, and needs while respecting those we talk to. It also means recognising that other people have the right to express the same. Thus, both individuals are equally important. Assertiveness is also the ability to communicate and behave:

- **H**onestly
- **A**ppropriately
- **R**espectfully
- **D**irectly

It can be **HARD** (see Fig. 14.1).

Nonetheless, it is a skill learned and developed through time and practice. To foster assertiveness, we can follow the steps stated by Bourne (2010):

1. Evaluate your rights.
2. Designate a time.
3. State the problem situation in terms of its consequences.
4. Express your feelings.
5. Use "I-statements."
6. Make your request.
    a. Use assertive nonverbal behaviour.

NonAssertive (Passive)		Assertive (Tactful)		Aggressive (Rude)	
☹	**H** onest	✓	**H** onest	✓	**H** onest
✓	**A** ppropriate	✓	**A** ppropriate	☹	**A** ppropriate
✓	**R** espectful	✓	**R** espectful	☹	**R** espectful
☹	**D** irect	✓	**D** irect	✓	**D** irect

Fig. 14.1 Assertiveness is simple but HARD. (Source: Center for Integrated Healthcare and Veterans Affairs (2013))

b. Stand squarely, establish eye contact, maintain an open posture, and work on staying calm and self-possessed.
c. Keep your request simple.
d. One or two easy-to-understand sentences will suffice.
e. Avoid asking for more than one thing at a time. Be specific.
f. Ask for precisely what you want—or the person you are addressing may misunderstand.

7. State the consequences of gaining (or not gaining) the other person's cooperation.

Likewise, we can use the *XYZ* Formula for Effective Communication* (Center for Integrated Healthcare & Veterans Affairs, 2013). This formula states that the goal is to express feelings (internal world) in response to others' behaviour (external world) in particular circumstances.

As such, assertiveness involves respecting our rights and the rights of others. Consequently, to be assertive, we must first learn our rights so as to exercise our right to be assertive.

Assertiveness is based on principles or rights, which include:

- The right to be respected
- The right to feel and express feelings
- The right to own values, beliefs, and opinions and to express them
- The right to change our minds
- The right to make mistakes
- The right to say no
- The right to ask questions and help
- The right to tell others how we wish to be treated
- The right to like and accept ourselves even though we are not perfect
- The right to negotiate and reach compromises when conflict exists

So, it is vital to recognise our rights when dealing with others. However, others have the same rights, too. Thus, we have the right to be ourselves, but so do others. What is important is how we choose to exercise these rights—and for assertiveness, that means thinking about how we choose to behave and communicate with others and knowing, understanding, and being honest with ourselves about the motives and intentions underlying our behaviour.

Knowing our assertive rights helps us understand how and when we can all be more assertive and how we can respond to others who are not assertive. They also point out that we have the right to choose not to be assertive if we do not want to be—but we also must accept the consequences of not being assertive. We must be assertive to ensure we live out and protect these rights. Our decisions about our rights and how and when we will use them should be made through assertive decision-making. The most appropriate response should be made through conscious and responsible choice, not emotion. Everyone else has the same rights as we do, meaning they must be assertive to exercise their rights fully. By becoming aggressive, we are violating their rights. If we become non-assertive, they can infringe on our rights. This is much more concerning our responses to others. We may choose to manipulate others when they use their rights. If we do, then we are not being assertive.

Therefore, assertive rights and being assertive the right way pave the way for building a culture of virtue, peace, and equity.

Being assertive involves defending personal rights and the rights of others. This can also mean taking personal responsibility for our actions and staying accountable for what we have said or done. This is how assertiveness helps promote a culture of virtue, peace, and equity because it implies:

- Self-control
- Honesty
- Respect
- Taking responsibility
- Constructive feedback

It also is based on justice since not only do we claim our rights but we balance our needs with the needs of others. We stand up for ourselves but not at the disadvantage of other people.

Hence, assertiveness is a virtue grounded in philosophical standpoints such as the Aristotelian view, Reflexivity, and social approaches. The latter alludes to interpersonal effectiveness, which requires thinking through whether it is appropriate to communicate and behave in specific ways considering the situation, the people involved, and the context, leading to a culturally appropriate method of conflict resolution and healthy ways of interacting with others. As a result, to be assertive the right way, developing intercultural competence and knowing and exercising assertive rights is necessary (see Fig. 14.2).

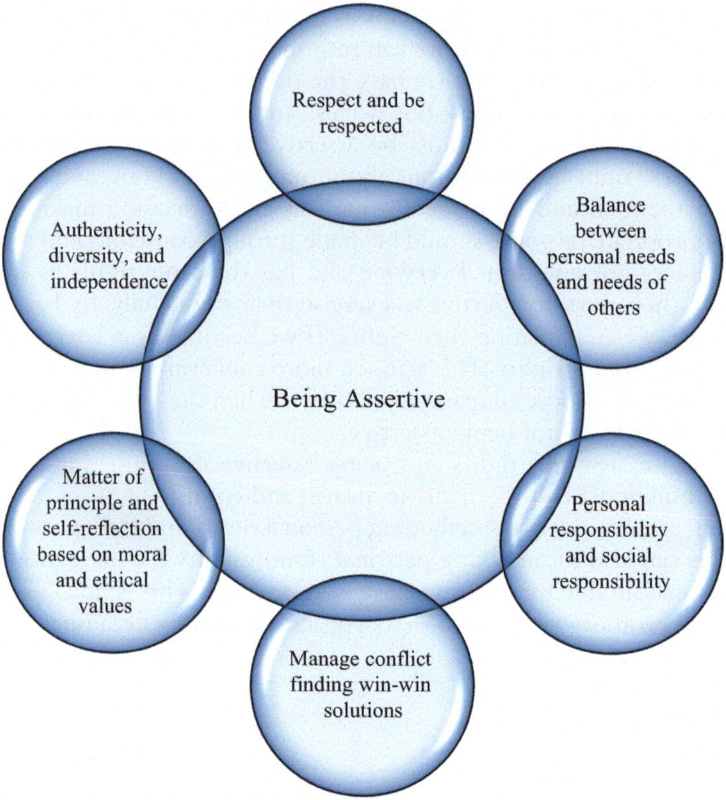

Fig. 14.2 Promoting a culture of virtue, peace, and equity through assertiveness. (Source: Author's own elaboration)

Moreover, to be assertive, it is fundamental to educate in assertive rights, which will facilitate exercising the right to be assertive, especially among vulnerable groups.

Educating in Assertive Rights to be Assertive

Why do some people have assertive communication and behavioural styles when others are more passive or aggressive? Some may fear the repercussions of acting assertively or lack the skills to express themselves effectively. They may believe that they do not have the right to be assertive. On the other hand, others may believe that it is their right to be heard and that their needs, wants, and desires are above everyone and everything else.

Being assertive is a matter of practising communication and behavioural skills and having the right inner attitude. As a core skill, assertiveness can help us express ourselves effectively and stand up for our points of view. It can also help us do this while respecting the rights and beliefs of others. However, being assertive will not guarantee that the other person will change his or her behaviour and give us what we want. Nevertheless, it will help us establish limits and boundaries with others. Thus, knowing and learning our assertive rights is the key to developing assertive behaviour, and this process takes place through education. Consequently, education provides the means for being assertive the right way. It paves the way for understanding assertive rights and our behaviour, specifically when believing that being pleasant and accommodating to others is the socially appropriate and the right way to communicate and behave (see Table 14.1).

Hence, educating in assertive rights sets the foundation for behaving and communicating assertively since one can only be assertive by knowing that we have the right to be assertive and what these rights imply. Furthermore, besides knowing and learning our assertive rights, we must understand that the same rights apply to others so we can build just, inclusive, and equal societies where all opinions matter and everyone's voice is essential. Such education in assertive rights should begin in the early stages, and these rights must be embedded in a society's legislation to guarantee their full exercise and be able to protect them as well as provide a strong foundation for the establishment of a community focused on ethics, virtue, and principles.

Finally, why does being assertive make sense? It makes sense because assertiveness is based on mutual respect, where what we say and how we say it and behave matters. It is an effective intercultural and diplomatic behavioural and communication style. Being assertive implies respecting ourselves since we are willing to stand up for our wants, desires, and interests and express our thoughts and feelings firmly, fairly, honestly, and clearly. It also denotes that while doing so, we are not only aware of others' rights but we strive to protect and promote such rights, seeking to work on resolving conflicts based on win-win solutions or at least on solutions where everyone is satisfied.

Assertiveness is necessary for the society in which we live because only thanks to it will we be able to behave ethically and communicate effectively with others. In reality, assertiveness is considered the most efficient

Table 14.1 Assertive rights and assumptions

Assumptions	*Rights*
It is selfish to put your needs before others' needs.	You have a right to put yourself first sometimes.
It is shameful to make mistakes. You should have an appropriate response for every situation.	You have a right to make mistakes.
If you cannot convince others that your feelings are reasonable, then the feelings must be wrong, or maybe you are going crazy.	You have a right to be the final judge of your feelings and accept them as legitimate.
You should respect the views of others, especially if they are in a position of authority. Keep your differences of opinion to yourself. Listen and learn.	You have a right to have your own opinions and convictions.
You should always try to be logical and consistent.	You have a right to change your mind or decide on a different course of action.
You should be flexible and adjust. Others have good reasons for their actions, and it is not polite to question them.	You have a right to protest unfair treatment or criticism.
You should never interrupt people. Asking questions reveals your stupidity to others.	You have a right to interrupt to ask for clarification.
Things could get even worse; do not rock the boat.	You have a right to negotiate for change.
You should not take up others' valuable time with your problems.	You have a right to ask for help or emotional support.
People do not want to hear you feel bad, so keep it to yourself.	You have a right to feel and express pain.
When someone takes the time to give you advice, you should take it very seriously. They are often correct.	You have a right to ignore the advice of others.
Knowing that you did something well is its own reward. People do not like show-offs. Successful people are secretly disliked and envied. Be modest when complimented.	You have a right to receive formal recognition for your work and achievements.
You should always try and accommodate others. They will not be there when you need them if you do not.	You have a right to say no.
Do not be antisocial. People will think you do not like them if you say you would rather be alone than spend time with them.	You have a right to be alone, even if others would prefer to spend time with you.
You should always have a good reason for what you feel and do.	You have a right not to justify yourself to others.
When someone is in trouble, you should help them.	You have a right not to take responsibility for someone else's problem.

(*continued*)

Table 14.1 (continued)

Assumptions	*Rights*
You should be sensitive to the needs and wishes of others, even when they cannot tell you what they want.	You have a right not to anticipate others' needs and wishes.
It is always a good policy to stay on people's good side.	You have a right not to worry about the goodwill of others constantly.
It is not pleasant to put other people off. If questioned, answer.	You have a right to choose not to respond to a situation.

Source: From Counselling Center (n.d.)

communication and behavioural style. It allows us to regulate thoughts and emotions and build and maintain healthier relationships with ourselves and others. It facilitates the achievement of personal and professional goals, and it helps improve our lifestyles. It is the path towards independence of thought, authenticity, and living in a harmonious society where justice, equity, diversity, and inclusion prevail.

For the first time in emerging and developing countries such as Mexico, this book studied assertiveness from a human rights perspective and as a core skill fundamental for behaving and communicating righteously and virtuously that should be taught since infancy and embedded in laws and regulations. We hope researchers, scholars, and people can add to the growing body of literature on this matter based on the analysis and results provided, thus contributing to the ethical improvement of societies.

References

Bourne, J. (2010). *The anxiety and Phobia workbook* (5th ed.). New Harbinger Publications, Inc.

Center for Integrated Healthcare & Veterans Affairs. (2013). *Assertive communication.* https://www.mirecc.va.gov/cih-visn2/Documents/Patient_Education_Handouts/Assertive_Communication_Version_3.pdf.

Counselling Center. (n.d.). *Assertive assumptions and rights.* James Madison University. https://www.jmu.edu/counselingctr/self-help/relationships/assertive-assumptions-and-rights.shtml.

Glossary

Chapter 1

Assertiveness (Authors' elaboration based on Alberti & Emmons, 1974): Human rights in which people appropriately and objectively express their ideas, feelings, and boundaries without resorting to manipulation or pretence while respecting others' rights, maintaining positive affect in the receiver, and considering potential consequences of the expression.

Belonging (Authors' elaboration based on Allen et al., 2021): Creating an environment where people can be themselves, feel appreciated, valued, useful, needed, and respected, interconnect with others, and become a part of something bigger and more significant.

Diversity (Authors' elaboration based on UNICEF, n.d.): People are different through the lenses of race, ethnicity, age, nationality, disability status, religion, ability, gender, sexual orientation, neurodiversity, and beyond.

S. Castaños-Cervantes, C. Atristain-Suárez (eds.), *Assertiveness in the Context of Human Rights, Ethics, and Classical Virtues*,
https://doi.org/10.1007/978-3-031-60962-6

Equity	(Authors' elaboration based on UNOPS, 2022): Recognising that each person has different circumstances and may need additional resources and opportunities to reach an equal outcome.
Inclusion	(Authors' elaboration based on UNOPS, 2022): Valuing people's unique ideas and experiences ensures they feel involved, respected, and connected, and that their voice is heard and considered.
Intercultural Competence	(Authors' elaboration based on Leeds-Hurwitz, 2013): Set of skills based on diversity and inclusion that foster equity, justice, and peace through assertiveness and lead to belonging.
Justice	(Authors' elaboration based on OECD/ Open Society Foundations, 2019): Continuous attunement of a society to ensure equal access to opportunities for growth, development, and promotion to all its members.
Peace	(Authors' elaboration based on Royce, 2009): Is a stress-free state of security and calmness when coexisting in constructive and adaptive harmony and freedom.

References

Alberti, R., & Emmons, M. L. (1974). *Your perfect right: A guide to assertive behaviour* (2nd edn). Impact Press.

Allen, A., Kern, M. L., Rozek, C. S., McInereney, D., & Slavich, G. M. (2021). Belonging: A review of conceptual issues, an integrative framework, and directions for future research. *Australian Journal of Psychology*, *73*(1), 87. https://doi.org/10.1080/00049530.2021.1883409.

Leeds-Hurtwitz, W. (2013). *Intercultural competences: conceptual and operational framework*. UNESCO. https://unesdoc.unesco.org/ark:/48223/pf0000219768.

Organization for Economic Cooperation and Development/ Open Society Foundations. (2019). *Overview of legal needs surveys and access to justice", in Legal Needs Surveys and Access to Justice*. OECD Publishing. https://doi.org/10.1787/001fafb8-en.

Royce, A. (2009). A definition of peace. *Peace and Conflict: Journal of Peace Psychology, 10*(2), 101–116. https://doi.org/10.1207/s15327949pac1002_2.

United Nations Children's Fund. (n.d.). *Mission #9-respect for diversity. Plan 12-Learn to transform*. https://www.unicef.org/lac/en/mission-9-respect-diversity.

United Nations Office for Project Services. (2022). *Gender equality and social inclusion mainstreaming in projects strategy 2022–2025*. UNOPS. https://content.unops.org/publications/UNOPS-GESI-Mainstreaming-in-Projects-Strategy_EN.pdf.

Part I

Chapter 2

Exercise of a Right — The possibility of enjoyment of a right by an individual or group. It is one thing to be entitled to a right and another to exercise it. In any case, the exercise of a right can be passive, assertive or aggressive, depending on the individual or group's behaviour. It also depends on the circumstances or capacities to flourish as a human being (Donnelly, 1989).

Human Dignity — It is a value, principle and right that acknowledges the intrinsic value of all human beings just for the sake of sharing a common nature. It is considered the source of human rights and duties (Universal Declaration of Human Rights, Preamble, Article 1).

Human Duties	These are correlated to human rights. They are human duties that we as human beings have towards other persons. According to the author, to express rights assertively, it is crucial to consider that we also have duties towards other individuals, groups, the community or the human family. One of our first duties is a brotherhood, contained in Article 1 of the Universal Declaration of Human Rights (Jones, 2021; American Convention on Human Rights, Article 32).
Human Rights	Those rights to which everyone is entitled only for the fact of being human. They have their source in human dignity (Universal Declaration of Human Rights, Preamble, Article 1).
Human Rights Education	A set of tools and perspectives that communicate and promote the importance of human rights to different sectors of society. Human Rights Education needs to promote the mechanisms for an assertive exercise of human rights, capable of creating the conditions for the recognition of everyone, everywhere and everywhen, as "a person before the law." It also promotes liberty, morality and human solidarity, such as the capacity to establish assertive relationships with other human beings (Al-Daraweesh and Snauwaert, 2015).

International Human Rights Law The field of International Law originated after World War II with the foundation of the United Nations. It studies the content, processes and application of human rights internationally. In this sense, States ratify treaties or recognise other sources that contain human rights. They must respect, protect and guarantee human rights to all persons under their jurisdiction. Individuals obtain the capacity to bring cases to international tribunals (CO-26, Inter-American Court of Human Rights, 2020).

Responsible Subject A point of view on exercising human rights and duties that considers the person an active and autonomous actor who can bear legal duties and assert legal rights. When considering legal personality, one of the main objectives of a culture of assertiveness is to create responsible subjects who can not only claim but assert their rights and duties properly. It is an ideal but an aspiration for the exercise and education on human rights that promote human flourishing. The origins of this field of International Law are connected to situations where a lack of respect for human rights can be identified and circumstances that did not permit an assertive exercise of rights (Chowdhury, 2020).

References

Al-Daraweesh, F., & Snauwaert, D. T. (2014). *Human rights education beyond universalism and relativism: A relational hermeneutic for global justice.* Palgrave Macmillan.

Chowdhury, T. (2020). *Time, temporality and legal judgement.* Routledge.

Donnelly, J. (1989). *Universal human rights in theory and practice.* Cornell University Press.

Inter-American Court of Human Rights Advisory Opinion OC-26/20 on November 9, 2020. Requested by the Republic of Colombia. *The obligations on matters of human rights of a state that has denounced the American Convention on Human Rights and the Charter of the Organization of American States.*

Jones, C. (2021). Are human rights enough? On human rights and inequality. *Ethics & Global Politics, 14*, 1991138.

Chapter 3

Assertive Rights	Do not have a formal definition. However, based on Smith (1985), we define them as the declaration of our rights and the establishment of their limits while respecting the rights of others.
Assertiveness	Has been defined in several ways, from the ability to express feelings, desires, and thoughts to the capacity to defend one's rights and those of others (Naranjo, 2008). It can also be understood as avoiding putting oneself or others through demeaning behaviours.
Human Rights	These are universal values inherent to all human beings. Each person seeks the protection of such rights and freedoms that allow individuals to achieve a desirable quality of life (Castilla, 2011).
Legal Socialisation	Encompasses how individuals encounter the law and associated values and attitudes (Trinkner & Tyler, 2016). LS also refers to developing adherence and respect towards legal normativity or laws (Baz Cores & Fernández-Molina, 2022).

Self-competence	Consists of considering oneself a capable being who can promote the common good within society (Honneth, 1995).
Self-confidence	Refers to considering oneself as kind, loving, or sympathetic and acknowledging emotional needs (Renger, 2018).
Self-regard	Related to self-esteem (Renger, 2018), and its definition is based on the self-recognition theory (Honneth, 1995) and the positive self-regard theory (Murphy et al., 2020). It refers to the attitudes toward oneself, the satisfaction of self-experiences, the development of identity and the self-concept of dignity, capacity, confidence, and autonomy within legal and social frameworks.
Self-respect	Ability to see oneself as an entity that possesses rights and deserves to be treated fairly within social or legal contexts. It includes perceiving oneself with the same dignity and rights as others and equity in exercising rights (Renger, 2018).

References

Baz-Cores, O., & Fernández-Molina, E. (2022). An empirical approach to the study of legal socialisation in adolescence. *European Journal of Criminology, 19*(2), 237–258. https://doi.org/10.1177/1477370819896212

Castilla, K. (2011). Un nuevo panorama constitucional para el derecho internacional de los derechos humanos en México (A new constitutional panorama for international human rights law in Mexico). *Estudios Constitucionales, 9*(2), 123–164.

Honneth, A. (1995). *The struggle for recognition*. Polity Press.

Murphy, D. Joseph, S. Demetriou, E., & Karimi Mofrad, P. (2020). Unconditional positive self-regard, intrinsic aspirations and authenticity: pathways to psychological well-being. *Journal of Humanistic Psychology, 60*(2), 258–279. https://doi.org/10.1177/0022167816688314.

Naranjo, P. (2008). Relaciones interpersonales adecuadas mediante una Comunicación y conducta asertivas (Appropriate interpersonal relationships through assertive communication and behaviour). *Actualidades Investigativas En Educación, 8*(1), 1–27.

Renger, D. (2018). Believing in one's equal rights: Self-respect as a predictor of assertiveness. *Self and Identity*, *17*(1), 1–21. https://doi.org/10.1080/15298868.2017.1313307.

Smith, M. J. (1985). *When I say no, I feel guilty*. Bantam Books.

Trinkner, R., & Tyler, T. R. (2016). Legal socialisation: Coercion versus consent in an era of mistrust. *Annual Review of Law and Social Science*, *12*, 417–439.

Chapter 4

Arete (Virtue or Excellence) "Is a settled disposition of the mind determining the choice of actions and emotions, consisting essentially in the observance of the mean relative to us, this being determined by principle, that is, as the prudent man would determine it. It is a mean state between two vices, one of excess and one of defect" (Aristotle, 1926, 1106b36–1107a16).

Assertiveness A social competence of "advocating for yourself to achieve your objectives and overcome difficulties" (Peneva & Mavrodiev, 2013, p. 3) by spontaneously expressing one's feelings, ideas, needs or rights without being aggressive or violating other people's rights. Also, people "express their desires and feelings openly, positively, and directly so that others will respond to them in more satisfying ways" (Matsumoto, 2009, p. 53).

Episteme Politike (Political Science or "Philosophy of Human Affairs") "The principal care of this science is to produce a certain character in the citizens, namely to make them virtuous, and capable of performing noble actions" (Aristotle, 1926, 1099b8).

Eudaimonia (Happiness/ Flourishing/Well-being)	"… doing and living well' (Aristotle, 1926, 1095a15–22). The ultimate human goal, according to Aristotle.
Hamartia (Tragic Error)	"To miss the mark, to err". "Failure" (Liddell & Scott, 1968, p. 77).
Hexis (Habit)	Second nature or developed spontaneous behaviour (Aristotle, 1926, VII, 11, 1152a29-33). "…from the standpoint of psychology, is a more or less fixed way of thinking, willing, or feeling acquired through previous repetition of a mental experience" (Andrews, 1903, p. 121).
Hybris (Thinking too Big about Oneself)	"Wanton violence, arising from the pride of strength or passion, insolence…" (Liddell & Scott, 1968, p. 98).
Phronesis (Prudence or Practical Wisdom)	"Is that virtue of the intellect by which men can deliberate well about the good and bad things we have mentioned, to achieve happiness." (Aristotle, 1995b, 1366b13).
Prohairesis (Rational Long-life Choice)	Is a purposive choice (Aristotle, 1995a, 1331b and Chamberlain, 1984).

References

Andrews, B. R. (1903). Habit. *The American Journal of Psychology, 14*(2), 121–49. https://doi.org/10.2307/1412711. ISSN 0002-9556. JSTOR 141271.

Aristotle. (1926). *Nicomachean ethics* (NE) (H. Rackham, Trans.). Loeb Classical Library 73. Harvard University Press.

Aristotle. (1995a). *Politics.* In J. Barnes (Ed.), *The complete works of Aristotle Princeton.* Princeton University Press.

Aristotle. (1995b). *Rhetoric.* In J. Barnes (Ed.). *The complete works of Aristotle Princeton.* Princeton University Press.

Chamberlain, C. (1984). *The meaning of prohairesis in Aristotle's ethics, transactions of the American Philological Association (1974–2014)* (Vol. 114, pp. 147–157). The Johns Hopkins University Press.

Liddell, H.G & Scott, R (1968). *A Greek-English Lexicon.* Clarendon Press.

Matsumoto, D. (Ed.). (2009). *The Cambridge dictionary of psychology.* Cambridge University Press.

Peneva, I. & Mavrodiev, S. (2013). A historical approach to assertiveness. *Psychological Thought*, *6* (1), 3–26.

Part II

Chapter 5

Assertiveness Social skill or communication style that has been considered a pendulum behaviour, oscillating between passive and aggressive attitudes (Castanyer, 2021; Vargas, 2012).

Culture Social way of life which has a holistic character and is therefore defined as the totality of learned behaviour (Harris, 2001; Salzmann, 1991).

Interculturality Suggests a process of interaction between various cultures (Nivón, 2012; Sandoval, 2013).

Multiculturality Implies parallel lives between different cultures (Kymlicka 1996; Nivón, 2012).

Otherness A complex process through which a group builds an identity and differentiates itself from other social groups; it is vital in anthropology to be aware of the existence of the "other" (Cansino, 2002).

Social Anthropology Branch of anthropology that studies cultural diversity in the past and present (Harris, 2001).

Social Conflict Process inherent to the human being that can have adverse effects such as violence but has the potential to be regulated peacefully (Slapsak, 2001; Turner, 1974; Valencia et al., 2005).

References

Cansino, C. (2002). *Esteban Krotz, La otredad cultural. Entre utopía y ciencia. Un estudio sobre el origen, el desarrollo y la orientación de la antropología (Esteban Krotz, Cultural otherness. Between utopia and science. A study on the origin, development, and orientation of anthropology)*. Fondo de Cultura Económica and Universidad Autónoma Metropolitana-Iztapalapa.

Castanyer, O. (2021). *Asertividad, sana autoestima (Assertiveness, A healthy self-esteem)*. Desclée Brouwer.

Harris, M. (2001). *Antropología cultural (Cultural anthropology)*. Alianza editorial.

Kymlicka, W. (1996). *Ciudadanía multicultural, Una teoría liberal de los derechos de las minorías (Multicultural citizenship, A liberal theory of minority rights)*. Paidós.

Nivón, E. (2012). Néstor García Canclini y las políticas culturales (Néstor García Canclini and cultural policies). In E. Nivón (Ed.), *Voces híbridas, Reflexiones en torno a la obra de García Canclini (Hybrid voices, Reflections on the work of García Canclini)* (pp. 31–47). Universidad Autónoma Metropolitana and Siglo veintiuno editores.

Salzmann, Z. (1991). *Antropología; Panorama general (Anthropology: General overview)*. Editorial Patria.

Sandoval, E. (2013). *Educaciones interculturales en México (Intercultural education in Mexico)*. Estudios Sociológicos.

Slapsak, S. (2001). The use of women and the role of women in the Yugoslav War. In I. Skjelsbaek & D. Smith (Eds.), *Gender, peace & conflict* (pp. 161–183). SAGE Publications, Ltd.

Turner, V. (1974). *Dramas, Fields & Metaphors: Symbolic Action in Human Society*. Cornell University Press.

Valencia, P., Jiménez, J., & Muñoz, F. (2015). Complejidad, conflictividad y paz, Una perspectiva global (Complexity, conflict and peace, A global perspective). In P. Valencia, F. Muñoz, & C. Flores (Eds.), *Conflictos y paces (Conflicts and peace)* (pp. 13–49). Editorial Universidad de Granada.

Vargas, H. (2012). "Ahimsa y Satyagraha: Principios de actuación que buscan la justicia basada en la fuerza de un corazón compasivo y osado" ("Ahimsa and Satyagraha: Principles of action that seek justice based on the strength of a compassionate and daring heart"). In M.H. Fernández (Ed.), *Ciencias sociales, humanidades y salud, Metodología y análisis (Social sciences, humanities and health, Methodology and análisis)* (pp. 279–288). ECICUSXXI, Editorial Centro de Investigación campus Universitario Siglo XXI; Centro de Investigación de Investigación de Estudios Comparados de América Latina, CIECAL; Instituto de Estudios Históricos y Económicos de la Universidad Complutense de Madrid.

Chapter 6

Assertivate ("Asertivar" in Spanish)	Assertiveness practice in social interaction (concept proposed from reflexivity).
Assertiveness	It is a behaviour based on recognition, truthfulness, affirmation, dignity, courage, and honesty, using the strong ability to say *yes* or *no* according to one's conviction (Wolpe, 1993).
Reflexivity	It is an intellectual practice that represents the consciousness of the researcher, in which he critically examines his effect on the study and the impact of his interaction.
Sociology	It is a critical study of social interaction.
Social Interaction	A social practice based on culture in two or more individuals (Author's elaboration)

Reference

Wolpe, J. (1993). *Practice of behavior therapy.* Trillas.

Chapter 7

Assertiveness	Refers to a technique to accomplish self-realization in people; assertiveness implies to accept and value oneself, having respect for other people, stand firm on one's own choices, communicate on a clear and direct way and in the right moments (Egúsquiza, 2000).

Social Work	Is a profession based on science; an academic discipline that privileges and values change and social development; social cohesion, the strengthening and liberation of people; seeks to better the wellbeing of people, beginning with facing challenges of life by meeting needs and reducing or eradicating social problems (International Federation of Social Workers [IFSW], 2018).
Social Intervention	Process that involves the subjects for their participation and collaboration in actions that let them change the way of being, thinking and acting; implies changes and collective, group or individual transformations; has the goal of achieving changes in the living conditions of their members to reach a quality of life that corresponds with their historical moment and social context (International Federation of Social Workers [IFSW], 2018).
Humanist and Existential Models	There are models of intervention that consider essential the fact that human beings seek to give sense to the world in which they live; and the professionals, from their practice, can contribute to people with training to analyze themselves, also by finding individual signification that the world imprints, and the person perceives and is impacted by (Fernandez, 2008).

References

Egúsquiza, O. (2000). Asertividad: Modelo de comunicación en las organizaciones (Assertiveness: Model of communication in organizations). *Quipukamayoc, 7*(14), 119–121. https://doi.org/10.15381/quipu.v7i14.5704.

Fernández, T. (2008). *Trabajo Social con casos (Social work with cases)*. Alianza.

International Federation of Social Workers [IFSW]. (2018). *Global social work statement of ethical principles*. https://www.ifsw.org/global-social-work-statement-of-ethical-principles/.

Part III

Chapter 8

Assertive Communication A person can speak and interact in a way that considers and respects others' rights and opinions while defending their own personal rights, needs and limits, staying in the middle of two extreme poles: passivity and aggressiveness (Alberti et al., 1977, as cited in Caballo, 1983).

Decision-making A psychological process of choosing an action among possible alternatives leads to the best result according to preferences (Aguiar, 2004).

Ethics of Responsibility The ethical theory originated in Germany at the beginning of the twentieth century by Max Weber, subsequently developed by Hans Jonas, who raised a new imperative of responsibility, which dictates that people should act in such a way that the effects of their actions are compatible with the permanence of an authentic human life (García, 2021).

Ethics of Care	American psychologist Carol Gilligan initially proposed ethical theory in the 1980s. It focuses on real situations where it is necessary to consider others' needs, avoid harm, be responsible and care for each other (García et al., 2018).
Four-Component Model of Morality	American Psychologist James Rest created a model that identified four phases of moral decision-making through empirical research: (a) moral sensitivity, (b) moral judgement, (c) moral motivation, and (d) moral character (Bebeau et al., 1999).
Phronesis	Also known as prudence or practical wisdom, it represents the ability to discern how to act ethically in each situation, according to Aristotle (349 B.C.E./1926).
Responsibility	Consideration of actions' consequences and adverse effects' prevention so that one must rationally deliberate about the consequences and choose based on obtaining the most ethically desirable consequences before acting (Jonas, 1984).
2 Systems Theory	A theory developed by psychologists such as Daniel Kahneman considers that two mental processes can lead to decisions after perceiving a situation, one related to intuitions and the other to reasoning (Kahneman, 2003).
Virtue	An excellent character trait that is a disposition ingrained in its pos-

	sessor to notice, expect, value, feel, desire, choose, act, and react in specific ways (Hursthouse & Pettigrove, 2018).
Virtue Ethics	The ethical theory originated in ancient Greece and was mainly developed by Aristotle. The theory focuses on Virtue, through which happiness and good life can be achieved (Hursthouse & Pettigrove, 2018).

References

Aguiar, F. (2004). Teoría de la decisión e incertidumbre: modelos normativos y descriptivo (Decision theory and uncertainty: normative and descriptive models). *Empiria. Revista de Metodología de Ciencias Sociales, 8*, 139–160. https://doi.org/10.5944/empiria.8.2004.982.

Aristotle. (1926). *Nicomachean ethics* (H. Rackham, Trans.). https://doi.org/10.4159/DLCL.aristotle-nicomachean_ethics.1926. (Original work published ca. 350 B.C.E.)

Bebeau, M. J., Rest, J. R., & Narvaez, D. (1999). Beyond the promise: A perspective on research in moral education. *Educational Researcher, 28*(4), 18–26. https://citeseerx.ist.psu.edu/viewdoc/download?doi=10.1.1.637.7940&rep=rep1&type=pdf.

Caballo, V. E. (1983). Asertividad: definiciones y dimensiones (Assertiveness: Concept and dimensions). *Estudios de psicología, 4*(13), 51–62. https://dialnet.unirioja.es/descarga/articulo/65876.pdf.

García, C., Preciado, M., Ángel, M., & Luna, A. (2018). El desarrollo moral y la toma de decisiones éticas del psicólogo (Moral development and ethical decision making of the psychologist). *Investigación y Práctica en Psicología del Desarrollo, 4*. https://doi.org/10.33064/ippd41993.

García, C. (2021). Fundamentos teóricos para una distinción clara entre el comportamiento ético y el normativo-moral en el desempeño profesional del psicólogo (Theoretical foundations for a clear distinction between ethical and normative-moral behavior in the professional performance of the psychologist). *Avances en Psicología Latinoamericana, 39*(3), 1–16. https://doi.org/10.12804/revistas.urosario.edu.co/apl/a.10321.

Hursthouse, R., & Pettigrove, G. (2018). Virtue ethics. *The Stanford Encyclopedia of Philosophy (Winter 2018 Edition)*. https://plato.stanford.edu/archives/win2018/entries/ethics-virtue/.

Jonas, H. (1984). The *imperative of responsibility: In search of an ethics for the technological age*. The University of Chicago Press.
Kahneman, D. (2003). A perspective of judgement and choice. *American Psychologist*, *58*(9), 697–720. https://doi.org/10.1037/0003-066X.58.9.697

Chapter 9

Community	"The community is not that which protects the subject by enclosing it within the confines of collective belonging, but rather that which projects in outward, exposing it to contact" (Esposito, 2009, p. 16).
Governance	"Governance is the enactment of political relations among diverse actors involved in the process of deciding, executing, and evaluating decisions on matters of public interest, a process that can be characterized as a power game, in which competition and cooperation coexist as possible rules; and that includes both formal and informal institutions. The form and interaction among the various actors reflect the quality of the system and affect each of its components, as well as the system as a whole" (Whittingham Munévar, 2010, p. 222).
Pacification	"Pacification' is often thought to have been developed as a term during the America–Vietnam war, following its adoption in 1964–1965 as a substitute term for 'counterinsurgency" (Neocleous, 2010, p. 14).
Pain	The pain is a secure means to be accompanied, commiserated, loved, and above all recognized within the particular status that pain itself offers (Le Breton, 1999, p. 231).
Pre-political	"An everyday embryonic form, as yet unthematized but no less pressing, of social suffering and moral injustice" (Honneth, 2006, p. 92).
Witness/Testimony	"The witness usually testifies in favor of truth and justice, which lend consistency and completeness to their words. But in this case, the tes-

timony holds essential value for what is lacking within it; it contains, at its very core, something that is untestifiable" (Agamben, 2014, p. 34).

Victimal Invisibility Governmental, criminal organisation, or specific social group strategies that conceal the causes and consequences of victimisation processes (Author's elaboration).

References

Agamben, G. (2014). *Lo que queda de Auschwitz. El archivo y el testigo. Homo Sacer III. (Remnants of Auschwitz: The Witness and the Archive. Homo Sacer III)*. Pre-textos.

Esposito, R. (2009). *Comunidad, inmunidad y biopolítica* (*Community, immunity and biopolitics*). Trad. Alicia García Ruiz. Herder.

Honneth, A. (2006). Redistribución como reconocimiento. Respuesta a Nancy Fraser (Redistribution as recognition. Response to Nancy Fraser). In N. Fraser, & A. Honneth (Eds.), *¿Redistribución o reconocimiento?: un debate político-filosófico (Redistribution or recognition: a political-philosophical)* (pp. 89–148). Ediciones Morata.

Le Breton, D. (1999). *Antropología del dolor (Anthropology of pain)*. Editorial Seix Baral.

Neocleous, M. (2010). War as peace, peace as pacification. *Radical Philosophy*, *159*, 8–17.

Whittingham Munévar, M. V. (2010). ¿Qué es la gobernanza y para qué sirve? (What is governance and what is it for?). *Revista Análisis Internacional* (2), 219–236.

Chapter 10

Assertive Leadership Assertive leadership is characterised by expressing opinions, needs and rights clearly and respectfully, without assaulting or subjecting others. In the cognitive approach, assertive behaviour consists of expressing what is believed, felt, and desired directly and honestly, asserting one's rights and respecting the rights of others (Gaeta-González & Galvanovskis-Kasparane, 2009, p. 404).

Human Rights	The United Nations has mentioned that Human Rights are inherent rights of all human beings, without distinction of race, sex, nationality, ethnic origin, language, religion, or any other status. Human rights include the right to life and freedom; freedom from slavery and torture; freedom of opinion and expression; education and work, among many others. These rights belong to all persons without any discrimination.
Gender Inclusion and Perspective	Inclusion refers to ensuring that all members of the university community have equal opportunities and access to resources, regardless of gender, disability, sexual orientation, race, or any other difference. Social inclusion ensures that all people without distinction can exercise their rights and guarantees, take advantage of their skills and benefit from opportunities in their environment. On the other hand, the gender perspective involves analysing how power structures and gender norms influence people's lives and how actions should be taken to generate a parity consciousness (Authors' elaboration).

References

Gaeta González, L., & Galvanovskis Kasparane, A. (2009). Assertividad: Un análisis teórico-empírico (Assertiveness: A theoretical and empirical anaylsis). *Enseñanza e Investigación en Psicología, 14*(2), 403–425.

Part IV

Chapter 11

Assertiveness	Personality trait whose purpose is to establish and maintain functional interpersonal relationships, invariably with positive results, achieve personal goals and increase respect, situated in a specific sociocultural context.
Human Dignity	A particular understanding of each culture of the moral value intrinsic to the human person and its political relations with society.
Human Rights	Rights inherent to all human beings, regardless of race, sex, nationality, ethnicity, language, religion, or other status.
Legal Hermeneutics	Studies the interpretation and meaning of written law.
LGBTQI+	Lesbian, gay, bisexual, transgender, queer, intersex, and asexual. (Authors' elaboration)

Chapter 12

Homeless Females	(Author's elaboration based on Castaños-Cervantes & Sánchez-Sosa, 2016): Teen girls between 10 and 19 years old that are sheltered, unsheltered, and emergency sheltered, as well as those at risk of homelessness because they lack stable housing and are victims of domestic violence and neglect.
Sexual Assertiveness	(Author's elaboration based on Loshek & Terrell, 2015): Ability to effectively communicate sexual desires and sexual consent and no consent, to develop and establish healthy sexual interactions, to exercise one's sexuality with responsibility and to exert one's sexual rights.
Sexual Attitudes	(Author's elaboration based on Armstrong et al., 2020): Individual cognitions about sexual and reproductive health, sexuality, the exercise of one's sexuality, sexual behaviours, and intimate relationships.

Sexual Education (Author's elaboration based on INSP & CENSIDA, 2014): Provision of information about physical development, sex, sexuality, and relationships, along with skill-building to enable people to protect and advocate for their health, well-being and dignity for exercising full bodily autonomy, which requires not only the right to make choices about one's body but also the information to make these choices in a meaningful way, to make healthy decisions, and to take personal responsibility for their health and overall well-being.

Sexual Empowerment (Author's elaboration based on Erchull & Liss, 2014): The ability to be sexually assertive, to exercise one's sexuality with responsibility, to exert one's sexual rights, to make safe and informed sexual decisions, and to establish healthy intimate relationships.

Sexual Health (Author's elaboration based on Wight et al., 1998): The exercise of one's sexuality founded in accurate knowledge, personal awareness, and self-acceptance, where one's behaviour, values and emotions are congruent and integrated within a person's broader personality structure and self-definition. It involves the ability to be sexually assertive, to act intentionally and responsibly, and to set appropriate sexual boundaries. For sexual health to be attained and maintained, the sexual rights of all persons must be respected, protected, and fulfilled.

Sexual Rights (Author's elaboration based on López-Alvarado et al., 2020):The right to enjoy healthy intimate relationships and a healthy, developmentally appropriate sexuality free of sexual violence, sexual coercion, sexual compliance, and risky sexual behaviours.

Sexual Violence (Author's elaboration based on Basile et al., 2014): Sexual act committed or attempted by another person without the victim's consent or against someone unable to consent or refuse.

References

Armstrong, J., Thorpe, S., & Williams, D. (2020). Sexual attitudes, religious commitment, and sexual risk behaviours among college-aged women: A feminist theory approach. *Journal of Gender Studies,* 1–12. https://doi.org/10.1080/09589236.2020.1838888.

Basile, K. C., Smith, S. G., Breiding, M., Black, M., & Mahendra, R. (2014). *Sexual violence surveillance: Uniform definitions and recommended data elements, version 2.0.* Centres for Disease Control and Prevention.

Castaños-Cervantes, S., & Sánchez-Sosa, J. (2016). Towards a psycho-social and cultural definition of Mexican homeless girls: A qualitative approach. *Anales de Psicología, 32*(2), 516–527. https://doi.org/10.6018/analesps.32.2.204721.

Erchull, M., & Liss, M. (2014). The object of one's desire: How perceived sexual empowerment through objectification is related to sexual outcomes. *Sexuality & Culture, 18*(4), 773–788. https://doi.up.elogim.com/10.1007/s12119-013-9216-z.

INSP & CENSIDA. (2014). *Análisis sobre educación sexual integral, conocimientos y actitudes en sexualidad en adolescentes escolarizados. Informe Final (Analysis of holistic sexual education, sexual knowledge and attitudes in shool adolescents).* INSP and CENSIDA.

López-Alvarado, S. L., Van Parys, H., Jerves, E., & Enzlin, P. (2020). Development of sexual assertiveness and its function for human sexuality: a literature review. *Revista Interamericana De Psicología/Interamerican Journal of Psychology, 54*(2), e948. https://doi.org/10.30849/ripijp.v54i2.948.

Loshek, E., & Terrell, H. K. (2015). The development of the sexual assertiveness questionnaire (SAQ): A comprehensive measure of sexual assertiveness for women. *The Journal of Sex Research, 52,* 1017– 1027. https://doi.org/10.1080/00224499.2014.944970.

Wight, D., Abraham, C., & Scott, S. (1998). Towards a psycho-social theoretical framework for sexual health promotion. *Health Education Research, Theory and Practice, 13*(3), 317–330.

Chapter 13

Assertive Education It is a transformation rewiring of the behaviour and the foundations on an individual level to achieve significant conversions in the macro strata by teaching forms of conscious autonomy that instill in students the mental clarity to relocate motivations. Author's elaboration based on a descriptive term used over time by various professionals in the field of education and psy-

	chology, so it cannot be specifically attributed to a unique source or a single person.
Assertive Rights	It is a mix of human rights and psychology, which would deal with understanding assertiveness in all its capacities and being agents of change who control thoughts and actions, as these are the source of new cerebral patterns and connections. Author's elaboration based on a descriptive term, meaning it was not coined in the sense of inventing a new expression, but its conceptualization is associated with the work of Manuel J. Smith in his book "When I say no, I feel guilty"—properly cited in the chapter-.
Assertive Synergies	The mental model's interaction is based on aligning values with the meanings given to things and with the efforts to understand others (Author's elaboration).
High-end Professionals	Experts in top-quality thinking who contribute to social change and shared value via the elevated status of their jobs (Author's elaboration).
Kama Muta	The most profound emotion that human beings can experience when they are allowed to be moved to tears when faced with triggering factors that originate above all in the exterior and on an internal plane. Author's elaboration based on a Sanskrit term whose usage is attributed to Alan Page Fiske—properly cited in the chapter—to conceptualize a certain type of very specific emotion.
Rigid Mental Models	Stereotypes and prejudices that impoverish thinking, undermine autonomy and self-esteem, and crush the value of individual growth of all types of personalities. Author's elaboration of a descriptive term that cannot be attributed specifically to a unique source or a specific author.

Social Pressure	Influence that determines the behaviour in the face of fear of the consequences of failing to follow the rules, be they just or otherwise. Author's elaboration of a descriptive term that cannot be attributed specifically to a unique source or a specific author.

Index[1]

[1] Note: Page numbers followed by 'n' refer to notes.

S. Castaños-Cervantes, C. Atristain-Suárez (eds.), *Assertiveness in the Context of Human Rights, Ethics, and Classical Virtues*, https://doi.org/10.1007/978-3-031-60962-6

e manufacturer's authorised representative in the EU is Springer
ure Customer Service Centre GmbH, Europaplatz 3, 69115 Heidelberg,
many. If you have any concerns regarding our products, please
act ProductSafety@springernature.com

d and bound by CPI Group (UK) Ltd, Croydon, CR0 4YY
01/10/2026
02225852-0006